ISLAM
IN BANGLADESH

INTERNATIONAL STUDIES
IN
SOCIOLOGY AND SOCIAL ANTHROPOLOGY

General Editor

K. ISHWARAN

VOLUME LVIII

U.A.B. RAZIA AKTER BANU

ISLAM
IN BANGLADESH

ISLAM
IN BANGLADESH

BY

U.A.B. RAZIA AKTER BANU

E.J. BRILL
LEIDEN • NEW YORK • KÖLN
1992

The paper in this book meets the guidelines for permanence and durability of the Committee on Production Guidelines for Book Longevity of the Council on Library Resources.

Library of Congress Cataloging-in-Publication Data

Banu, U. A. B. Razia Akter.
   Islam in Bangladesh / by U.A.B. Razia Akter Banu.
     p.   cm.—(International studies in sociology and social
anthropology, ISSN 0074-8684; v. 58)
   Includes bibliographical references and index.
   ISBN 90-04-09497-0 (pbk.)
   1. Islam—Bangladesh. 2. Bangladesh—Religious life and customs.
I. Title. II. Series.
BP63.B3B36   1991
297'.095492—dc20   91-19061
                                            CIP

ISSN   0074-8684
ISBN   90 04 09497 0

PRINTED IN THE NETHERLANDS

For my Husband: Dr. Talukder Maniruzzaman

CONTENTS

LIST OF TABLES

PREFACE

History speaks. Literature speaks. So do numbers and tables. Together these constitute the most formidable tools of socio-political analysis. In the present study we have tried to use these incisive methodological weapons to construct perhaps the first socio-political study of Islam in Bangladesh.

Although Bangladesh is the second largest Muslim state in the world, with Muslims in 1981 constituting 86.6 per cent of her 90 million people[1] (today the total population is well over 100 million), Islam in Bangladesh has not drawn much academic attention. The scholarly studies on Islam in Bangladesh are limited in number, scope, and method, as well as the period covered. There have only been four major studies on Bengal Islam—Muhammad Enamul Haq's *A History of Sufi-ism in Bengal,*[2] Asim Roy's, *The Islamic Syncretistic Tradition in Bengal,*[3] Muin-ud-din Ahmad Khan's, *History of the Faraidi Movement,*[4] and Rafiuddin Ahmed's *The Bengal Muslims, 1871–1906: A Quest for Identity.*[5] These studies all reflect one particular approach to the study of Bengal Islam—"cultural interaction between an intrusive religion [Islam] and an indigenous culture".[6]

Haq's work shows "how Islam under the garb of Sufiistic movements, which were in their full swing up to the sixteenth century AD in India, entered Bengal, and how it underwent many momentous changes in the hands of the Bengali Sufis. . . ."[7] Roy interprets Islam in Bengal during the sixteenth century to the eighteenth century as "an uncommon paradigm of one religion's containing two great traditions juxtaposed to each other, one exogenous and classical, and the other endogenous and syncretistic".[8] Khan's study deals with the nineteenth-century Faraidi movement whose aim was "to purge the Muslim peasantry of their age long un-Islamic beliefs and practices".[9] Ahmed argues that it was because of the inherent strength of the Bengali linguistic and cultural traditions that the Bengali Muslims' quest for Islamic religious identity which began in the last quarter of the nineteenth century and culminated in the creation of Pakistan in 1947 proved illusory.[10]

All the four studies mentioned above are based on qualitative methods. The scholars concerned partly use the historical researches already done on Bengal. But the major original sources of all four are the Bengali Puthi[11] literatures of the periods with which they are concerned.

In the present study we have tried to get away from the fixation of the scholars on Bangladesh Islam with the conflicts between "exogenous" Islam and "endogenous" Bengali culture and with Puthi literature. We have carried out the present research within a larger and comprehensive Weberian framework, focused on religion and social change in Bangladesh, through, we believe, an imaginative use of qualitative as well as quantitative methods of modern social research.

This study thus belongs to what is usually called the sociology of religion.

The sociology of religion does not involve speculating on the respective merits of different religious beliefs and practices, nor even on the legitimacy of belief in the hereafter. The sociological studies of religion do not simply describe religious beliefs and practices.[12] The sociologists are primarily concerned with three basic aspects of the study of religion. First, they want to understand the conditions under which the various religious beliefs appear. Secondly, they seek to explain the variations of religious beliefs among societies, groups and individuals. Lastly, they are concerned with the consequences of religious beliefs on society.[13]

It is the third aspect of the sociological study of religion, the impact of religion on social change, which has been the most challenging field for the social scientists. Karl Marx, who is usually regarded as a greater sociologist than economist, could hardly be oblivious of the consequences of religion in the process of social change,[14] although he argued that religion, as an epiphenomenon, was "used as a weapon for various historically relative, and usually established, social and political forces",[15] and therefore was caused only on a very low level. It was Max Weber who first brought into sharp focus the mutual influence of religious change and social change as the central question in the sociology of religion.[16]

> Is religion a prime mover in history, or perhaps, as some contend *the* prime mover, 'the clue to history'? If this is true, how does one explain changes in religion itself? Oppositely, is religious change a mere reflection of other changes, a symbol, but not a part of the causal interaction? Or is religion one of several 'levels of causation', a force that once set in motion is part of a complex of causes that mutually condition each other?[17]

These are some of the seminal questions with which sociology of religion deals. Max Weber blazed the trail by trying to wrestle with these questions, sometimes explicitly and sometimes implicitly in his voluminous works on the sociology of religion.[18] All these questions are particularly relevant for the study of religion in the present-day developing nations which are in the process of change and transformation. These questions are even more important for the study of Islam in a transitional society as,

> The traditional Islamic world view provided a holistic approach toward life, a life in which religion was intimately and organically related to politics, law and society.[19]

The primary purpose of our present study is, therefore, two-fold. First, we have tried to provide a sociological analysis of Islamic religious beliefs and practices in contemporary Bangladesh. Secondly, and more importantly, we have tried to understand the impact that the Islamic religious beliefs have on the socio-economic development and political culture in present-day Bangladesh.

However, to put our study in proper perspective and to understand better the interactions between religious change and social change in contemporary Bangladesh, we have tried to provide in the first two chapters of our study a sociological interpretation of the origin of Islam in Bengal in the thirteenth century and of the transformation within Bengal Islam throughout its long history stretching over some eight centuries. This part of our study is based on historical and literary works on Indian and Bengal Islam and some of the original writings in Bengali by twentieth-century Bengali Islamic thinkers.

The second and more original part of our study (Chapter III to Chapter IX) is based on two sample surveys that we conducted in May-July 1983 in the rural and urban areas of Bangladesh. For the rural sample we selected twenty villages from the four regions of Bangladesh according to probability proportional to the number of households. First we selected five police stations randomly from each of the four regions of Bangladesh. In the second stage one village was randomly selected from each of the selected police stations so that the total number of households in the selected villages would be approximately 500 in each region. The rural sample is thus representative of the whole rural population of Bangladesh.

We purposively selected an urban sample from three areas in Dhaka, the metropolitan city of Bangladesh, which were likely to have a high incidence of modernisation not only in terms of urban-rural differentiation but also with respect to indices like high income, higher education and modern professional occupations. We thought that a comparison between such a highly modernised urban sample and a representative sample of rural Bangladesh, sometimes called "a vast rural slum", would help us to gain a better understanding of interactions between religious change and social change in present-day Bangladesh. We are struck by the high level of consistency among the mutually reinforcing character of the tables that have emerged and from the mechanised tabulation of the data collected by both the rural and urban surveys. This points, perhaps, to the relevance of the sample survey method for measuring and interpreting religious beliefs and practices.

In the second part of our study we have first tried to have a rough quantitative determination of the extent of the spread of different types of Islamic religious beliefs (modern, orthodox and popular) and levels of observance of Islamic religious practice (high, medium and low) in Bangladesh today, and to find out whether the differences in religious beliefs and levels of religious practice can be explained in terms of their social correlates.

To test empirically the Weberian hypothesis that religion can play a crucial role in creating a work ethic among its adherents, we have tried to find out whether Bangladeshis do have a work ethic and how far different Islamic religious beliefs are related to this work ethic. We have also sought to ascertain the level of interpersonal trust among the Bangladesh Muslims and to see how the level of trust is related to Islamic religious beliefs, as a high level of interpersonal trust is regarded as essential for the co-operative efforts needed for development. We have also tried to understand the impact of Islamic religious beliefs on social change by examining their relations with belief in and practice of family planning, demand for increased rights for women equal with men and adoption of modern methods of agricultural production.

Lastly, we have tried to understand the impact of Islam on the political culture in Bangladesh in terms of the extent of Islam's influence on the day-to-day temporal activities of Bangladesh Muslims and on the Muslim-Hindu relationship in Bangladesh. In this regard we have particularly tried to examine the relationship of Islamic religious beliefs with the proclivity of Bangladeshi Muslims to separate religious and political leadership and with the largely secular symbols of present-day Bangladesh national identity.

Religion, of course, is not the only intellectual force affecting social change in Bangladesh. Many recent social scientists argue that the intellectual forces emanating from the West and now being diffused all over the world are major factors inducing change and transformation in the developing countries. Of all the exogenous forces of social change, Western education is usually considered as the primary one. For gaining a relatively more accurate understanding of the role of religion on social change in Bangladesh, we have tried to see how Islam compares with Western education in "transformative capacity".

Our study of the role of ideational factors in social and political change in Bangladesh, we believe, has wider relevance. Bangladesh, "the poorest of the poor countries"[20] in the present-day world, is regarded as "the test case of development".[21] Moreover, it is now being realised that the role of "culture and belief systems" has not been given adequate attention in the voluminous developmental literature produced by Western social scientists in the last three decades.[22] A comparative analysis of the roles of two major ideational factors—religion and education—in social change in Bangladesh will help deepen our understanding of the processes of development common to many parts of the Third World.

The pages that follow this Preface speak for themselves. Here I want only to acknowledge the debt I owe to many outstanding scholars and academic administrators without whose help, understanding and guidance I could never have completed the present study. Marcus F. Franda, a long-time scholar of South Asian social and political change first urged me to undertake a comprehensive scientific and systematic study of the virtually unexplored subject of contemporary Bangladesh Islam.

My participation in the International Conference on "Islam, Communalism and Modern Nationalism" at Bellagio, Milan, Italy, held in April 1981, exposed me to the provocative ideas of scholars of modern Islam like Ernest Gellner, Charles Gallagher, Richard W. Cottam, Dennison I. Rusinov, Marcus F. Franda, Iliya Harik, Saad Eddin Ibrahim, de Sulejman Grozdanic, Mark Tessler, and Mushirul Hasan. Learning about Islam in other societies whetted my appetite for deciphering Bangladesh Islam.

I could not have undertaken and completed the survey on which the present study is primarily based without a financial grant from the Asia Foundation, Dhaka. I am grateful to Fazlul Halim Choudhury, Vice-Chancellor of the University of Dhaka, for recommending my application for the research grant, and James J. Novak, the Representative of the Asia Foundation in Bangladesh, for promptly approving it.

Anwar Hossain Talukder, Professor of Statistics, University of Dhaka, acted as the statistical consultant for the survey project. Sudhir Das Gupta of the Bangladesh Institute of Development Studies, and Mallick Shamim Ahsan of the Computer Centre, Bangladesh University of Engineering and Technology, contributed their expertise in the computerisation of data.

I must also mention that the Asia Foundation awarded me a supplementary travel grant. As I started my research, reflecting on the usual poverty of libraries in the developing world, I felt an acute need to travel somewhere to work in a first-rate, world-class library. Fortunately, I was able to spend a year at the Library of Congress, Washington, D.C., one of the largest libraries in the world, to delve into the past of Bangladesh Islam and to improve my grasp of recent social science research tools. While in Washington, besides working in the Library of Congress I gained considerably by occasional attendance at the open seminars of the Woodrow Wilson International Center for Scholars of the Smithsonian Institution, where my husband, Talukder Maniruzzaman, was a Fellow at the time.

The book is the revised version of my doctoral dissertation at the University of London, and my greatest indebtedness is to Dr. David Taylor, Director, Centre of South Asian Studies, School of Oriental and African Studies, University of London, and my advisor, whose thoughtful suggestions led to both substantive and stylistic improvements of the work. I am grateful to J.M.S. Baljon, whose valuable comments and suggestions helped me to make the dissertation fit for publication in the present form. I am also grateful to Dr. F. Th. Dijkema, Oriental Editor, E.J. Brill, for his continuing interest in the manuscript.

Finally, I must express my gratitude to my family. My Children— Raguib Muneer, Sayema Parveen and Sadid Muneer—suffered a lot because of my work. My husband provided me with the inspiration that sustained me in the arduous process of data collecting, data analysing and the writing of the study over the six year period. He took full responsibility of maintaining the whole family while I was in London to finish my thesis. I am so glad that I could present the book to him.

NOTES

1 See *Statistical Year Book of Bangladesh, 1986* (Dhaka: Bangladesh Bureau of Statistics, December 1986). These population figures of Bangladesh are provisional counts of the 1981 census. Muslims constitute 90 per cent of the 158 million people of Indonesia, the largest Muslim state in the world. See A.S. Banks and W. Overstreet (eds.), *Political Handbook of the World: 1982-1983* (New York: McGraw Hill, 1983), pp. 221-2. Banks and Overstreet also quote the Bangladesh 1981 provisional census figures for the Bangladesh population. See *ibid.*, p. 37.

2 Dacca, Asiatic Society of Bangladesh, 1975. The present military government of Bangladesh changed the spelling Dhaka for Dacca in 1982. So the sources published in the capital city of Bangladesh before and after 1982 use the spelling Dacca and Dhaka respectively. In our bibliographical references throughout the book we shall use Dacca or Dhaka as it appears in the sources cited.

3 Princeton, Princeton University Press, 1983.

4 Karachi, Pakistan Historical Society, 1956; second edition, Dhaka, the Islamic Foundation, 1984.

5 Delhi, Oxford University press, 1981.

6 Roy, *op. cit.*, p. 249.

7 Haq, *op. cit.*, p. iv.

8 Roy, *op. cit.*, p. 250.

9 Khan, *op. cit.*, second edition, 1984, page m.

10 See Ahmed, *op. cit.*, p. 190.

11 Puthi literally means a book or manuscript. It refers generally to all ancient and medieval Bengali works.
12 See J. Freund, *The Sociology of Max Weber* (translated from the French by Mary Ilford) (London: Allen Lane, the Penguin Press, 1968), p. 74.
13 See "Social Aspects of Religion", in *The New Encyclopaedia Britannica*, Vol. 15, 15th edition (Chicago: Encyclopaedia Britannica, 1981), p. 604.
14 See the compendium of writings of Karl Marx and Friedrich Engels on religion, *Karl Marx and Friedrich Engels on Religion* (New York: Schocken Books, fifth printing, 1974).
15 See "Introduction" by Reinhold Niebuhr, *ibid.*, p. vii. As Niebuhr states, Marx himself became "the revered prophet of a new world religion, as potent in the twentieth century as was Islam in the seventh", *ibid.*, p. xi.
16 For an excellent discussion on the interaction between religious change and social change as the main theme of the sociology of religion, see J.M. Yinger, *Religion, Society and the Individual* (New York: Macmillan, 1957), pp. 265–312.
17 *Ibid.*, p. 265.
18 See M. Weber, *The Protestant Ethic and the Spirit of Capitalism* (translated by Talcott Parsons) (New York: Charles Scribner's Sons, 1958); *The Religion of China: Confucianism and Taoism* (translated by Hans H. Gerth) (New York: Free Press, 1951); *Ancient Judaism* (translated and edited by Hans H. Gerth and Don Martindale) (New York: Free Press, 1952); *The Religion of India: The Sociology of Hinduism and Buddhism* (translated by Hans H. Gerth and Don Martindale) (New York: Free Press, 1958); *From Max Weber: Essays in Sociology* (translated, edited and with an Introduction by H. Gerth and C. Wright Mills) (London: Routledge and Kegan Paul, paperback, 1977), *passim*.
19 J. L. Esposito, "Introduction: Islam and Muslim Politics", in J.L. Esposito (ed.), *Voices of Resurgent Islam* (Oxford: Oxford University Press, 1983), p. 5.
20 J.F. Stepanek, *Bangladesh—Equitable Growth?* (New York: Pergamon Press, 1979), p. xii.
21 Just Faaland and J.R. Parkinson write: "Bangladesh is the world's most difficult problem of economic development. If the problem of Bangladesh can be solved, there can be reasonable confidence that less difficult problems of development can also be solved. It is in this sense that Bangladesh is to be regarded as the test case". J. Faaland and J.R. Parkinson, *Bangladesh: The Test Case of Development* (New Delhi: S. Chand, 1977), p. 5.
22 See M. Weiner, "Introduction", M. Weiner and S.P. Huntington (eds.), *Understanding Political Development* (Boston, Mass.: Little, Brown, 1987), pp. xiv, xvii–xx.

CHAPTER I

SOCIAL ANOMALIES, A PROPHETIC BREAK,
AND THE GROWTH OF ISLAM IN BENGAL
(FROM AD 1201 TO 1757)

The spectacular growth and expansion of Muslim political power during the centuries following the advent of Islam in Arabia is one of the most important phenomena of world history. Scholars of Islam explain this dazzling expansion of Muslim political power in terms of two factors. The first was the decadence of the two gigantic empires of Byzantium and Persia, which alone could have checked the onslaught of the virile Muslim army. Both empires were "exhausted by incessant mutual wars and corroded from within by spiritual and moral stagnation", and thus failed to block the swift Muslim advance.[1]

The second and most important factor was internal and intrinsic to the religion itself. It was the very structure of religious thought of Islam. The Koran promises that Islam will be victorious over all other religions (S.LXI.9), and that believers in Islam will inherit the world (S.XXIV.55). The Koran urges believers repeatedly to fight for God's cause or against those "who do not believe in God and the Last Day" (S.II.190–3; S.IV.74, 76, 84; S.IX.29). The Koran also promises the believer who fights in God's cause repeatedly that he will have "the highest rank in the sight of God" and will be greatly rewarded "whether he is slain or gets victory" (S.IX.20; S.IX.111; S.IV.74).

With such religious beliefs at the core of Islam, the urge for political power can be seen to be inbred in Islam. This, perhaps, is the key factor giving rise to the celebrated political genius of the religion of the Arabian desert. Early Muslims considered themselves to be the instruments of Allah for establishing His rule on earth through seizure of political power. Like modern communist ideology, Islam consciously and deliberately sought the assumption of political power.

While explaining Islam's expansion to India and Bengal in the thirteenth century two other factors should be mentioned. One is a variant of the so-called "sword theory" of the spread of Islam as expounded by some Western scholars. Islam came to India and Bengal by way of Muslim conquest. The Turanian *Völkerwanderung*, which began with the migration of the Kara Khitai hordes from the borders of Mongolia in a south-westerly direction in the second half of the twelfth century AD, caused dislodgement of nomadic tribes of the Trans-Oxus region. Two of these dislodged Turkoman tribes—the Ghuzz and the Khilijis—overran Khorasan, Seistan and Afghanistan. Joined by other Muslim adventurers from the conquered territories, these tribes continued their victorious march from east of the Indus until they reached the fertile and rich plains of Bengal.[2]

A distinction has to be made here between the expansion of the political

power of the Muslims and the establishment of Islam as the religion of the
conquered people. The nature of the preaching of Islam is obviously different
from that of Buddhism and Christianity, and the extent and geographical
distribution of the spread of Islam in India at least proves the partial validity
of the "sword theory". At the same time, however, the "sword theory" can
only be a partial explanation of an extremely complex process that has
resulted in the spread of Islam.

The political expansion of the Muslim power in India did not mean that
Islam spread in India primarily through violence. One can, of course, point to
some examples of the conversion of non-Muslims by official pressure or force
during the long period of Muslim rule, beginning with Muhammad Ghori's
conquest of Delhi in AD 1192–93, and ending with the British conquest of
Bengal in 1757. Muhammad Ghori's influence in converting the Ghakkars, a
barbarous people in the mountainous districts of Punjab; Firuz Shah Tughlaq's offer of exemption from *jiziah* (poll tax) to the converts; conversion of the
Rajas of Kharagpur by one of Akbar's generals, and Aurangzeb's proselytiz-
ing in the eastern districts of the Punjab, all provide instances where state
power was used to spread Islam. There were also deeds of violence and
outbursts of fanaticism during many of the Muslim invasions and triumphs.[3]

Delhi and Agra had been the major centres of Muslim power in India for
over 500 years. In modern times, the Muslims constituted barely one-tenth of
the population of Delhi and one-fourth of the population of Agra. These
figures of the Muslim populations of Delhi and Agra clearly indicate that the
spread of Islam in India and Bengal was not primarily effected by violence on
the part of the Muslim rulers of India.[4]. The more important factor in the
spread of Islam was the appeal of the religion itself as well as the work done
by the Muslim missionaries. As Arnold argues,

> ...whatever the truth there may be in the assertion that 'it is impossible even to
> approach the religious side of the Muhammedan position in India without surveying first
> its political aspect', we undoubtedly find that Islam has gained its greatest and most
> lasting missionary triumphs in times and places in which its political power has been
> weakened as in Southern India and Eastern Bengal.[5]

The growth of one of the largest Muslim concentrations in the world
(second only to Indonesia) in the Eastern Bengal areas (now constituting
Bangladesh) is a particularly striking phenomenon. How could a small pocket
develop with a high Muslim concentration while all surrounding areas
remained heavily populated by Hindus? Why did this phenomenon take place
in Bengal, a province bordering on the periphery of the successive Muslim
empires where the writ of those empires did not hold sway? How did Islam
spread so extensively and so quickly in East Bengal? To what extent did
Islam, as an ideology of the ruling political power and as a social force,
transform the economic and political life of medieval Bengal?

Controversies Concerning the Method of Spread of Islam in Bengal

The Census of 1872 was the first in modern India. It revealed large
concentrations of Muslims in the alluvial plains of Bengal. The Rajshahi,

Dacca and Chittagong divisions (now constituting Bangladesh) had respectively 56, 59.1 and 67.4 per cent Muslim population in 1872.[6] According to the 1881 Census, the Muslims of Bengal (of which the vast majority were in Northern and Eastern Bengal) constituted more than one-third of the total Muslim population of India.[7]

British administrative and census officers were quick to interpret the large-scale presence of Muslims of Northern and Eastern Bengal as the result of mass conversions of low-caste Hindus. As Beverley wrote,

> ...probably the real explanation of the immense preponderance of the Mussalman religious element in this portion of the delta is to be found in the conversion to Islam of the immense low castes (the Chandals and Rajbansis) which occupied it.[8]

Similarly, Risly, through an anthropological examination of 185 low-caste Muslims, concluded that the Bengali Muslims were converts from the Chandaos, Pods and Rajbansis.[9]

The conversion theory is stoutly opposed by some of the Muslim writers of whom Khondkar Fuzli Rubbee at the end of the nineteenth century was the leading spokesman. Rubbee claimed that the Muslim community of Bengal was formed mainly by aristocratic immigrants from all over the Muslim world who came to Bengal in successive waves during over five-and-a half centuries of Muslim rule there. He argued that the Muslim immigration to Bengal was larger than in any other part of India. Rubbee explained the immigration to Bengal in terms of Bengal's natural defences, its fertile soil, and the settlement in Bengal of the vast majority of 71 assorted Muslim governors, kings and nizams with most of their nobility, retinues, soldiers and administrators. Rubbee argued that it was the natural urge of Muslim foreign rulers to bring followers with them and to help settle in Bengal immigrants of similar culture after political disturbances in other parts of India and the Muslim countries further west.[10]

A more recent historian, Muhammad Abdur Rahim, also claims that a large portion of the Bengal Muslims were of immigrant origin. He has tried to identify the major waves of immigration to Bengal and the probable number of immigrants in each wave during the period 1220–1620. Assuming a 100 per cent increase in the Bengal Muslim population every 100 years—an assumption based on census figures which show a 50 per cent increase of Bengal Muslims during the forty years 1872–1911—Rahim comes out with statistics indicating that there were probably 10.6 million Muslims in Bengal in 1770, of which about 3.2 million (30 per cent) had foreign blood.[11]

The claims of Rubbee and Rahim, while interesting historically, can be put to rest by census figures. The very fact that only 1.52 per cent of the Muslims of Bengal and 1.2 per cent of the Muslims in the Eastern Bengal areas (Rajshahi, Dacca and Chittagong divisions) claimed foreign ancestry in the 1872 Census goes far to demolish the force of Rubbee's arguments and Rahim's far-fetched statistics.[12]

Thus the contention that mass conversion alone explains the presence of the large Muslim population in Bengal seems incontrovertible. But the question still remains: Why did this mass conversion take place? One line of

explanation could be in terms of the diffusion of the culture of the ruling elite. This line is particularly favoured by those scholars who believe that a sizeable percentage of converts came from the upper strata of the Hindus and Buddhists. It has been claimed, for example, that the culture of the elite occupying the commanding heights in politics, administration, the economy and defence gradually but inevitably percolated and ultimately saturated the educated, status and power-seeking upper crust of the conquered people. During the period of British rule, for example, upper-class Hindus and Muslims became Westernised or "Anglicised" so as to ensure for themselves jobs and other advantages from the British Raj.[13] In a similar fashion, it is argued, upper-class Hindus and Buddhists consciously emulated the culture of the Muslim elites during the earlier period. Since Christianity was not the dominant element of the British elite political culture, conversion to the rulers' religion was not an important part of a process of upward mobility for Bengalis during British rule. However, since Islam was a core element in the political culture of the Bengal Muslim rulers, it has been argued, status-seeking and job-seeking Hindus and Buddhists had to accept the Islamic religion in order to enter into the Muslim elite circles. Usually, the observations of the Portuguese merchant Barbosa, who visited Bengal in AD 1518, are quoted to strengthen this theory of the extension of Islam through political patronage.
Barbosa wrote:

> The King who is a Moor is a great lord and very rich; he possesses much country inhabited by the Gentiles (Hindus), of whom everyday many turn Moors (Muslims) to obtain the favour of the King and the Governors.[14]

While it is important to note the conversion of some important elites in Bengal to Islam, we shall argue below that the number of non-Muslims who could achieve high position was quite small and, barring only a few, non-Muslim office-holders did not generally change their religion. Thus the vast extension of the Muslim society in Bengal cannot be explained simply in terms of the diffusion of elite culture.

Social Tensions and Mass Conversions

Large-scale conversion in any society must reflect its "disharmony and anomalous condition". The explanation of mass conversion in Bengal thus has to be sought in the social structures of Bengal. A traditional society with rigid social structures legitimised by a sacred system of beliefs, can successfully resist the onslaught of even aggressive and fresh ideas. A society susceptible to a new set of ethical and spiritual values must necessarily be a society in turmoil. Both functionalist and Marxist sociologists agree that change and innovation are the results of social conflict.[15] Changes of values and religion are basically psychological processes and the receptive and innovative frame of mind is generally the result of prolonged and pervasive tension and conflict in the whole social order.[16] Thus it was only when Indian Hindu society experienced prolonged conflict among its various castes, par-

ticularly between Brahmins and Kshatriyas, that new religions like Buddhism and Jainism arose, securing the allegiance of large segments of Hindu
society. Having undergone a renaissance during the Gupta period, and after
having won a victory over Buddhism, its main rival in India, the Hindu
religion established its full and unreserved sway over Northern Indian society
by the end of the fifth century. Northern Indian society could, therefore,
withstand penetration by the conquering Muslims. In Bengal, however, the
situation was quite different. Research on ancient and medieval Bengal
provides convincing evidence for our main thesis in this chapter, i.e., that
tensions and conflicts had developed in Bengal society over centuries, creating a "unique syndrome of historical antecedents". These became all-
pervasive at the time of the Muslim conquest, predisposing the bulk of the
population to accept the new faith. The major factors providing empirical
support for this thesis are outlined in the remainder of this chapter.

Perhaps the most distinguishing feature of ancient Bengal was its non-
Aryan population and culture. Bengal was not a part of *Aryavarta*, the
eastward march of the Aryans having stopped near Bhagalpur in Bihar.[17] The
original inhabitants of Bengal had been primitive people now known as Kol,
Sabara, Polinda, Hadi, Dom, Chandala, and the like. Linguistic evidence
suggests that they belonged to the stock of Austric and Austro-Asiatic people
also known as *Nishadas*. They were later joined by Dravidian and Tibeto-
Burman linguistic groups. Lastly came the Alpine Aryans. They originated
from the deserts of Pamir and Taklamakan and were different from the Vedic
Aryans who were similar racially to the European Aryans. Most of the
upper-class Hindus of Bengal—Brahmans and Kayasthas—seem to be de-
scendants of these Alpine Aryans, whose numbers at the time of immigration
were not very large.[18]

Recent archaeological discoveries clearly indicate the growth of a comparatively advanced civilisation in parts of pre-Aryan Bengal. The Proto-
Bengali dialect and alphabet, preference for the goddesses representing
female energy (culminating in the worship of Durga as the national festival),
the growth of Tantrism, the peculiar laws of inheritance codified by Jumuta-
vahana (which were quite different from those in force in other parts of India)
are among those distinctive features of Bengal that were developed by
non-Aryans.[19]

Casual and intermittent contacts between the Aryans and the original
inhabitants of Bengal, which took place after the fourth century BC, served
primarily to widen the gap between the two cultures. The Aryans despised
the early settlers in Bengal for their alien culture and distinct physical
features.[20] The first serious contact between the two peoples took place during
the rule of the Maurya Emperors 324 BC to AD 187), when the Mauryas were
at the peak of their rule and had annexed all of Bengal west of the Brahmaputra. Systematic and large-scale settlement of non-Alpine Aryans took place
first during the reign of the Guptas (AD 320–496), when the Guptas
conquered North and West Bengal. The Guptas established Vedic Hinduism
as the state religion and brought about a renaissance of Hinduism all over
their empire. The Guptas brought into Bengal a large number of Brahmins

from *Aryavarta* and granted them land for settlement. They patronised the building of temples, the worship of Vedic deities, the performance of Vedic rituals, and cultivation of the Aryan language (Sanskrit). The Guptas also brought into Bengal a large number of Kayasthas to help run the administration.[21] In the declining period of the Guptas, Sasanka (probably AD 606 to 637) established an independent kingdom in Northern and North-western Bengal with its capital at Karna Subarna (in the present district of Murshidabad in West Bengal). Sasanka also patronised Brahminism as jealously as the Guptas.[22]

Buddhism, which seemed to have spread in Bengal some time before the reign of the great Maurya emperor Asoka (273–236 BC), was in its flourishing stage when the Aryan Brahmins and Kayasthas were colonising North and Western Bengal under the Guptas. Bengal thus became the final place in India for a long and drawn-out confrontation between Vedic Brahminism and Buddhism.

The Chinese traveller Fahien, who visited Bengal in the first decade of the fifth century AD, left an account of the prosperous state of Buddhism in Bengal. The accounts of subsequent Chinese travellers—Hsuan Tsang, Sheng-che and I-tsing—indicate some decline of Buddhism, at least in Temralipta (in West Bengal), but Buddhism continued to flourish in Samatata (South-east Bengal) where the Buddhist Khadaga dynasty ruled throughout the fifth, sixth and seventh centuries AD.[23] Perhaps it was the rule of the Guptas that took its toll on Buddhism in general. Because of the late Aryanisation of Bengal and the existence of an already developed non-Aryan culture, the Brahminising programmes of the Guptas and King Sasanka were not fully successful. Anarchical conditions that prevailed in Bengal for about one hundred years (AD 750–850, called the *matsyanyayam*) clearly indicated that no rigid hierarchical social structure on the pattern of Aryan North India had emerged in the aftermath of Gupta-Sasanka rule.

Anarchical conditions in Bengal were ended with the emergence of Gopal (AD 750–770) as a strong ruler and the establishment of the Pala dynasty, which with vicissitudes of fortune ruled North and West Bengal for over four centuries (AD 756–1161). The Palas gave a fresh lease of life to Buddhism after it had been badly mauled by Gupta-Sasanka rule, because the Pala kings openly professed Buddhism.[24] As in the Gupta period, south-east Bengal maintained its separate identity during the Pala era but most of the rulers of the Deva and Chandra dynasties who ruled South-east Bengal and were contemporaries of the Palas, like the Khadaga rulers during the Gupta period, were Buddhists. During the tenth century AD, the Kambojas seized power from the Palas in North and West Bengal as a consequence of internal upheavals. The Kambojas then limited the Pala authority to South Bihar until the end of the tenth century when the Palas reasserted themselves and regained their territory. Since the Kamboja rulers were also Buddhists, almost the whole of Bengal was ruled by Buddhists for the better part of four centuries. Because Brahmanism had already made itself felt strongly, at least over North and East Bengal during the Gupta period, the Pala kings had to extend royal support to it as a matter of political expedience if not as a matter of a catholic and tolerant religious policy.

The most influential Pala kings, Dharmapala, Devapala, and Mahipala I, were engaged almost exclusively during their reigns in extending their dynastic rule in North India. Because the Palas were dependent on the resources of the powerful Brahminical landed and official interests created by the Guptas for their foreign ventures, they had to court Brahminical power centres. The Brahmins were also important to the Palas for keeping the peace at home while extending the frontier of their domain westward. It was no wonder that the ministers, officials, and court poets of the Pala kings were primarily Hindus, or that many of the Pala kings married into aristocratic Brahmin families.[25] Brahminical influence in the Pala court became so overwhelming that the latter-day Pala kings (from the second half of the eleventh century AD) became disposed more towards Hinduism than to Buddhism.[26]

As Barrie M. Morrison has discovered from an analysis of the donations recorded in the Bengal epigraphs (from the fifth century AD through the thirteenth century), most of the donations were made to Brahmins and Brahminical establishments.[27] Thus the Pala kings not only maintained the Brahmin-dominated *Samanta* (feudal) system developed by the Guptas, but also increased Brahminical ascendancy through the creation of additional feudal rulers from among the Brahmin caste.

The Pala kings did patronise their own religion (Buddhism) as well, but such patronage was limited to the fields of religion and education and did not result in the creation of dominant social classes among the Buddhists. Some of the most prominent examples of support for Buddhism by the Pala kings include the establishment by Gopal of a *Vihara* (monastery) at Nalanda, the famous Odantapuri *Vihara*. Gopal also established numerous schools for the spread of Buddhist education. Dharmapala (AD 770–810) renovated the decaying Nalanda *Vihara* and established a new *Vihara* at Vikramsila which, with 114 teachers in different subjects, became one of the most influential Buddhist education centres in India from the ninth century to the twelfth century AD. Dharmapala established a second *Vihara* at Somapura (now Paharpur in North Bangladesh) which was probably the largest *Vihara* in all of India. According to Taranatha, Dharmapala established a large number of Buddhist schools and patronised the famous Buddhist scholar Haribhadra.[28]

Dharmapala's son and successor, Devapala, was famous for his extensive patronage of Buddhist religion. He continued his predecessors' tradition of looking after the Nalanda and other *Viharas*. At the request of Balaputradeva, the Sailendra King of Java and Sumatra, Devapala helped to build an additional *Vihara* at Nalanda and donated five villages for its maintenance.[29] The third greatest Pala king, Mahipala I, as the Sarnath copper plates bear evidence, built a large number of Buddhist establishments, including two temples at Bodh-Gaya. He also renovated many Buddhist institutions, including Nalanda and Somapura. Mahipala's extensive public welfare services, particularly the digging of large ponds for drinking water and the establishment of new towns, made his name (as folk songs still extant in North Bangladesh indicate) a household word.[30]

All of these general pro-Buddhist and public service works of the great Pala kings no doubt increased the appeal of Buddhism among the general people. But their particular cultivation of the Hindu feudal class had more crucial consequences for the stability and the very existence of the Pala dynasty. Whenever a Pala king proved inadequate and ineffective, the feudal rulers would declare themselves independent and conspire to dethrone the king. *Ramacharita* (Life of Rama), an epic written by Sandhyakara Nandi, son of a highly placed officer of the Pala court and the major literary source of ancient Bengal, gives a detailed and vivid account of how the weaker Pala kings were at the mercy of the feudal rulers.[31] Ultimately one of the feudal rulers, Vijayasena, established a new dynasty in Bengal by defeating the last Pala king of North and North-western Bengal. One of the legacies of the Palas was, no doubt, popular Buddhism, approximating, as Trevor Ling suggests, "closely to the popular culture of Bengal".[32] The other legacy of the Palas was a powerful social base for Brahminism, the arch-rival of Buddhism, in the shape of the Hindu-dominated feudal class. The Palas were dethroned in Bengal by Vijaysena, the scion of a deeply religious Brahma-Kshatriya Carnatic family, who first created his power base in the area of the family's settlement—*Radha* (West Bengal), the *Aryavarta* of Bengal. Vijaysena first drove the Palas from North Bengal, silenced other pretentious *Samantas*, and then conquered South-east Bengal. This brought almost the whole of Bengal under common rule for the first time in history. This common rule lasted for half a century and ended with the defeat of Lakshmanasena by Bakhtyar Khilji in AD 1204, after which Lakshmanasena moved to South-east Bengal.

The Senas seem to have surpassed the Guptas in their zeal for Brahmin-ising Bengali society. Halayudha, the all-India famed Brahmanic scholar, prime minister and head of the religious department under Lakshmanasena, in his work *Brahmana-Sarvasya* (The Entire Brahmana), clearly articulated the mood and philosophy of the Sena ruling class—the spirit of the Upanishads. The Senas and their nobility doubted the purity of the Brahmins of the *Radha* and *Varendra* (North Bengal) areas, not to speak of those of East Bengal. Thus began possibly the largest ever programme of immigration of Aryan Brah-mins into Bengal. The copper plates of the Sena period show that countless Vedic Brahmins, even from such faraway places as the Deccan, Madhyadesh and Lata (Gujarat), were brought in to settle in Bengal. These Vedantic Brahmins produced the first work on *Smriti* (Law) and *Bayabahara Sastras* (Jurisprudence). Under state patronage, Vedic ablutions, great sacrificial rites and religious festivals were performed with a kind of pomp and grandeur that had never before been seen in Bengal.[33]

The Senas did not fail to strengthen the social base already created for continued Brahminical ascendancy in Bengal society. We have already seen that a landed aristocracy of the Brahmins was first created by the Guptas, and that the Palas for reasons of political expediency, further expanded this class. The Senas continued expansion of the Brahminical aristocracy as a matter of state policy. According to Niharranjan Ray, the greatest historian of ancient Bengal, countless numbers of Brahmins received large land grants from members of the Sena royal family and from their high officials.[34] These Brahmins were settled all over the Sena kingdom. South-east Bengal, which had so far managed to ward off formal Aryan penetration, now came under the full impact of the Brahminising programme of the zealous Senas.[35]

In conformity with the policy of Brahminisation, the Senas transformed their court into a formidable platform of Sanskrit, the language of the Vedas. Vallalasena himself authored the work *Dana-Sagara* (Sea of Gift), and left another, *Adbhuta-Sagara* (Sea of Peculiarities), half done. Lakshmanasena, also a scholar of stature, completed the *Adbhuta-Sagara*. A large number of Sanskrit poets—Dhoyi, Sarana, Jaya Deva, Govardhana, Umapatidhara to name a few—adorned the Sena court. Sanskrit and Vedic scholars like Bhavadeva, Misra, Aniruddha, Purushottama, Pasupati and Isana as well as the great Halyudha were other luminaries of the Sena court.[36] Indeed, it can be argued that the Bengali language, inchoate at the time, would have had a premature death had Sena rule continued for a longer period.

One social consequence of Brahminist expansion under the Senas was the acute polarisation of Hindu society. The caste structure in Bengal Hindu society had not developed on the Rigvedic pattern, possibly because the Bengali Aryans were Alpine, different from those of the Rigvedas. Two of the four Vedic castes—the Kshatriyas and Vaisyas—seem to have been virtually absent in ancient Bengal. Bengali Hindus did not appear to care for the *Smriti* regulations framed in the Deccan and North India, with the result that during the Pala period there was considerable flexibility in the caste system. For example, the Pala plates show only the Brahmins as a group and do not name other allottees of land by caste. But the *Smriti* regulations formed under the Senas provided for rigid, inflexible and specific caste regulations which are extant among the Bengali Hindus even today. Under the Senas, the functions of the Kshatriyas were usurped by Brahmins. In addition to their own caste and religious functions, the Brahmins monopolised positions in the royal court, army and administration—positions traditionally held by Kshatriyas in Aryan North India. As we have already mentioned, the Brahmins dominated the landed class. The only other caste to share positions in the court and administration was the immigrant *Karana Kayasthas* who specialised in fields like land surveys, land revenue administration, accounting and correspondence. Literary works of the Sena period, including the *Vallalacharita* (Life of Vallalasena) indicated that the Senas were very disdainful of the *Vaisyas* and the latter were counted by the Senas among the traditional lower-caste Hindus. The Sena policy of exclusive expansion and development of Brahminic landed class and state officials, at the expense of both the merchants and the peasantry, depressed the latter two classes and alienated them both from the Brahmins. Thus during the Sena period the duality between the Brahmins (and some *Karana Kayasthas*) and non-Brahmins, coincided with the division between the haves and have-nots.[37]

Sena policies eventually drove the Buddhists into positions occupied by non-Brahmin lower caste Hindus and made the vertical polarisation in the whole society complete. Partly for reasons of political expediency and partly

because of the basic "humanist character of ancient Bengal", the Bengali
Palas followed the policy of equal opportunity and equal share of state
patronage to all religions. The non-Bengali Senas, upholding Brahminism
and having immigrated from the conservative and orthodox Deccan, could
hardly follow the liberalism of the indigenous Palas. The Senas did not try to
hide their contempt for Buddhism. Vallalasena himself expressed his disdain
for the Buddhists in his work *Dana-Sagara*. It became customary on the part of
the Sena ruling class to refer to the Buddhists as *Pashandas* (inveterate
sinners).

We have seen that the liberal policy of the Palas had initially weakened
the upper-class bases of Buddhism. The withdrawal of all patronage by the
Senas from Buddhism threatened its very existence. Statues of Buddha were
hardly visible during the Sena period. The number of *Viharas*, Buddhist
Schools and *Acharyas* fell drastically.[38] The Buddhists had at least one strong
social base in Bengal at the end of Pala rule, i.e., the Buddhist merchant class
in South-east Bengal that flourished from the eighth to the thirteenth centuries, following the loss of commercial viability of the urban centres of North
and North-west Bengal, but Sena hostility towards the business community
and the shift to an agrarian economy on which thrived the official and
Brahmin classes, all of this led to the decay of the Buddhist trading and
commercial community.[39]

In the face of an "all-embracing and all-consuming" Brahmanist expansion, to use the words of Niharranjan Ray, the Buddhists under the Senas
developed a severe sense of identity crisis and turned inwards. Buddhist
self-searching led to the growth of a number of new cults, like *Vajrayana*,
Shahajayana, *Kalachakrayana Natha*, and *Avadhuta*, of which *Shahajayana* seems to
have been the most popular. Because of their emphasis on flesh, body and sex
as a means of spiritual exercise these new cults were generally viewed as a
degeneration of Buddhism. But one could hardly find anywhere in the world
during that age a greater manifestation of rationality and humanism than in
the mystic songs and verses composed mostly by the Shahajayana *Siddhacha-
rayas* (Buddhist religious teachers), and collected in *Dohakosa* and
Charyapadas.[40] A few statements from the *Dohakosa* of Saroyovajra indicate this
rationality and humanism as follows: (a) Whether the sacrificial fires bring
out salvation, no one knows, but the smoke produced by them certainly
troubles the eyes; (b) They say that Brahmanas were originally born from the
mouth of the Brahma, but what then? Now they are born exactly as a man of
any other caste. Then wherein lies the superiority of Brahmana?; (c) If you
argue that Brahmana became superior by virtue of the *Samskaras* (rites and
ceremonies), I would say, let the *Chandalas* have those *Samskaras* and become
Brahmana. If that knowledge of the Veda makes one a Brahmin, let the
Chandalas read the Veda.[41] In all of the above and throughout the Dohakosa,
Saroyovajra expresses his deep sense of humanism, equalitarianism and
anti-casteism.

One of the great difficulties in reading the earliest Bengali writings
results from the imperfectly developed words and phrases used by the
so-called "mystics", who were primarily responsible for the early establish-

ment of Bengali as a language. For example, Dhandhana states the following in Charya No. 33 in *Charyapadas*: (a) My house is in the town, I have no neighbour, I have no rice in the pot, I serve always; (b) He who is wise is surely foolish. He who is a thief is surely an honest man; (c) Day by day the jackal fights the lion. Few understand the song of Dhandhania.[42]

Experts on Bengali linguistics interpret the above statements of Dhandhana in the following way: the first statement depicts the absolute helplessness of poverty-stricken womenfolk at the time. They did not have even daily food, and their abject poverty was taken advantage of by wealthy libertines who came to make love to them. The second quotation indicates the absence of any sense of justice in society, which rewarded the wicked rather than honest people. The third quotation refers to the oppressions carried out by the Hindu kings on Buddhists, which forced many of the latter to flee to Nepal and Tibet. The king became so tyrannical, the Buddhist poet said, that even his smallest subject had to fight hard battles against the king for sheer survival, just as a small jackal had to fight the tyrannies of the lion for his existence.[43]

Other early Bengali literature reflects the strong antipathy of the people towards Brahmins. Ramai Pandit, a Buddhist poet, found Brahminical oppression going strong even as late as the fourteenth century AD. He wrote in his famous poem, *Niranjaner Rushma* (The Wrath of Niranjana),

> There are sixteen hundred families of the Brahmins in Jaipur. They go to different places demanding *dakshina* (perquisites); where they do not get any, they pronounce their curse and thus burn the world. At Malda they levy a regular tax upon all without distinction. There is no end of their knavery. They have grown very strong; ten to twenty come together and destroy the worshippers of *Dharma*. They pronounce the *Vedas*; fire issues forth incessantly, everyone trembles before them. Being aggrieved at heart, people say, 'O *Dharma*! Protect us. Who is there other than yourself to rescue us?' Thus do the Brahmins destroy creation. This is the worst form of injustice.[44]

The celebrated poet Chandidas, who belonged to the Shahajayana cult, expressed the spirit of Bengal at the cross-roads of Brahminical dominance and Muslim expansion when he wrote: "Listen, brother man, man is truth above all; there is no truth above man".[45]

The period at the end of Sena rule proved to be a great watershed in the history of ancient Bengal. Centuries-old attempts at penetration of Bengal by Aryan culture and religion clashed fiercely with the resistance to such penetration by the indigenous Bengalis. Aryan Brahminism, with its alien religious forms and inequitable social prescriptions, seemed to be making desperate attempts to establish its sway all over Bengal. The Bengalis, and especially those in East Bengal who were Buddhists, resisted assimilation to Aryanism and, as we have seen, developed, in protest at Aryan expansion, a sublime form of humanism and egalitarianism. The Bengali Hindus also asserted their identity *vis-a-vis* the Aryans by developing and worshipping a host of goddesses, in contrast to the male gods of the Aryans, as sources of energy and power.[46]

The coincidence of religious and racial cleavages, reinforced by the economic class distinctions and landed base of Aryan expansionism, helped spread conflict throughout Bengal society, creating extreme tension, anxiety and suppressed anger on the part of the depressed majority. As Niharranjan Ray argues, Bengal society at the end of the Sena period had developed all its full potential for great and deep revolutionary change.[47]

The traditional peasant economy could not produce the social and economic leadership required to rival the landed aristocracy, but accumulated feelings of discontent had no outlet but to explode. This created the threshold for what Max Weber calls a "prophetic break". The revolution that occurred in Bengal was not a social one. It was ideological and religious. The non-Brahmin, non-Aryans rediscovered their identity through their mass conversion to Islam, which was fully compatible with their egalitarian and humanist yearnings.[48]

This climacteric confrontation between Aryanism and non-Aryanism had a geographical dimension. Historians are in agreement that it was *Radha* (West Bengal) where Aryan colonisation had been early and deep enough to strike some roots. Thus West Bengal continues to have a majority Hindu population. In contrast, Aryan penetration to the areas north and east of the Ganges was thin, but was sufficiently visible that it roused the deepest fears among indigenous people about being swamped by "Aryans and half-caste Aryans". It is little wonder that mass conversion of Buddhists to Islam took place mostly in Northern and Eastern Bengal.[49]

The Role of the Sufis: Charisma and Adaptation

As Max Weber has suggested in his celebrated three-fold typology of authority (traditional, charismatic and legal-rational), in times of change and stress it is charismatic leadership above all others that can play the most effective role.[50] The psychic, economic, religious and racial stress generated by Sena rule in Bengal helped create the ground where charismatic authority could have absolute sway. As the indigenous leadership failed to throw up such authority, opportunity was created for an immigrant group to provide the leadership demanded by the times. Thus began the story of the Sufis (Muslims mystic saints) who effected the most indelible change in Bengali history by creating a new Muslim society in this part of the subcontinent.

Legends have it that a few eminent Sufis from places like Mecca, Balkh, Yaman, Bistam, Ghazni and Delhi came to Bengal even before the conquest of North-west Bengal by Bakhtyar Khalji. Historically speaking, it was after the Muslim conquest that a large number of Sufis, originating from Arabia, Mesopotamia, Persia, Samarqand, Bukhara and Northern India, flocked to and settled in Bengal to preach Islam. The phenomenal proselytising success of pioneer Sufis of the thirteenth century encouraged a larger influx into Bengal of saintly preachers from the West and Central Asian heartland of Islam in the fourteenth century, the peak period of immigration by the Sufis. This movement of Sufi mystics to Bengal continued uninterrupted up to the seventeenth century. Even a casual observer cannot fail to notice today the *Dargahs* (mausolea of the saints where devotees come to pay respect to their spiritual guides and offer votive prayers) in every nook and corner of Bangladesh. One scholar has actually listed the names of 408 Sufis who preached Islam in Bangladesh from the thirteenth century through the nineteenth century.[51] But most scholars agree that the actual number is much larger.

The most distinctive aspect of the Sufis was their charismatic appeal. Max Weber, in elaborating his concept of charismatic authority, writes:

> . . .the term 'charisma' shall be understood to refer to an *extraordinary* quality of a person, regardless of whether this quality is actual, alleged, or presumed. 'Charismatic authority', hence, shall refer to rule over men, whether predominantly external or predominantly internal, to which the governed submit because of their belief in the extraordinary quality of the specific person. . . . The legitimacy of charismatic rule thus rests upon the belief in magical powers, revelations and hero worship. The source of these beliefs is the 'proving' of the charismatic quality through miracles, through victories and other successes, that is, through the welfare of the governed.[52]

We can understand the type of authority that the Sufis of Bengal exercised by examining some typical legends widely prevalent among the general mass about the Sufis. A few legends are given below:

1. Shah Sultan Balkhi, whose *mazar* (tomb) is in Mahasthana in Bogra district, reached Sandvipa (in the Bay of Bengal) after having crossed the sea riding on a huge fish. . . . Having reached Mahasthana, he appealed to Raja Parasuram, the local king, for a piece of ground measuring only a cubit and a quarter outside the palace, so that he might spread his small prayer-carpet over it . . . to the utter amazement of all, when the saint spread his prayer-carpet, it began gradually to expand and cover the whole place around the palace.[53]

2. The powerful Koch King in Mymensingh district sent for Shah Muhammad Sultan Rumi, who settled in the king's territory to test miraculous powers attributed to the saint. As the saint arrived, the king ordered deadly poison to be administered to him. He quaffed the whole glass of poison, reciting the formula of "Bismillah" (lit., in the name of Allah I begin). To the bewilderment of the king and courtiers, the poison had no effect on the saint. All present there, including the king, then voluntarily accepted Islam. The king also donated the whole village in which the saint settled to maintain his *khanqah* (mystic convent).[54]

3. One day, while some fishermen were fishing in the river Padma (Ganges), they noticed a strange phenomenon: an unusually tall man, wearing a turban and an "alkhella" (a loose garment), was crossing the river on foot . . . the fishermen hurriedly reached the bank. As the strange man came near the fishermen, the latter respectfully offered him some food. He sat down on the ground, took off his turban, and covered the food with it. He then raised his hands in a praying mood, muttered something for a few minutes, and removed the turban from the dishes. Lo! the meagre food turned into fishes and the earthen dishes had become gold. Such was the *kiramat* (miraculous power) of Shah Makhdum. People who visit the tomb of this saint in Rajshahi, always find their wishes fulfilled.[55]

4. When Makhadum Shaykh Jalalud-Din Tabrizi reached Bengal, he sat

down by the side of a stream to rest, but suddenly rose and performed his ablutions. In explanation he said to those around him that he was saying prayers for the Shaykhu-'l-Islam who had just died, and subsequently this turned out to be a fact. . . . He purchased some land. There had been a few ancient temples in that place. He demolished them by his miracles and erected a mosque in that very place and all worshippers in the temples were converted to Islam.[56]

5. Makhdum Shah Zahiruddin had the miraculous power to cure every disease.[57]

Revelation and the sword are the two typical charismatic powers. Some Sufis, dubbed "warrior-saints", wielded both. This combination of "the oracles of the prophet and the edicts of the warlord" brought large areas and large segments of the population of Bengal under the sway of Islam. There are a number of historical examples of the exploits of the warrior Sufis. One was Khan Jahan, who conquered Khulna-Jessore and colonised the Sundarban areas during the reign of Nasir at-Din Mahmud Shah (AD 1442–1459). One of Khan Jahan's famous converts was a Brahmin who took the name of Pir Ali Mohammad Taher. The relatives of Pir Ali were ostracised by the Hindu community because of Pir Ali's conversion to Islam. From that time onwards the relatives of Hindus converted to Islam were called Pir Ali Hindus.[58] Khan Jahan also left behind a number of *dighis* (large and deep ponds), towns and mosques, including the 60-dome mosque at Bagerhat which is perhaps still the largest mosque in Bangladesh.

A second warrior Sufi was Shah Ismail Ghazi, who commanded the army of Sultan Barbak Shah (AD 1459–1474) in conquering Kamrupa.[59] According to legend, Shah Sultan Balkhi fought and killed a Kali worshipper, King Balarama, at Hariram Nagar, while the king's minister accepted Islam. Balkhi also fought against King Parasurama and his sister, Sila Devi. The king was killed and Sila Devi committed suicide.[60] Baba Adam Shahid and Makhdum Shah Dawlah Shahid fought against the local Hindu kings of Rampal and Shahzadpur respectively, thus achieving martyrdom.[61]

The latter-day Sufis were fortunate in being able to count on Muslim governors, sultans and even emperors of Delhi in facing militant and oppressive Hindu chieftains and local kings. The reverence and respect afforded by Muslim sultans to the Sufis can be gauged from Shamsu-d-Din Ilyas Shah's veneration for Shaikh Raja Biyabani. When Ilyas Shah was staying at Ekdala fort, besieged by Emperor Firuz Shah Tughlaq, he heard about the death of Shaikh Raja Biyabani. Ilyas Shah risked his life and kingdom to come out of the fort in disguise, in order that he might participate in the last rites of Biyabani. The veneration of most sultans for Sufis was similar. They did not hesitate to send troops to uphold the prestige and influence of their *gurus*, the Sufis.[62]

Sultan Husain Shah (AD 1493–1519) sent a large body of troops to defeat and kill Mahes Raja of Hematabad at the request of Pir Badhru-d-Din.[63] Again, in the first half of the thirteenth century, Mahmud Shah Ghaznawi was being harassed by Raja Bikramakesari of Mangalkot in Burdwan, so he sent a message appealing for help from the Emperor of Delhi.

The emperor did not delay in sending a large army, under the command of a warrior-saint, with sixteen other Sufis accompanying the army. The warrior *darvishes* (saints) were responsible for freeing Mangalkot from the Hindu grip.[64] Troops sent by the the Emperor of Delhi, Jalaluddin Firoz Shah Khalji, to punish the Hindu King of Chota Pandua in Hughly (between AD 1290 and 1295), at the instance of Shah Safiu-d-Din Shahid,[65] and the successive despatch of two contingents of the army by Samsu-d-Din Firoz Shah, Sultan of Gaur (AD 1302–1322), to help Shah Jalal and his 300-strong dervish army in their fight against Raja Gour Govinda of Sylhet, are two examples of state power propping up the spiritual power of the Sufis.[66] Armed support, plus the lavish patronage by the Muslim rulers for the Sufis (including the building of *khanqahs* (mystic convents), erection of mausolea, large endowments of lands for *khanqahs*, tombs and the like) created the impression that the temporal powers at the time were at the beck and call of the Sufis. Thus the extraordinary powers of the Sufis were authenticated and the appeal of the Sufis among common men increased in phenomenal ways.

There seems to have been a degree of design on the part of the Sufis to increase their mass appeal. The Sufis usually established their *khanqahs* in places that had long been sacred to Hindu and Buddhist rites. Thus the *dargah* of Shah Sultan Balkhi at Mahasthana was on the top of a Hindu temple while Muslim relics were found at the famous monastery at Paharpura. Both the *dargah* of Bayazid Bistami at Chittagong and the *khanqah* of Shah Jalal at Sylhet are located on ancient sacred mounds. Medieval Bengali literature often refers to disputes between Hindu *sadhus* (hermits) and Sufis, the discomfiture of the *sadhus*, and the conversion of *sadhus* to Islam. In this atmosphere it is only logical that the victorious Sufis would have taken over the hermitages and clientele of both Hindus and Buddhists in many instances.[67]

The transformation of Hindu and Buddhist religious sites into *khanqahs* and *dargahs* was not the only kind of adaptation wrought by the Sufis. The more important adaptation was carried out within Islam itself.[68] One fundamental difference between the Semitic and Aryan religions is that while the Semitic religions emphasise ethical aspects the mystical aspects predominate in Aryan religions. The original Sufis from Arabia and Mesopotamia, like al-Hasan of Basra (AD 643–728), developed Sufism as a form of austerity and asceticism to discipline the soul. As Sufism reached the Aryan lands— Persia, Bukhara, Samarkhand, Afghanistan and India—it became enmeshed in metaphysical conceptions developed among Hindus, Buddhists and Jaina religions. The Sufis discovered two meanings of the Koran—one manifest and the other esoteric or hidden. They later adhered to the esoteric knowledge of the Koran called *marifat*. The Sufi creeds that developed in Persia and Central Asia, which came to Bengal via Northern India, were vastly different from the dogmatic creeds of Islam, but suitable to the Bengal environment.

While orthodox Islam stands for one, and absolutely one God only, being transcendent and all-powerful over everything, the Indian Sufis, on the other hand, preached the immanent unity of God. They conceived of God manifesting himself throughout the universe in manifold ways. The Sufis of India preached the unity of God in the plurality of phenomena. The Indian Sufi conception of *tawhid* was thus different from that of pristine Islam, but it was compatible with local pantheistic and animist beliefs.

Similarly, the Indian Sufi doctrine of soul was vastly different from that of orthodox Islam. According to the Koran, the soul is created by God (S.XVII.85). It is subject to punishment. It will ultimately return to God and will not merge with Him. The Indian Sufis held that the human soul was a part of the Divine soul, and that a man's soul could be united with the Divine soul if he developed his soul to its utmost. The stage of the union of the human soul with the Divine soul is called *fana* (absorption of the individual self into the divine). The concept of *fana* or *baqa* is compatible with Buddhist and Hindu mystic concepts—*nirvana* and *mukti* respectively.

The Indian Sufi doctrine of infusion of divine spirit into the body of man, transforming him into a god and inspiring him to declare "ana-l-haqq" or "I am the real", is a blasphemy in orthodox Islam, but quite consistent with the theory of *avatar* (incarnation of God in the form of man)—a popular doctrine of Hinduism. To many Hindus in Bengal, the Sufis were, no doubt, the *avatars*.

From the Koranic verse, "We are nearer to him (man) than his jugular vein", (S.L.16), the Indian Sufis came to the conclusion that God was within the body and He pervades it. The body is "more than a thousand *Ka'bas*. Ka'ba [The centre of the great mosque at Mecca and the main object of pilgrimage by the Muslims] is only a cottage of Abraham. But heart is the very home of God". How close is this doctrine to the Sahajaya assertion: "The Pandit explains the *sastras* (scripture) but does not know that Buddha resides in the body. There is no place of greater pilgrimage than the body".

The central doctrine of Sufism in general and Sufism in India in particular, was, of course, love. The Sufis consider love as the cause of creation and as the only relation between man and God. The Koran mentions 99 attributes of God. But Sufism divested God of his sterner qualities. For the Sufis God was shorn of all kinds of grandeur, majesty and pomp—those things that had kept Him away from man. The Sufi God could be approached only with a loving heart, and God would similarly reciprocate. This feminine conception of God is, again, fully compatible with the goddesses of Hindu Bengal and with feminine divine symbol of love (Sahajaya) of latter-day Buddhists.

In addition to Sufi doctrines, Sufi practices were also adapted to the environment of Bengal. According to the Sufis, a man had to acquire the esoteric doctrines of Sufism and techniques of the unknown journey (*tariqa*) towards union with God only under a spiritual guide, a *murshid* or *pir* or *shaykh*. The *salik* (traveller) who placed himself under the guidance of a *pir* was known as a *murid* (disciple). The *pir-murid* relationship virtually repudiated the intercessionary role of Prophet Muhammad and was more akin to the "Guru-Chela" relationship among Bengali Hindus and Buddhists. The Sufi processes like *dhikr* (repetition of God's name in a technical manner), use of *tasbih* (rosaries), mechanical processes like the controlling of breath, and *latifahs* (centres of light in the human body), mystic meditation, and the like, were based on Hindu *Yoga* theory. The *maqamat*, or stages leading to the union of God, had close parallels to the Buddhist *Yoga* system. The Sufi stages of *malkut* entering the spiritual world), *jabrut* (realising the attributes and essence of God), and *lahut* (union with God), are similar to the three stages of Buddhist sainthood: (i) Satapannabhava, the stage in which one is put on the right current; (ii) Sakadagamibhava, or stage when one has only one more birth to undergo, and (iii) Arhat, when one attains *nirvana*. Lastly the Sufi practice of *kashful-i-qubur*, the psychic power to receive revelation from the dead buried in graves, was borrowed from the Hindu Tantrik exercises through the medium of a corpse known as *sava sadhana*. The Sufis claimed that while orthodox Islam provided only the ordinary form of spiritual attainment, Sufism helped man to achieve the highest stage of spiritual development. Whether Sufism was a higher form of Islam or simply degeneration of it will continue to be debated. It is, however, certain that one factor that considerably helped Islam to spread rapidly and extensively in Bengal was that it took the form of Sufism. Islam, in Sufi garb, was intelligible and psychologically acceptable to the people of Bengal—people who had been steeped in mysticism, animistic beliefs and Tantric practices.[69]

Thus the conversion of the people of Bengal to Islam was not conversion to the pure, pristine Islam. Bengali Muslims retained some of their pre-Islamic beliefs and practices. The Sufi form of Bengal Islam made it easier for the Bengali Muslims to retain those practices.

Changing Social Bases of Islam in Medieval Bengal

If Bengal Muslim society was ushered in by the charisma and design of the Sufis (with the shadow of the sceptre always behind them), it was consolidated through the institutionalisation of Islam and the building up of strong and stable social bases for the Muslim community. Of course, the *khanqahs* and *dargahs* of the Sufis turned into great institutions and have survived to the present as the meeting grounds for Muslims of all classes and occupations in hours of crisis as well as celebrations. But the important institutions of Bengal Islam resulted from the creation of the very dynamics of a socialisation process enjoined by Islam itself. The centre of the group life for Muslims was the prayer place. Whenever a group of families and workers in a common profession clustered together permanently, the prayer place became a prayer house. If the prosperity of the community increased, the prayer house turned into a mosque, on permanently endowed land. Surrounding the mosque there developed a complex of educational institutions—such as maktabs, madrassas and high madrassas (colleges) for imparting religious and other types of education to Muslim children and adults. The Muslim rulers performed their religious obligation to establish the rule of the *Shariah* by setting up an *Adalat*, or Court of the *Qadi*, in the area for strict enforcement of Islamic regulation.[70] The Muslim rulers of Bengal helped immensely in the process of Muslim community-building by establishing innumerable mosques and madrassas all over the country and by permanently endowing lands for their maintenance. These mosque-madrassa complexes have provided the

nerve centres of Bengali Muslim society and culture.[71] Many of the mosques
built by the Muslim rulers are still extant, and some of them (like the Adina
Mosque at Pandua and Khan Jahan's Mosque at Bagerhat) are among the
largest and most splendid mosques of the subcontinent.[72]

While building of the mosque-madrassa complexes by Muslim rulers
strengthened the process of Islamic socialisation in Bengal, Islam needed a
strong social and economic base if it were to strike roots permanently in
Bengal society. Any religious community dependent upon another rival
religious group for both economic and status considerations could not sustain
its original purity and virility for long. Even if there was perfect religious
toleration through cumulative penetration of influence, as with Hinduism/
Buddhishm, the religion of the dominant community would debilitate that of
the non-dominant community. The possibility of this decay of Islam in
Bengal was all the greater because of the peasant character of Bengal society.

As Max Weber has pointed out, peasants are not usually the carriers of
an "ethical and rational religion". Peasants usually develop a "magical frame
of reference". Dependent absolutely on nature and engaged in struggles for
immediate survival, peasants believe in sorcery, directed against the spirits
who control natural forces, or they simply want to buy divine benevolence.
Peasants do not usually feel the "need for salvation" or "an ethical rational
religion".[73] Given the innate irrational religious behaviour of peasants, an
ethical rational religion like Islam could not maintain its original character
for long if the "natural" leadership of Bengali peasant society remained in the
hands of Hindus who had already incorporated most of the sorcerous practices, animist beliefs and methods of propitiation of local gods controlling
nature (Laksmi, Manasa, Sitala, Ola Bibi, Sasthi, and the like) into their own
religion.

Like any other medieval society in the East, the natural leaders of
Bengali peasant society were those who owned or controlled land. It is true
that a European-type feudal system did not develop in Bengal or India.[74]
Juridically, the supreme ruler, the king, or the emperor, owned all the land.
The class generically known as *zamindars* acted only as revenue farmers.[75]
While the *zamindars* did not have legal ownership of land, they had more
control over the fate of the peasants than the feudal lords of the West because,
unlike the latter, the former had no legally or conventionally prescribed
obligations toward peasants. The *zamindars*, or their equivalent functionaries,
held tenants in Bengal at their beck and call. The absence of elaborate and
prescribed procedures for eviction, or for redress of complaints, particularly
when coupled with an overwhelming pressure on the *zamindar* to pay rent to
the government, led the *zamindars* to be highly capricious and unpredictable
with their tenants. Having a primitive but highly repressive revenue collection machinery, and with little penetration of the formal government into the
countryside, the *zamindars* were the real government for the tenants. The
zamindars were seen as a direct and effective evil spirit that the peasants had to
gratify. One way of propitiating the *zamindar* was to emulate him in social
behaviour which, given the traditional nature of the society, meant religious
observances. Thus the *zamindar* class became the crucial social base for the

ascendance of the two basically antithetical religions of medieval Bengal—Islam and Hinduism. If either of these two religions failed to dominate the strategic social summit occupied by the *zamindars*, that religion could not but be affected and overwhelmed by the other.

As we have already shown, a Brahmanical samanta (feudal) class steadily arose in Bengal, beginning in the Gupta and Sena periods. For practical administrative reasons—constraints of personnel and expertise, the unknown nature of the land and its people, and the like—the early Muslim governors of Bengal allowed Hindu *samantas* to govern their territories as tributaries. However, with the passage of time, increasing portions of land came under Muslim revenue farmers. First, officers of the state were given *jagirs* (fiefdoms) as emoluments and the officers themselves arranged collection of revenues for their *jagirs*. Since the state officers at the upper levels during early Muslim rule (AD 1201–1338) were almost all from the conquering race, the *jagirs* became the exclusive preserve of Muslims during that period. Most probably, some of these *jagirs* became hereditary. Moreover, patronage considerations must have led some governors to create a few *zamindaris* (hereditary rights for revenue farming) for Muslim noblemen. Thus we find the mention of some Muslim *zamindaris* existing at the time of Chaitanya Deva (AD 1484–1533) in the Chaitanya Kavyas (poetical literature) and in the Vaishnava Kavyas.[76]

Sher Shah, the Emperor of Delhi (AD 1540–1545), drastically altered the administrative structure of Bengal in 1541, and initiated the process of growth of a powerful Afghan landed aristocracy there. To pre-empt any attempt at rebellion, which had become "second nature" with all the imperial governors of this most intractable part of India, Sher Shah divided Bengal into a number of fiefs (*jagirs*) under his favourites and vested the general superintendance of the province in a Muslim doctor of law, Qazi Fazilat. The freebooting Afghan chiefs were settled as vassals by the greatest Afghan adventurer-statesman—Sher Shah—thereby founding landed houses that survived in Bengal for centuries. Many of these houses remained intact until the revenue reforms of Murshid Quli Khan in 1717. Even in the first half of the twentieth century, traces of this Afghan landed class could be found in such historic names as Ghazvani, Pani, Yusufzai, Sur, and Lohani.[77]

The phenomenon of the "Bara Bhuiyans" ("Twelve Landlords") was largely the immediate effect of Sher Shah's creation of Afghan vassals. The "twelve landlords" emerged as bloated *zamindars* usurping neighbours' territories and establishing virtually independent principalities, in the twilight period between the decline of Afghan rule and the rise of Mughal power in Bengal.[78] The "twelve landlords" formed a confederacy under Isa Khan (and, after his death, under his son Musa Khan) which, for a quarter of a century, tested the nerves and skills of the most talented soldier-administrators of the great Mughal Emperors Akbar and Jahangir, including Khan-i-Jahan, Shahbaz Khan, Man Singh, and Islam Khan.[79] Although these rebellious *zamindars* were usually designated as the "twelve landlords", the descriptions provided by the contemporary chronicles—*Bahristan* (Land of Spring), *Akbarnama* (Biography of Akbar), and *Rajmala* (Garland of Kings)—

about the members, families and activities of this parvenue landed class showed that these *zamindars* numbered at least thirty-three. The effect of Sher Shah's new land administrative order on the religious composition of the Bengal landed class can be gauged from the fact that of these 33 *zamindars*, 19 (58 per cent) were Muslims (mostly Afghans), and 14 (42 per cent) were Hindus.[80]

The resistance to the Mughals of the "Bara Bhuiyans" finally collapsed under the weight of dogged determination, shrewd diplomacy and the relentless and inexhaustible armed pressure by the Mughal Viceroy Islam Khan. Again from contemporary chronicles, we find that Islam Khan, at the end of his five-year-long (1608–1613) successful campaign, stripped at least nine *zamindars* of their estates. The remaining twothirds or so of the *zamindars* were allowed to retain their lands as *jagirs*. Of the nine *zamindars* whose territories were confiscated, six were Muslims and three Hindus.[81] The annexed territories were distributed as *jagirs* among Mughal officers, almost all of whom came from the cultured Muslim families of North India. Islam Khan's final dispensation brought some changes in the personnel of the landed class but, on the whole, strengthened further the recently dominant position of the Muslims in that class, since vast areas held by three of the largest Hindu rajas (big landlords)—Pratapaditya (Jessore), Ram Chandra (Bakla, Barisal), and Ananta Manikya (Bhalua, Noakhali)—came under Muslim *jagirdars*.

To comprehend the total extent of the Muslim hold on land in Bengal, we should mention that besides *zamindaris* and *jagirs* there were two other types of landownership—*aima* and *madad-i-ma'sh*—during the period of Muslim rule in Bengal. Under *aima* and *madad-i-ma'sh*, rent-free land was granted in perpetuity to persons of noble birth, holy men, mosques and other religious and educational establishments. By 1613, Bengal had already four centuries of Muslim rule and the accumulated land granted to Muslim scholars, saints, mosques, *dargahs* and *madrassas* must have been quite extensive. At the end of the eighteenth century, the British government found rent-free lands amounting to about one-fourth of the total in many places.[82] The amount could not have been much less at the beginning of the seventeenth century.

Thus, by the start of the seventeenth century, Bengal Muslims had finally achieved the predominant position in the landed class. For about a century (1612–1717) thereafter, a stable and prosperous Mughal rule flourished. The migration of Sufis, which ebbed a little during the turbulent period of the Afghan ascendancy and the "Bara Bhuiyans", now became, as Jadunath Sarkar says, "ampler in volume". The peak period of Mughal power was possibly also the golden age of Islam during the 550-year period of Muslim rule in medieval Bengal. With Sufis active, Muslim *jagirdars* set the religious and social tone of the up-country regions, and Muslim rulers and officers dominated the towns. Islam was now becoming predominant in many parts of Bengal over Hindu culture, religious beliefs and practices.

It was during the period of Murshid Quli Khan as Subadar (lieutenant of a province) (1717–1727), and during the period of Murshid's successors in the independent *nizamat* (administration), that Muslim society and Islam began to be affected by Hindu practices. The main reason for this Hindu influence was Murshid Quli Khan's drastic alteration of the land settlement pattern in favour of the Hindus, as Sher Shah had effected previously for the Muslims. Murshid Quli Khan had excelled under the Mughals as a revenue administrator, but as a Subadar he looked at the total administration from the narrow perspective of an aggressive revenue management officer. He did not have the breadth of vision and political talent to understand that the Muslim *nizamat* could not survive for long without the creation and support from strong social bases of Bengal Muslims.

Murshid Quli Khan replaced the Mughal *jagirdari* system with what was called the *mal jasmani* system. Under this system, which was similar to the *fermiers generals* in France, Murshid Quli Khan took security bonds from *ijaradars* (contractors) who then collected the land revenue. Murshid Quli Khan had had long service (1700–1717) in revenue administration in Bengal as *Diwan*, with only short interruptions in his tenure. In his positions he came to know many pusillanimous, but honest lower-ranking Hindu revenue officers. Since many Muslim *jagirdars* had been found to have embezzled their collections, Murshid Quli Khan appointed the honest Hindu revenue officers he knew and some other Hindus as *ijaradars*. Many of the older *jagirdars* remained, but were shortly crushed out of existence by the new contractors. In time, these contractors came to be called *zamindars*. Murshid Quli Khan thus created a new Hindu landed aristocracy in Bengal, whose position was confirmed and made hereditary by Lord Cornwallis under the Permanent Settlement in 1793.[83]

The twenty big *zamindaris* created during Murshid Quli Khan's time covered about 1,000 out of a total 1,600 parganas, and accounted for two-thirds of the revenue of the *nizamat*. Of these twenty *zamindaris*, one was held by a Muslim family (the *zamindar* family of Birbhum).[84] The process by which the remaining nineteen *zamindaris* came into existence can be understood by examining a few case studies. Raghunandan was a *Varendra* Brahmin and trusted counsellor of Murshid khan in revenue matters. When the Devinagar *zamindari* was terminated because of disobedience to the nizam by the *zamindar* concerned, Raghunandan acquired the estate in the name of his brother Ramjiban, and established the nucleus of the Natore estate. Later, when the neighbouring *zamindaris* of Bengachi, Bhaturia, Sultanpur, Saruppur and a few other places fell because of irregular revenue payments, parts of these latter territories were added to the Natore estate. Raghunandan also grabbed the greater portion of the large estate of Bhusan after the fall of its *zamindar*. Thus arose the Brahminical Natore estate, the premier *zamindari* of eighteenth-century Bengal. Daya Ram Ray, a Teli caste servant of Raghunandan, founded the *zamindar* family of Dighapatia through the acquisition of parts of the Bhusna *zamindari*.

The two largest *zamindaris* of Mymensingh district—those of Mymensingh and Muktagacha—also arose during the time of Murshid Quli Khan. Srikrisna Havladar, a *Varendra* Brahmin, was a loyal revenue officer of Murshid Quli Khan. The latter rewarded him with a revenue farm of the Mymensingh *pargana*. Srikrisna's son, who served in the *khalsa* (crown land) department of Murshid Quli Khan's successor, Alivardi, secured for his father

Zafarshahi *pargana* (west of Brahmaputra). Similarly, Srikrisna Acharya Chowdhury, again a *Varendra* Brahmin and a revenue officer of Murshid Quli Khan, got the *ijaradari* of Alaphshahi *pargana* and founded the Muktagacha family, later known as the Maharajas of Mymensingh. The Hindu *zamindars* of Bardawan and Navadip, who traced their origins from the time of Jahangir, added many *parganas* to their estates as a result of Murshid Quli Khan's revenue reorganisation. The *zamindar* of Dinajpur and many other smaller Hindu *zamindars* similarly enlarged their estates during the Murshid Quli Khan's *nizamat* and emerged as influential persons in Bengal's social life.[85]

The *zamindars* of the *nizamat* period kept their own armed forces and were in charge of law and order in their *zamindaris*. These rajas and maharajas overwhelmed the people by their wealth, power, pomp and grandeur. As Bharat Chandra's depiction of the court of Maharaja Krishna Chandra of Navadip shows, the courts of these big *zamindars* rivalled the majesty and pageantry of the Murshidabad court. Naturally these *zamindars* emerged as the most influential social leaders of Bengal. The social activities of the *zamindars* eventually affected the religions of Bengal as well. While the Brahmin *zamindars* were naturally inclined to establish the supremacy of the Brahminical religion, non-Brahminical and low status Hindus who acquired *zamindaris* compensated for their low origins by their over-enthusiasm in religious rites and festivals. Zealous patronage of their religion by the Hindu *zamindars*, *pundits* and Brahmins of their courts, the vast chain of the subinfeudated retinues and officials, and the splendourous celebration of *pujas* and other religious festivities, deeply affected the Muslim community, which was now absolutely dependent on the Hindu *zamindars* economically.[86] By 1793, when the Permanent Settlement officially made these *zamindaris* hereditary, the Hindu landed aristocracy was already about a century old. It is little wonder that Muslim scholars of Bengal have found the zenith of Hindu influence on the beliefs and practices of Bengal Islam to have been reached in the first half of the nineteenth century.[87].

Attempts at Building Multi-religious Coalition Elites

Bengal has long been known as fertile ground for political factionalism. Because of the traditional nature of the socio-economic condition of Bengal, the making and unmaking of the supreme rulers (when they were not imposed from Delhi) was limited exclusively to courtiers, nobility and high state officials. Until the establishment of the independent sultanate in Bengal in the middle of the fourteenth century, these courtiers, nobility and state officials seem to have all been immigrant Muslims. Muslim elite groups in Bengal were so riven by acute factionalism, personal animosities and intrigues against the Delhi emperors, that contemporary historians referred to Bengal as Bulghakkhana ("House of Strife").

As Diya al-Barani wrote,

> ...Any *wali* that the Sultan of Delhi appointed for Lakhnawati... disobeyed and revolted (against the King of Delhi). If the *wali* did not revolt, others revolted against him and killed him and the country was captured. For many years the revolt has become their

second nature and habit. And every *wali* appointed there was turned away against the king by the trespassers and balghakians (rebels).[88]

Babar's reflection on the political culture of Bengal at that time is also worth noting:

> It is a singular custom of Bengal that there is, in like manner, a seat or station assigned to each of the *amirs*, *wazirs* and *mansabdars*. *It is this throne and station which engages the reverence of Bengali chiefs* . . . whoever kills the king and succeeds in placing himself is immediately acknowledged as king . . .[89]

Abul Fazl argued that "owing to the climate's favouring the base, the dust of dissension is always rising" in Bengal.[90] While it is difficult to ascertain the cause of intrigues among the Bengal political elite at that time, it is easy to see that Islam alone was not sufficient to ensure horizontal or vertical elite cohesion, either at the all-India or provincial level.

It was during the period of the independent sultanate that several attempts were made to create multi-religious elites. Like the earlier independent Pala kings, the sultans felt the political necessity to ensure support from Hindus in order to safeguard the independence of Bengal and for ventures abroad. The fear of invasion from the powerful emperors of Delhi compelled the sultans to create a sense of what might be called in modern terms "a territorial nationalism" in Bengal by ensuring participation of major religious groups in the state machinery. Thus, to thwart the invasion by Emperor Firoz Shah Tughlaq, Shams-ud-din Ilyas Shah (1342–1357), who founded the first independent Muslim dynasty of Bengal, built up a multi-communal (including both Muslims and Hindus) elite structure. Shahdeo, one of his Hindu generals, commanded large forces against the Delhi emperor. We find in the contemporary chronicles that Ilyas Shah appreciated the service of Brahmin *zamindars*, chiefs and military officers by decorating them. The fact that several Brahmin *zamindars* also sided with the Delhi emperor, and were rewarded by him, only lays bare the typical vulnerability of Bengal rulers from within and the critical need for them to guard their rear.

In order to continue the policy of co-opting talented Hindus to high positions in the state, Ilyas Shah appointed Jayananda Bhaduri, a Brahmin, to the important office of *diwan* (collector of revenue). Jayananda's three brothers also held important positions in the state and were granted *jagirs*. These *jagirs* later flourished as the *zamindaris* of Etatia and Bhaduris. Sikandar Shah, Ilyas Shah's successor, also had to face a massive invasion of Bengal by Firuz Shah Tughlaq and similarly adopted his father's policy as the key to state-building in Bengal.

But the inclusion of large numbers of influential Brahmins into the nobility created tensions in the Ilyas Shah court even when Sikandar Shah was alive. Muslim nobles, supported by influential shaikhs and the *ulama*, Shaikh Ala al-Haq and Hazrat Muzaffar Shams Balkhi, opposed the policy of appointing non-Muslims to responsible offices of the state and argued that this policy was against both the Koran and the Sunnah. The Hindu group was led by Raja Khan, a Brahmin, with the able support of another Brahmin official named Narasingh Narail. Ultimately taking advantage of the youth of

Sultan Ghias-ud-Din Azam Shah and a series of intrigues among members of the royal family, Raja Khan seized power after having crushed the Islamic party for the time being. Shaikh Nur Qutb Alam, the leader of the Islamic party, had to seek the support of Sultan Ibrahim Sharqi of Jawnpur to humble Raja Khan and to hand power to his son (who converted to Islam under the name of Jalal-ud-Din Mohammad).[91]

Despite the Raja Khan episode, the strategy of creating composite elite structures for defence and expansion of the kingdom of Bengal continued to appeal to the independent sultans. Thus, Alauddin Husain Shah, fearful of invasion by Emperor Sikandar Lodi and bent on recovering Bengal's military prestige, needed the loyalty and support of both Hindu and Muslim communities. Similarly, Husain Shah, often compared to the great Mughal emperor, Akbar, had a whole array of Hindus in such positions as *wazir*, private physician, chief of the bodyguards, private secretary and superintendent. One of his important generals was a Hindu. Husain Shah was very respectful to Chaitanya Deva and directed his *qadi* at Navadip to show proper consideration to the saint.[92]

Some tensions did develop in the multi-religious court of Husain Shah, although they did not take on the disastrous proportions of the Raja Khan phenomenon. Two very scholarly Brahmin brothers and confidants of Husain Shah, Rup (private secretary) and Sanatan (superintendent of state), ultimately deserted the sultan. Sanatan even suffered incarceration for disobedience to the sultan on a matter of religious sentiment. Both these brothers joined Chaitanya Deva's movement and repented their association with the Muslim sultan.[93]

The Kayastha-Muslim partnership at the state level seems to have worked better than the Brahmin-Muslim coalition. This was possibly because of the technical nature of the Kayastha's job—accounting, revenue and agricultural administration. Neither the Muslims nor Brahmins had much expertise or liking for complicated and tough technical jobs. The Kayasthas, therefore, virtually monopolised such jobs in the revenue department. Kayasthas like Maladhar Basu and his son, Lakshminath Basu, served under the later Ilyas Shahi sultanate and Habshi and Husain Shahi sultans. Gopinath Basu held the highest posts in the revenue department (*wazir*, i.e., finance minister) under Husain Shah. Two brothers of Gopinath Basu and his five sons were also employed in Husain Shah's government. Three other Kayastha brothers—Rambhadra, Ramanth and Banikanta served in the revenue department of Husain Shah. Of these, Banikanta rose to the position of *ray rayan*, one of the highest posts in the revenue department. Several members of another Kayastha family, that of Ramananda Guha, served under Sulaiman Karrani. Ramananda's grandson, Srihari, was the *wazir* of Daud Karrani.[94] As the Kayastha technocrats posed no political threat to the Muslim sultans, the latter could easily place confidence in them. Given the Brahminical domination of Hindu society, the Kayasthas might have preferred the Muslim rule, under which they had been thriving. Partly because of their dominance in the revenue department and partly due to the sultan's satisfaction, most Kayasthas serving the Muslim rulers ended up as *jagirdars* and *zamindars*. As Abul Fazl wrote, most of the Hindu *zamindars* in Bengal were Kayasthas.[95]

The imperial Mughals, who had to conquer Bengal piece by piece, did not have to worry about the "communal arithmetic" indulged in by the independent sultans. During the entire Mughal period (1574–1717), 32 *subahdars* and about the same number of *diwans* and *bakhshis* (paymasters-general) ruled bengal. All of them came from metropolitan North India. Only one of them—Raja Man Singh (1594–1606), who was said to be more Mughal than the Mughals themselves—was Hindu.[96] Like all conquered peoples, the Hindus had to remain satisfied with secondary jobs in the personal establishments of *subahdars*, *diwans*, *bakshis* and other high officials.

The cycle turned full-wheel with the establishment of the independent *nizamat* of Murshid Quli Khan. While Hindu participation in the government of the independent sultans preceding the Mughal conquest was limited to influential Brahmins and Kayasthas, now Vaidya and confectioner castes found their entry into the Muslim court. We have already seen how Murshid Quli Khan, with efficiency in revenue collection as his prime administrative goals, helped the growth of a powerful Hindu landed aristocracy. After Murshid Quli Khan, some of the influential Hindu *zamindars* took their due places in the nizam's court.

During the Mughal period, there had been a massive flow of administrative and military talent from Delhi to Bengal. This virtually prevented the development of local Muslim talent. The drying up of migration from North India during the twilight of the Mughal empire might also have led Murshid Quli Khan to depend on the Hindus. Thus we find Hindus like Darpanarain, Raghunandan, Alamchand and Kinkar Sen at the top of the revenue department, with Bhupat Ray and Kishen Ray as private secretaries; Dilpat Singh Hazari and Lahirimal were generals in Murshid Quli Khan's administration.[97]

In the meantime, because of the changes in the economy of Bengal under the Mughals, new influential Hindu groups emerged to press for their share in the government. During Mughal rule, "the outer world came to Bengal and Bengal went out of herself to the outer world".[98] The result was the growth of a seaborne trade in Bengal. Bengal's export trade—in silk stuffs, indigo and cotton goods—was carried on mainly by Dutch, French and British traders. The trade earned phenomenonal profits.

The Hindu trading class were quick to take advantage of this trade boom as subsidiaries of foreign companies, particularly the British East India Company. All of the 52 native merchants associated with the East India Company in Calcutta during the years 1736–1740 were Hindus. Similarly, all of the 25 native merchants who acted as agents of the Company at Kashimbazar in 1739 were Hindus. In Dacca, ten out of twelve such native merchants belonged to the Hindu community. The Hindus who acted as the Company's trusted bankers in Calcutta also made quick profits.[99] This Hindu *nouveau riche* class had enough wealth to make their power felt at the *nizamat* court. Their representative, Jagat Seth, soon secured an influential position in the Court of Shuja-ud-Din, the successor of Murshid Quli Khan, along with

Hindu *zamindars* and officials. Hindu influence at the *nizamat* court reached its high points at the time of Alivardi Khan and Siraj-ud-Daulah in the middle of the eighteenth century, when the highest positions even in the military intelligence services passed out of the hands of Muslims.[100]

Fear of Maratha plunder led the Hindu landed class, official aristocracy and the *nouveau riche* to prop up Alivardi's regime in the eighteenth century. As the Maratha menace disappeared, however, Hindu elite groups met at the house of Jagat Seth and, on the recommendation of Maharaja Krishna Chandra, the *zamindar* of Navadip, decided to overthrow Alivardi's successor, Siraj-ud-Daulah, with the help of the British.[101] As the Muslim hold on all important social bases of power—land, trade, administration and armed services—had been unwittingly destroyed by the *nizamat* rulers themselves, the withering away of Muslim political power in Bengal was a foregone conclusion.

Islam and the Growth of a Vernacular Language in Bengal

One development during Muslim rule, which took place particularly under the independent sultanate (1338–1538) and had an immense bearing on future political configuration, was the flourishing of Bengali from an inchoate language into a lingua franca for the whole of Bengal. Stemming from both religious and political considerations, the independent sultans patronised the Bengali language and ensured its due recognition as a literary medium.

Whether religion should go to the language of the people or the people should go to the language of the religion is a question always debated among the preachers of religions. The language of the scriptures, no doubt, helps stir within devotees the deepest feelings and passions during the most intensely religious moments. But if the language of the religion is not the indigenous language of the people, the preaching of the religion becomes extremely difficult. The Sufis, therefore, took up the vernacular Bengali, disdained by Hindu rulers and Brahmins, to spread the message of Islam among the masses in Bengal. The very first Muslim poet in Bengali, Shah Muhammad Saghir, who flourished in the reign of Ghias-ud-Din Azam Shah (1389–1409), had nothing but religious considerations in mind when he wrote his epic, *Yusuf-Zolekha*. Saghir says in the introduction, "I am afraid of writing religious subjects in Bengali because it might be a sin. But after much thought I find my fear baseless. Language does not make any difference if subject matter is true".[102] Similarly, Muzammil, a poet of the mid-fifteenth century, wrote at the beginning of his *Nitisastra* (On Morals) that as the people did not understand Arabic, he felt the necessity of writing religious books in Bengali.[103]

For the sultans, political reasons undoubtedly weighed more than religious reasons in their support of Bengali. The very considerations which led the independent sultans persistently to follow the principle of Hindu-Muslim coalitions at the elite level also inspired them to take up the cause of the vernacular language. They had to understand and communicate with the people to build permanent rapport with them. This could best be done in the vernacular language. Thus we find from the Chinese account compiled by Ma Huan (between AD 1425 and 1432) that Bengali had already become a universal language for the nobility in the capital of Bengal, although Persian was also spoken.[104]

One independent sultan welcomed a Bengali poet with garlands in his court while others had eminent Bengali poets and scholars in the services of their courts.[105] Sultans like Ghias-ud-Din Azam Shah, Ala-ud-Din Husain Shah, Nusrat Shah and firuz Shah actively encouraged and patronised Bengali literature.[106] As D.C. Sen remarks, Bengali would scarcely have got an opportunity to find its way to the courts of the kings if the Hindu kings had continued to enjoy independence.[107]

Although Persian was the state language, the revenue accounts during the sultanate period were kept in Bengali. Thus for all practical purposes Bengali emerged as the second state language under the sultans. After the Mughal conquest, the constantly changing officers from Northern India found no time to learn Bengali, and their subordinate indigenous staff had to acquire mastery over Persian. But by that time the Bengali language had acquired enough vitality to be self-sustaining.

Conclusion

To sum up our discussion, an acute multi-dimensional conflictual situation at the close of the Sena era, with intense feeling raging between Brahmins and Buddhists, Brahmins and non-Brahmis, upper-class Aryans and non-Aryans, produced the opportunity for a prophetic break in Bengal society. The Muslim Sufis, with their charisma and adaptive skills and occasional armed support from Muslim rulers, took full advantage of the climacteric situation, and converted a major section of the Bengal population to Islam.

The proximity and juxtaposition of the two antithetical religions, Hinduism and Islam, particularly in light of the recentness of conversion, created problems for both religions, with both being affected by each other's rites and practices. Under the circumstances, the religion that could dominate the social and economic heights of Bengal society could alone avoid penetration by the other. Muslims gradually supplanted Hindus in the landed aristocracy by the seventeenth century, and maintained their domination on land throughout that century. At the beginning of the eighteenth century, Murshid Quli Khan, in an unwitting and utterly self-destructive move, destroyed this important power base of the Muslims and brought into being about twenty large Hindu *zamindar* houses that came virtually to control almost all of the land of Bengal.

Even before the rise of the new Hindu landed aristocracy, a totally Hindu dominated wealthy mercantile class had already grown in Bengal in the seventeenth century as a result of the enormous growth of trade between Bengal and European countries during the golden age of the Mughal peace in India.

This Hindu trading class, in collaboration with their co-religionists in the landed aristocracy, turned the later Muslim nizams into a tool in their hands, conspired with the imperial trading interests for the fall of Muslim power, and ultimately handed over political power to the imperial interests in return for the maintenance of their own status as the proteges of the imperialist sceptre and interests. Thus Hindu domination of the upper echelons of the Bengal society and economy, which began at the start of the eighteenth century and continued through British rule, resulted in the much talked about Hindu influence on Bengal Islam (often dubbed as "degeneration, corruption and contamination of Islam" in Bengal by subcontinental Muslim scholars) in the eighteenth and nineteenth centuries.

It should be noted in passing that syncretistic religious movements—like Chaitanya Deva's Vaishnavism, which created much intellectual and religious ferment in the mid-fifteenth and mid-sixteenth centuries—did not survive even another century, primarily because these movements could not find a mooring in any stable socio-economic base of Bengal society.

The independent sultans of Bengal began to follow the strategy of composite nation-building about two centuries ahead of the great Mughal emperor, Akbar. In a uniform pattern, the Muslim shaikhs and *ulema* in Bengal and North India opposed the policy of Hindu-Muslim elite coalition-building on grounds of its being contrary to the principles of Islam. It is quite suggestive that Brahmin-Muslim coalitions during the sultanate usually ended disastrously for the Muslims, but Kayastha-Muslim unity worked reasonable well. On the other hand, all-caste Hindu coalitions brought about the final eclipse of Muslim power in Bengal in the first half of the eighteenth century.

A singular development that took place during the independent sultanate was the growth of Bengali as the lingua franca for the whole of the Bengal province. This development took place partly because of Islam's need for the vernacular medium to reach the Bengali people effectively, and partly due to the sultans' need for effective political control of their kingdom, and had profound effects on the future subcontinental political configurations, because where language tended to unite Bengali Muslims and Hindus, religion and economic disparity tended to separate them. Again, where common religions tended to bring about a coalition of Bengal and North Indian Muslims, language created ethnocentric disdain between the two. After many vicissitudes, the Bengalis possibly finally solved the conundrum by choosing the Bangladesh phenomenon—i.e., a union of language and religion.

NOTES

1   F. Rahman, *Islam* (London: University of Chicago Press, second edition, 1979), p. 2.
2   See J.N. Sarkar, *History of Bengal*, Vol. 2, *Muslim Period (1200–1757)* (Dacca: University of Dacca, 1948), p. 1.
3   See T.W. Arnold, *The Preaching of Islam: A History of the Propagation of the Muslim Faith* (Lahore: Shirkat-i-Qalam, n.d.), pp. 256–78.
4   *Ibid.*, p. 262.
5   *Ibid.*, p. 263.

6   See Table A in R. Ahmed, *The Bengal Muslims 1871–1906: A Quest for Identity* (Delhi: Oxford University Press, 1981), p. 2.
7   K.F. Rubbee, *The Origin of the Musalmans of Bengal* (Calcutta: Thacker, Spink and Co., 1895), p. 1.
8   *Census Report of Bengal, 1872*, p. 132.
9   Quoted in M.A. Rahim, *Social and Cultural History of Bengal*, Vol. 1, 1201–1576 (Karachi: Pakistan Historical Society, 1963), p. 56.
10 Rubbee, *op.cit.*, pp. 11–65. During the entire period of Muslim rule, there were 76 governors, kings and nizams in Bangladesh. Of these, only three—Raja Ganesh and his son and grandson (Jalal-at-Din Muhammad and Shamsal-Din Ahmed Shah)—were probably of Bengali origin. Two—Todermal and Man Singh—were of non-Bengali (but of Indian) origin. The remaining 71 were of either Afghan, Mughal, Iranian or Arab origin. *Ibid.*, pp. 22–3.
11 See Rahim, *op.cit.*, pp. 61–4.
12 See Table C in Ahmed, *op.cit.*, p. 17.
13 A. Ahmed, *Studies in Islamic Culture in the Indian Environment* (London: Oxford University Press, 1964), p. 105.
14 Quoted in Rahim, *op.cit.*, p. 67.
15 See S.M. Lipset, "Social Structure and Social Change", in P.M. Blau (ed.), *Approaches to the Study of Social Structure* (London: Open Books, 1976), pp. 172–209.
16 See E.E. Hagen, *On the Theory of Social Change: How Economic Growth Begins* (Homewood: The Dorsey Press, Inc., second printing, January 1963), pp. 86–122.
17 Land of the Aryans, meaning North India.
18 See B. Gosh, *Bangali O Bangla Shahitya* (Bengalee and Bengali Literature) (Calcutta: New Age Publishers, 1981), pp. 2–4; A.K. Chattopadhyaya, *Introduction to Ancient Bengal and Bengalis* (Howra: Locknath Pustikalaya, 1957), pp. 11–12.
19 See A.M. Choudhury, "Aspects of Ancient Bengal Society and Socio-religious Attitudes: Tradition and Continuity", *The Dacca University Studies*, Vol. XXXVII, December 1982, pp. 148–60; N. Ray, *Bangalir Itihas: Adi Parbo* (History of Bengalees: The Ancient Phase) (Calcutta: Lekhak Somobay Samiti, 1950), pp. 850–63; R.C. Majumdar, *History of Ancient Bengal* (Calcutta: G.K.R. Mukherjee, 1974), p. 413 ff.
20 Chattopadhyaya, *op.cit.*, p. 13.
21 Ray, *op.cit.*, p. 309.
22 Chattopadhyaya, *op.cit.*, p. 28.
23 Ray, *op.cit.*, p. 315.
24 The Palas were probably the first indigenous dynasty to have ruled the whole of Bengal (excepting the South-east region). The Palas most probably came from Varendra (North Bengal) and had their capital at Ramabati, near the present Malda. See M.A. Rahim, A.M. Choudhury, A.B.M. Mahmud, S. Islam, *History of Bangladesh* (in Bengali) (Dacca: Nowroz Kitabistan, second edition, 1981), pp. 63, 107.
25 Ray, *op.cit.*, pp. 317–8.
26 *Ibid.*, p. 342.
27 Barrie M. Morrison, *Political Centres and Cultural Regions in Early Bengal* (Delhi: Rawat Publications, 1980), p. 84 ff.
28 Ray, *op.cit.*, pp. 328–9.
29 Chattopadhyaya, *op.cit.*, pp. 43–4; Rahim *et al.*, *op.cit.*, pp. 80–1.
30 *Ibid.*, p. 95.
31 *Ibid.*, pp. 100–06, 154–5; Chattopadhyaya, *op.cit.*, p. 101.
32 Choudhury, *op.cit.*, p. 158.
33 Ray, *op.cit.*, pp. 341–8.
34 *Ibid.*, p. 342; see also R.C. Majumdar (ed.), *The History of Bengal*, Vol. I, *Hindu Period* (Dacca: The University of Dacca, second impression, 1963), pp. 397–559.
35 South-east Bengal maintained its independence from the Guptas and Palas and came under Brahmini *Varmanas* rulers towards the end of Pala rule. Bijoya Sena conquered South-east Bengal from the Varamanas. The Senas ruled this riverine part of Bengal for about a century more after the Muslim conquest of North Bengal. Senas were followed by the Devas who continued the Sena policy of Brahminisation, *loc.cit.* South-east Bengal

thus had almost a century of Brahminical rule.

36   Rahim *et al.*, *op.cit.*, p. 146.
37   Ray, *op.cit.*, pp. 134–59.
38   *Ibid.*, pp. 341, 348.
39   *Ibid.*, pp. 198–200.
40   *Dohakosa* was an anthology of Buddhist mystic songs, and *Charyapadas* was a collection of verses. *Charyapadas* are regarded as the first literary compositions in Old Bengali. *Dohakosa* songs were written in *Sauresana Apabhamsa*, as used by the Buddhists of Eastern India during the period AD 600–1000. See Majumdar, *op.cit.*, pp. 380–1, 383–5.
41   Quoted in Gosh, *op.cit.*, p. 127.
42   M. Shahidullah, *Buddhist Mystic Songs* (Dacca: Renaissance Printers, reprint, June 1974), p. 94.
43   M.A. Hai and A. Pasha, *Charya Gitika* (in Bengali) (Dacca: Mowla Brothers, 1968), pp. 42, 51.
44   Quoted in A. Karim, *Social History of the Muslims in Bengal* (down to AD 1538) (Dacca: The Asiatic Society of Pakistan, 1959), pp. 143–4.
45   Quoted in Rahim, *op.cit.*, p. 317.
46   Ray, *op.cit.*, p. 451; Gosh, *op.cit.*, pp. 114–5.
47   Ray, *op.cit.*, p. 452.
48   It will be of interest to social scientists concerned with transnational comparisons to know that a similar conflictual situation between Hinduism and Buddhism in Brahminical Sumatra, Java and Malaya created opportunities for the spread of Islam in those places. See T. Ling, "Buddhist Bengal, and After", in D. Chattopadhyaya (ed.), *History and Society* (Calcutta: K.P. Bagchi, 1978), p. 322.
49   See J.N. Sarkar, "Transformation of Bengal under Mughal Rule", in J.N. Sarkar (ed.), *The History of Bengal*, Vol. II, *Muslim Period (1200–1757)* (Dacca: The University of Dacca, 1948), p. 227; Ray, *op.cit.*, pp. 444–5.
50   See H.H. Gerth and C.W. Mills, *From Max Weber: Essays in Sociology* (New York: Oxford University Press, 1958), pp. 245–52.
51   G. Saklayen, *Bangladsher Sufi Shadak* (Saint-Devotees of Bangladesh) (Dacca: Islamic Foundation, third edition, 1982), pp. 157–74.
52   Gerth and Mills, *op.cit.*, pp. 295–6.
53   See M.E. Haq, *A History of Sufi-ism in Bengal* (Dacca: Asiatic Society of Bangladesh, 1975), pp. 206–7.
54   *Ibid.*, pp. 209–10.
55   *Ibid.*, pp. 228–9.
56   *Ibid.*, pp. 162, 165–6.
57   *Ibid.*, p. 199.
58   Rabindra Nath Tagore, the greatest poet of Bengali literature, came from a Pir Ali Hindu family. For this information, and details of Khan Jahan's proselytising works, see Saklayen, *op.cit.*, pp. 67–76.
59   Haq, *op.cit.*, pp. 181–2.
60   *Ibid.*, pp. 205–9.
61   Karim, *op.cit.*, pp. 86–90.
62   Haq, *op.cit.*, pp. 177–8, 263–4.
63   *Ibid.*, p. 180.
64   *Ibid.*, pp. 185–96.
65   *Ibid.*, pp. 194–7.
66   *Ibid.*, pp. 218–24.
67   Karim, *op.cit.*, pp. 137–8; R.R. Qanungo, "Bengal under the House of Balban", in J.N. Sarkar (ed.), *The History of Bengal*, Vol. II, *Muslim Period* (1200–1757) (Dacca: University of Dacca, 1948), pp. 69–70.
68   The following discussion on the adaptation of Islam by the Sufis is based mainly on the very competent treatment of the subject by Professor Enamul Huq, the greatest Bengali Muslim scholar on Sufism. See Haq, *op.cit.*, pp. 52–142, 397–421.
69   Asim Roy, the author of the latest important work on Bengal Islam, also highlights the role of the Sufis in the mass conversion to Islam in Bengal. Roy argues that it was the

deltaic nature of the land of Bengal which helped the "disparate" Muslim Sufis to succeed "in appropriating the particular roles required by the exigencies of the local frontier situation". See A. Roy, *The Islamic Syncretistic Tradition in Bengal*, Princeton: Princeton University Press, 1983), p. 50. As we have seen above (pp. 11–2) it was the social tensions generated in Bengal society by inter-religious conflicts between Brahmins and Buddhists, intra-religious animosity between Brahmins and non-Brahmins, and inter-racial hostilities between Aryans and non-Aryans which provided the opportunity for the Sufis to play the prophetic role. We have also seen in Footnote 48 above, that a similar conflictual situation between Hinduism and Buddhism helped the spread of Islam in Sumatra, Java and Malaya.

70   M.A. Khan, "The Islamic Reform Movements in Bengal in the Nineteenth Century: Meaning and Significance", paper presented in the Symposium on Islam in Bangladesh: Society, Culture and Politics, Dacca, 24–26 December 1982, pp. 13–15.
71   See Karim, *op.cit.*, pp. 40–45.
72   Nazimuddin Ahmed, *Islamic Heritage of Bangladesh* (Dacca: Department of Films and Publications, Government of People's Republic of Bangladesh, 1980).
73   See Max Weber, *The Sociology of Religion*, translated by E. Fischoff (London: Social Science Paperbacks, 1965), pp. 80–4; see also Gerth and Mills, *op.cit.*, pp. 283–4.
74   For a discussion on the nature of and differences between the European and Indian feudal systems, see N. Karim, *The Changing Society in India, Pakistan and Bangladesh* (Dacca: Nawroz Kitabistan, 1976).
75   *Zamindars, ijaradars, jagirdars* and the like were various types of tenure holders of land in medieval Bengal. There were differences among these tenures which we shall comment on as we proceed with the discussion. But the common fundamental characteristic of these tenures was the revenue farming right, not the ownership title of the land.
76   A. Rahim, *Social and Cultural History of Bengal*, Vol. II (1576–1757) (Karachi: Pakistan Publishing House, 1967), pp. 185–7.
77   See N.B. Roy, "Bengal under Imperial Afghan Rule", and J.N. Sarkar, "First Muslim Conquest of Bengal", in J.N. Sarkar (ed.), *The History of Bengal*, Vol. II, *Muslim Period* (Dacca: The University of Dacca, 1948), pp. 177, 187–8.
78   *Ibid.*, pp. 225–6.
79   For details of the resistance by the "Bara Bhuiyans" to the Mughal Viceroys in Bengal, see J.N. Sarkar, "First Mughal Conquest of Bengal", and "Raja Man Singh Kachwa, Viceroy"; S.N. Bhattacharya, "State of Bengal under Jahangir", "Conquest of Islam Khan (1608–1613)", and "Last Achievements of Islam Khan", all in *ibid.*, pp. 187–206, 207–15, 234–46, 247–70, 273–88.
80   The figure about the number of *zamindars* in Bengal during the period of the "Bara Bhuiyans", is taken from M. Nathan, *Baharistan-I-Ghaybi* (translated by M.I. Borah) (Gauhati: Indian Government of Assam, 1936), Vol. I, and *Akbar Nama of Abul Fazl*, translated by H. Beveridge (Delhi: ESS ESS Publications, second edition, 1977).
81   *Ibid.*
82   A.R. Mallick, *British Policy and the Muslims in Bengal (1757–1856)* (Dacca: Bangla Academy, 1977), pp. 40–1.
83   See J.N. Sarkar, "Bengal under Murshid Quli Khan", in Sarkar, *op.cit.*, pp. 408–17.
84   The figures are culled from Rahim, *op.cit.*, pp. 202–6.
85   The details of the growth of these large Hindu *zamindaris* are given in *ibid.*, pp. 203–5, and Sarkar, *op.cit.*, pp. 408–17.
86   See Rahim, *op.cit.*, pp. 206–8.
87   See, for example, Mallick, *op.cit.*, pp. 3–40.
88   Quoted in Karim, *op.cit.*, p. 23.
89   Quoted in Rahim, *op.cit.*, p. 69 (emphasis added).
90   H. Beveridge, *op.cit.*, p. 427.
91   See Rahim, *op.cit.*, pp. 328–30; Karim, *op.cit.*, pp. 30–1; J.N. Sarkar and K.R. Qa-nungo, "Intervening Muslim Dynasty", in Sarkar, *op.cit.*, pp. 120–9.
92   See A.B.M. Habibullah, "Husain Shahi Dynasty", in *Ibid.*, pp. 142–65.
93   R.C. Majumdar (ed.), *The History of Bengal* (in Bengali), Part II, *Medieval Period* (Calcutta: General Printers and Publishers, 1946), p. 324.

94 See Rahim, *op.cit.*, pp. 306–11.
95 Abul Fazl, *The Ain-i-Akbari*, translation by H.S. Jarret (New Delhi: Oriental Books Reprint Corporation, third reprint, 1978), p. 141.
96 *Ibid.*, p. 16. The only other Hindu holding a high position was Jawharmal Diwan, who was appointed Diwan by Shah Jahan when he took possession of the province during his rebellion against Emperor Jahangir.
97 See Rahim, *op.cit.*, pp. 169–70.
98 J.N. Sarkar, "Transformation of Bengal under Mughal Rule", in Sarkar, *op.cit.*, p. 216.
99 See Mallick, *op.cit.*, pp. 70–2.
100 See Rahim, *op.cit.*, pp. 170–4.
101 See Rahim *et al.*, *op.cit.*, pp. 387–9.
102 Muhammad Enamul Haq, *Muslim Bangla Shahitya* (Muslim Bengali Literature) (Dacca: Pakistan Publications, second printing, 1965), p. 59.
103 *Ibid.*, p. 67.
104 See Karim, *op.cit.*, pp. 176–7.
105 Haq, *op.cit.*, p. 35.
106 See Rahim, *op.cit.*, pp. 214–9.
107 Quoted in *ibid.*, p. 214.

CHAPTER II

CHANGES IN ISLAM IN THE BENGAL AREA DURING THE BRITISH AND POST-BRITISH PERIODS

Changes in Islam in the Bengal Area: External Stimuli and Internal Dynamics

In the preceding chapter we have tried to understand the origin, growth and character of Islam in the thirteenth century through to the middle of the eighteenth century. This medieval Bengal Islam underwent profound changes during British rule. The changes were stimulated largely by forces external rather than internal to religion itself. First, the sense of Muslim frustration at the loss of political power to the British and the ideas of the Wahhabi movement in Arabia, brought in primarily by the pilgrims to Mecca, led to the growth of orthodox, revivalist movements among the Bengali Muslims in the first half of the nineteenth century. The spread of Western education under British rule caused the second wave of change in Bengal Islam, and a modernist Islamic movement grew to accommodate the Western ideas in the system of Islamic religious beliefs.

The timing and character of these two waves of change in Bengal Islam was determined by the nature and course of social change in Bengal Muslim society during British rule. Possibly because the British did not capture power directly from the Hindus, the Hindus in Bengal (as well as North India) could easily adapt themselves to British rule. Thus, during the first decades of British rule, the Hindus of Bengal moved fast to acquire European ideas by learning the English language and taking to English education and mixing with English people. Out of these contacts emerged a strong Hindu middle class with European liberal ideas. This new Hindu middle class, led by liberal reformers like Raja Ram Mohan Roy and Ishwar Chandra Vidyasagar, tried to redeem the Hindu religion from orthodoxy and superstition, and to infuse in their religion a dynamics that would enable the religion to cope with the modern scientific and technical world.

It was a long time before the Bengali Muslims (as well as the Muslims of North India) could reconcile themselves to British rule. Consequently they could not produce a strong middle class to lead their society and religion. In the absence of a Westernised middle class and in the face of a sharp decline of the Muslim aristocracy, the leadership of Muslim society in Bengal, as in the rest of North India, fell to the religious leaders educated in orthodox Islamic religious schools. Unable to understand the social, economic, political and technological reasons which led to the loss of power for all Muslims, the orthodox religious leaders confused the effect with the cause, interpreting the decline of Muslim power in terms of religious degeneration. These religious leaders therefore responded to the crisis of Muslim society that followed in the aftermath of British ascendancy by launching successive religious movements with the slogan, "Back to the glorious days of Islam".

In an atmosphere of intense frustration among the Muslims who had recently lost political power, religious movements led by the orthodox religious leaders transformed themselves into social movements, aimed at the restoration of Muslim power. However, since the British had superior arms and organisation, these attempts by the orthodox religious leaders to restore political power proved futile. The result was a period, lasting more than a century, when orthodox revivalism and Islamic modernism vied with one another for support among an increasing frustrated Muslim population.

Increasing Hindu Influence on Bengal Islam

As we have pointed out in the previous chapter, to increase the appeal of Islam the Sufis adapted Islam to local conditions and incorporated into Islam some of the local beliefs, rituals and practices. We have also argued that this adapted Islam came under intense Hindu influence as Hindus came to occupy in the twilight of Muslim power and the first decades of British rule, the commanding heights of Bengal's society and economy. As Hindu religious beliefs, customs and rites swiftly spread through Muslim society, the complete domination of the landed aristocracy by Hindus, from the very beginning of British rule, particularly affected rural Islam in Bengal.[1]

It has often been argued that Islam as developed originally in the deserts of Arabia, was too simple a religion to appeal to the minds and hearts of the people of Bengal. A religion more colourful than Arabian Islam was necessary for a region with varied and picturesque landscapes, changing seasons and varying climates. Something was needed that would have more appeal to the senses and imagination.[2] For example, Islam in Bengal had to incorporate some of the colourful Hindu festivities to sustain interest in Islamic ideas among those never previously exposed to such ideas. In this way, it is further argued, Bengal and its Hindu inhabitants "revenged" themselves on their conquerors.[3]

The depth and extent of accretion from Hindu society and religion to Bengal Islam at the end of the eighteenth century has been detailed by a number of Muslim Bengali scholars.[4] Stated in summary form, the salient aspects of Islam's accretions in Bengal can be described as follows.

First, belief in the principle of the unity of one, and only one omnipotent God (Allah) is the most fundamental belief in Islam. This concept of unity of God came to be diluted in popular Islam in Bengal when some sections of Bengali Muslim society committed *shirk* (attribution of partnership of godhood) by imputing godly powers to some of the Hindu deities. These Hindu gods were credited with the capacity to ward off trouble and sickness, or otherwise to have a personalistic impact on day-to-day life. The Hindu gods and goddesses like Satya Pir (a good natured god ready to respond to small prayers), Sitala (the goddess of smallpox), Olabibi (the goddess of cholera), Manasha (the goddess of snakes), and the like were worshipped by some of the lower classes of Muslims in Bengal.

Second, the doctrine of the unity of God was again violated when some Muslims, following the parallel of innumerable gods (*devtas*) among Hindus raised the Muslim *pirs* (holy saints) to the status of gods and began to worship their *dargas* (shrines). Following another Hindu custom, some Bengali Muslims venerated legendary personages like Zindha Ghazi (having power over wild beasts), Panch Pir (invoking danger, threats), Khwaj Khidr (the guardian spirit of seas and rivers), Pir Badar (sharing with Khidr the domination of water), or Madar Pir (controlling human breadth). Finally the Bengal Muslims also took up some of the religious customs and rites of Hindus. These included the *Rakhi* system, *Diwali* ceremonies, *Sraddha* (feasts in honour of the dead), *Muharram* festivities, and *Taziah* (following Ratha Jatra), Pir-Murid relationship (following Guru-Chela), the wearing of amulets, and many others.

In the social sphere, Bengali Muslims were affected by the Hindu caste system. Bengali Muslims developed and elaborated among themselves classes on the basis of birth, such as *ashraf* (the high born), and *atrap* (the low-born). There was also an articulation among many Bengal Muslims of a rudimentary caste-like system based on occupation (oil grinders, weavers, and so forth).

Religious Revivalism: the Faraidi Movement

The first religious movement that developed in Bengal in response to the increasing Hindu influence on Bengali Islam was called the Faraidi movement. Although the inspiration for this movement came from the puritanic Wahhabi movement that developed in Arabia towards the end of the eighteenth century, it was the first Islamic religious movement in Bengal to be launched and led by the Bengali religious leaders. The Faraidi movement spread widely and quickly among the rural Muslims in East Bengal.

The founder of the Faraidi movement, Haji Shariatullah, was born "of obscure parents" in 1781 in a village called Shamail in the district of Faridpur. He spent twenty years in Mecca and developed considerable proficiency as an Arabic scholar. In Mecca, he became a disciple of Wahhabi leader Shaikh Tahir al-Sumbal al-Makki. Haji Shariatullah also studied in al-Azhar University in Cairo. In 1818, after returning from Mecca, he quickly started preaching Wahhabi doctrines in the villages of Faridpur, his native district. Because of his remarkable personality, sincerity of conviction and exemplary character, Shariatullah developed a charismatic appeal for his countrymen. It was said that they "venerated him as a father, able to advise them in seasons of adversity and give them consolation in times of affliction". Shariatullah was succeeded by his son, Mohammad Mohsin, more commonly known as Dudu Miyan. Like his father, Dudu Miyan was educated in Mecca, but Dudu Miyan lacked the charismatic appeal of his father. This deficiency of Dudu Miyan was compensated for, however, by his superior organising capacity.[5] Dudu Miyan's organising ability was crucial to the spread of the Faraidi movement, the main tenet of which was "to adhere to the strict letters of the Koran". Both Shariatullah and Dudu Miyan urged Bengali Muslims, like the Arabian puritans, to go back to the pristine Islam that had been preached and practised by the holy Prophet.

The term Faraidi is derived from the Arabic word *faraid*, the plural of *farida*, which means obligatory duties enjoined by Islam. The Faraidi leaders thus emphasised the five fundamentals of Islam, that is, *Kalima* (the Doctrine of the Unity of God); *Salat* (prayer); *Roza* (fasting); *Hajj* (pilgrimage to Mecca), and *Zakat* (tax for the poor). The Faraidis insisted on the observance of these fundamentals by all members of the movement in an attempt to create in Bengal large numbers of practising Muslims, as opposed to mere believers.

The Faraidis urged Muslims to practise "self-correction", and to forsake forever the innovations and accretions that had trickled into Bengal Islam. They denounced the worship of Hindu gods and goddesses, the adoration of Muslim *pirs* (saints), attendance at festivals such as the *Muharram*, the use of a Hindu midwife to cut the umbilical cord of new-born children, and similar customs and religious rites which Bengali Muslims had acquired during their long association with Hindu society. The Faraidis insisted that Muslims practising these polytheistic and sinful accretions must express *towbah* (penance) and make a fresh vow to lead a perfect Muslim life. The most radical ideas of the Faraidis, from the point of view of subcontinental politics of the time, was their suspension of the *Juma* and the two *I'd* prayers in Bengal, and their contention that British rule was *Darul Harb* (the Abode of War). Shariatullah himself urged that the country had to be liberated through *jihad* (holy war), which, in his view, would involve two phases. In the first phase, Muslims had to develop themselves as perfect Muslims, in preparation for the second phase. The second phase was actual war against the British rulers. Shariatullah said that his own *jihad* was limited to the first phase, that is, "building soldiers of Islam". Above all else, the Faraidis proclaimed the equality of all Muslims.[6] To bring about such equality in practice Faraidi leaders urged reforms within the general parameters of the Hanafi Mazhab which covered the vast majority of the Muslims in Bengal.

The rural origin of the founding Faraidi leaders, their simplistic world view (based on an interpretation of the rise and fall of society in terms of religious changes), their Hanafi orientation and their egalitarian proclamations—all these appealed particularly to the lowest and most oppressed sections of rural East Bengal. With an appeal that spread to the bulk of Bengal's cultivators, weavers, oil grinders and other lower classes, Shariatullah became known among his detractors as the "Pir of Jolahas" (the "Saint of Weavers").

The Faraidi movement spread most extensively in those rural areas where Hindu *zamindars* and Christian indigo-planters held sway over the Muslim peasantry, or in areas where the Muslim aristocracy had lost control. According to James Taylor, writing in 1840, one-sixth of the population of the districts of Faridpur, Bakerganj and Mymensingh, and one-third of Dhaka district, belonged to the Faraidi sect.[7]

Predictably, as this powerful religious reform movement spread among the Muslim peasantry in the rural areas, it was transformed into a social protest movement. While the mobilisation of poorer classes began to frighten the oppressive Hindu *zamindars* and Christian indigo-planters, it simultaneously created confidence in the peasantry to assert its rights against vested interests.

The Faraidis soon came in conflict with the Hindu *zamindars*. On the instruction of their leaders, the Faraidi peasants refused to pay the *abwabs* (taxes imposed in excess of the original assessment by the *zamindars*), such as *Shrada Kharch* (levied on the death of a member of the *Zamindar's* family), *Poita Kharch* (levied when the Zamindar's son takes sacred thread), *Rath Kharch* (levied on Zamindar's car procession) and *Durga Vrithi* (levied for the festival in honour of the goddess Durga). Since taxes were spent only for Hindu festivals, the Faraidis contended that they were wrong and illegal. These taxes were especially objectionable to Muslim peasants since the payment of any of them meant encouragement of polytheism, a grievous sin on the part of a Muslim. The Faraidi peasants also came into conflict with the wealthy on secular grounds as well—with the indigo-planters and their agents who, to make huge profits through the export of indigo, forced the peasants to grow indigo and sell it to them at a price less than the cost of its production.

Despite Shariatullah's efforts to keep the Faraidi movement limited to the religious field, confrontations between Faraidi-inspired peasants and farm and plantation landlords continued. Responding to complaints from the *zamindars* and indigo-planters of Faridpur, Shariatullah was arrested by the police in April 1831, and was forced to give an undertaking that he would keep the peace in future.[8] However, when Shariatullah was succeeded by his son Dudu Miyan after Shariatullah's death in 1840, Dudu Miyan articulated a series of extremely radical economic ideas and developed a network of Faraidi organisations that covered almost the whole of Eastern Bengal.

Dudu Miyan quoted Koranic teachings that everything in heaven and earth belonged to God and that "man, being his most favoured creature, has equal claim to exploit this divine right". In Dudu Miyan's view, land belonged to those who exploited it. He strongly protested against hereditary rights to land and to the imposition of what he said was twenty-three kinds of illegal and unIslamic taxes by the Hindu *zamindars*. He asked the members of the Faraidi movement not to pay such taxes but instead to pay only the land revenue imposed by the Government of Bengal.[9]

Dudu Miyan's ideas were obviously extremely detrimental to the economic interests of the *zamindars* and indigo-planters. These vested groups attacked, harassed, assaulted and tortured the Faraidis. Innumerable legal suits were filed against them.[10] But Dudu Miyan sustained two main objectives in the face of such harassment: (a) protection of the Faraidi peasantry from the oppression of *zamindars* and indigo-planters, and (b) the securing of equal justice for the masses of the Muslims of Bengal. In order to promote the first of these objectives, Dudu Miyan raised a volunteer force of clubmen and arranged for their regular training in the art of affray fighting.

To advance the second objective, Dudu Miyan developed an elaborate system of administration for the followers of the Faraidi movement. His administrative reforms entailed the division of Faraidi settlement areas into small units consisting of 300–500 Faraidi families. Ten or more village units formed a "gird", or neighbourhood. In each of the village units Dudu Miyan appointed a unit khalifah. In each of the girds a superintendent khalifa was appointed. Each unit khalifa was subordinate to a superintendent khalifa.

At the apex of the above-described hierarchical structure was the *ustad*, ("master") i.e., Dudu Miyan himself. A few highly competent persons, styled *uparastra khalifas*, were appointed as advisers to the *ustad*. Each of the *uparastra khalifas* was given charge of various fields covered by the movement— religious doctrines, social problems, political affairs, security (affray fighters), and others.

The functions of the unit khalifas were manifold. They included teaching the Faraidis the *kalima* and other obligatory duties, making arrangements for congregational prayers, and administering justice according to the *Shariat*. The superintendent khalifas were to watch the activities of the unit khalifas, act as a court of appeal for decisions of the unit khalifas, to take an interest in the social and spiritual welfare of the Faraidis, and to look after political affairs in the "gird". One of the principal tasks of the khalifa was to raise a volunteer corps of clubmen, and to provide for their regular training. A member of the movement was not allowed to bring any disputes to the government courts without permission from the superintendent khalifas or *ustad*.[11]

As can be seen from the above, Dudu Miyan developed what amounted to a virtual parallel government to that of the British. This led some administrators to argue that Dudu Miyan's ultimate aim was to achieve the political independence of the country. According to Dampier, Commissioner of Dacca, Dudu Miyan had 80,000 active followers under his control. Dampier also said that "the real object of Faraidis was the expulsion of the then rulers in the land and the restoration of the Mahomedan power".[12] We do not know the source material of Dampier, on the basis of which he came to such a conclusion. Dampier certainly overestimated the strength and political motives of the Faraidis. There is no evidence either in the policies or actions of the Faraidis to suggest that they were engaged in a conspiracy to overthrow the British rule. At that time, such a policy or goal would have been simply impractical.

The Faraidi movement, like other movements in India at the time, was a purely local movement that started first as a religious movement, and later took on social and economic aspects. Its primary political goal was to protect the helpless Muslim masses from the miserable conditions created by despotic and capricious *zamindars* of rural Bengal. Contradicting the views of Dampier, Beveridge has argued that the Faraidis did not "share the dangerous political views of the Wahhabis. . . ."[13]

Radical Revivalism: Tariqah-i-Muhammadya

The Faraidi movement for the first time stirred the Bengal Muslim masses from their stupor, gave them new vigour, strengthened their Muslim identity, and prepared the ground for more radical socio-political movements. One of these more radical movements, *Tariqah-i-Muhammadya* (the Way of Mohammad), was launched in 1826, about a decade after the start of the Faraidi movement of Shariatullah, by Sayyid Ahmed Shahid in Delhi. The Tariqah-i-Muhammadya movement eventually spread all over North-west and Northern India, including Bengal.

Born in a respectable Sayed family of Rai Bareli (in U.P.) in 1786, Sayyid Ahmed was a spiritual inheritor of Shah Waliullah and his son Shah Abdul Aziz. These latter had tried to save Islam by emphasising *ijtehad* (individual judgment) in explaining the Koran and the Sunnah. They wrote profusely on Islamic theology, as well as on the prevailing social, political and economic problems of Muslim India. They tried, through the establishment of puritanical organisations and religious schools, to remove all the unIslamic customs, beliefs and practices that had crept into Islam.[14] Sayyid Ahmed was even more radical than Shah Waliullah and Shah Abdul Aziz in declaring India *Darul Harb* (Land of the Infidels). Sayyid Ahmed declared *jihad* (holy war) against the infidels—first against the Sikhs, and then against the British.

Economically depressed, politically uprooted, religiously fanatical and confused, thousands of Muslims in Bengal and Bihar were stirred to their depths by the preachings of Sayyid Ahmed and his associates. For attaining a better life in this world, and to gain rewards in the life hereafter, these Muslims directed their souls towards the path of God and the Prophet, in the spirit of *jihad*, as desired by Sayyid Ahmed. Having selected Patna (in Bihar) as the permanent centre of his propaganda, Sayyid Ahmed came into contact there with a number of important men, including two brothers—Inayat Ali and Wilayat Ali—who played an important role in Sayyid's movement.

Before leaving for Mecca to perform hajj, Sayyid Ahmed had established a sort of parallel government movement, similar in some ways to that of the Faraidis, which was based on the authority of five caliphs, including Muhammad Hussain as the chief khalifa. The other four khalifas were Maulvi Wilayat Ali, Inayat Ali, Marhum Ali and Farhat Hussain. Sayyid Ahmed also appointed innumerable principal and local agents to preach his doctrine and collect taxes from the profits of trade. These funds were used to support his parallel government, and to make preparation for *jihad*.

On his return from Mecca, Sayyid Ahmed was himself declared a khalifa, and "began to preach with renewed vigour, centring his attack on the abuses, seeking to free Islam from the corruptions".[15] According to European writers, including Hunter, Sayyid's close contact with the Arabian Wahhabis led him to urge—more directly and more emphatically—the Muslims of India to make up their minds in favour of *jihad*, which was at the time, thought to be a religious obligation in a country of *Darul Harb*.[16] In any event, Sayyid Ahmed asked the chiefs of different Indian native states to help him in a holy war against the Sikhs. With their assurances of help, Sayyid Ahmed left for the frontier.

Besides the preachings of the khalifas, the agents and other emissaries appointed by Sayyid Ahmed distributed pamphlets and seditious literature throughout India, seeking to fan the fires of *jihad* in the minds of Muslims. As one scholar has written,

> Bengal became the chief field of propaganda and recruitment. . . . Moulvi Karamat Ali of Jaunpur travelled through Chittagong, Noakhali, Dhaka, Mymensingh, Faridpur and Barisal, Inayat Ali of Patna confined his exertions to middle Bengal and preached in Faridpur, Pabna, Rajshahi, Maldah and Bogra. . . . [Thus] . . . the movement became to a great extent a Bengali Muhammadan revival.[17]

The khalifas and their agents established a strong organisational network throughout the whole of Bengal to recruit men and collect money and
arms, and to send them to the rebel camp. A regular system of correspondence was also established linking district centres with the frontier through
the Patna headquarters.

Youths under the age of twenty, from nearly every district of Eastern
Bengal, were sent, batch by batch, to sacrifice their lives to the cause of *jihad*.
These recruits were poor peasants. As Mallick has pointed out, these people,
ignorant and uninformed Muslims from educationally backward areas, had
been deprived of any facilities for self-education. They were dissatisfied with
the existing order of society, and could find no way out of their misery. It is
little wonder that they became easy converts to radical social and political
doctrines, preached in the name of religion.[18]

The main spirit of the movement, Sayyid Ahmed, did not lead the
movement for long. He died in 1831, in the battle of Balakot, warring against
the Sikhs. Although the ultimate aim of Sayyid Ahmed was to capture
political power in the whole of India in order to establish an Islamic state
there, he made it clear, for tactical reasons, that he had declared holy war
against the Sikhs and not against the British. Possibly he did not want to fight
both the enemies at the same time, preferring to seek elimination first of the
comparatively weaker enemy, the Sikhs.

After Sayyid Ahmed's death, when Punjab had been conquered by the
British, Sayyid Ahmed's followers turned against them too. Under the
leadership of Inayat Ali and Wilayat Ali, the movement gained momentum,
despite constant British harassment, arrests and trials of the preachers and
their agents. Money and men continued to flow from Bengal to the frontier for
the fight against the infidel, but by now the infidels were the British.

From 1850, however, when Inayat Ali began to preach in Rajshahi (in
North Bengal) with renewed vigour and zeal against the British, the authori-
ties began to take action against the Wahhabi preachers. The Wahhabi
fighters on the Punjab frontier, though not invincible, were not a negligible
force. During the years 1850 to 1863, the British government had to send a
total of 60,000 regular troops, besides irregular auxiliaries and police, to
combat the Wahhabis in a series of engagements.

No other puritanical movement in India was ever able to cover as vast an
areal of Bengal and India as the Wahhabis. Although like all other puritanical movements, the Wahhabi movement had to face a number of obstacles—
from the orthodox *mullahs* (who were fanatical about Islam without having
much knowledge of it), and from people who were accustomed to longstand-
ing practices, beliefs and customs—the movement definitely created a new
vigour and enthusiasm among the moribund and puzzled Muslims in Bengal.
The Wahhabis created a spirit of austerity in the minds of the Muslims of
Bengal, encouraging them to keep themselves away from all beliefs, customs,
and innovations that had penetrated into Islam from Hinduism and Buddhism during the long years of coexistence.

Revivalism: the Ta'aiyuni Movement

A second puritanical movement which was almost contemporary with the *Tariqah-i-Muhammadya* Movement, and was absolutely religious in character, was led by Maulana Karamat Ali, a resident of Jaunpur, the Province of Uttar Pradesh, Northern India. Maulana Karamat Ali was an ardent disciple of Sayyid Ahmed. He was also a student of Shah Abdul Aziz, under whom he had acquired expertise in Islamic theology. Although he worked for Sayyid Ahmed he neither took part in *jihad* nor went to the Afghan border to fight against the Sikhs. Karamat Ali termed his doctrine the Ta'aiyuni movement, through which he tried to revive Islam along purely orthodox lines. In his view, the Muslims of Eastern India, especially Eastern Bengal and Bihar, were plunged "so much in superstitious beliefs, customs and ceremonies that [they] became apprehensive of Divine retributions". In order to help rid Islam of superstitions in Eastern India, Karamat Ali came to Bengal in 1835 and spent the rest of his life there. He rejected all of the accretions and innovations in Islam that he found in East Bengal. He specially denounced music, dance and the raising of *tazia* on the occasion of *Muharram, Urs* and *Fatiha*.

In contrast to the views expressed by the Wahhabis and Faraidis, Karamat Ali declared that India was not *Darul Harb*, that the congregational prayers of *Jumah* and the two *'Ids* were lawful. He also criticised the intense political involvement of the Wahhabis and the radical programmes of the Faraidis. Karamat Ali conveyed "the true and pure teachings" to the hill people of Assam, the people of Eastern Bengal and residents of distant islands in the Bay of Bengal. His peaceful and moderate reform movement touched the hearts of the people of Bengal, without much opposition. In the view of Titus, Karamat Ali was "a skilful organiser . . . [who] showed great power throughout his life for regenerating Islam and revitalising Islamic life in Eastern Bengal". Surveying the Bengal of his time, Titus said that, "There was scarcely a village in Bengal that did not contain some of his [Karamat Ali's] disciples".[19] After his death in 1873, Karamat Ali's son, Maulvi Hafiz Ahmed, and his nephew, Muhammad Muhsin, assumed leadership of the movement.

Revivalist Movements: A Short Evaluation

The previous pages have examined the nineteenth-century revivalist movements in India, in which Bengal played the central part by providing most of the "soldiers of Islam" (recruits for the *jihad*). The discussion brings into bold relief the strengths and weaknesses of revivalist movements, particularly in the context of the confrontation between traditional and modern forces. The puritan movements failed to adapt Islam to the modernising forces generated by British rule. These movements could not show the Bengali Muslim community the way to shape their lives in conformity with changing social, political and economic conditions. Nor were these movements successful in eliminating all unIslamic beliefs, customs, local traditions and other accretions and innovations derived from the infidels.

Without a constructive programme, the Islamic-based protest movements were unable to upgrade the social position of lower-class Muslims of Bengal by emancipating them from the economic misery and distress caused by oppressive Hindu *zamindars*. But the movements did increase ideological conflicts within Islam. Except for the Wahhabi movement, which continued for over fifty years, all other movements either petered away with the death of their founder or lost direction, or became insignificant through a reduction of their followers or merger with other programmes. In these ways the Islamic-based protest movements of Bengal lost their earlier identities.

However, the consequences of these movements for Islamic revivalism were not entirely in vain. They did achieve some things, and these achievements have assured them a distinctive place in the history of Islam in Bengal. First among these achievements were the initial political organisations of the ignorant, superstitious and oppressed Muslims of the rural areas, who gained considerable consciousness of their potential as a social force. The religious spirit which penetrated the hearts of Bengali Muslims through the revivalist movements gave new life to people who otherwise lived in hopeless and helpless conditions. Although the recruits to these movements were ultimately crushed by the combined forces of the powerful *zamindars* and ruling authority, the revivalists did set an example for future generations as regards the appeal to ignorant masses of *jihad* in the name of religion. Later, during the Khilafat movement and the Pakistan movement, leaders like Gandhi and Jinnah were to take advantage of that religious spirit, although the contexts and motives of these later movements were quite different.

Although these reform movements did not gain much success in purifying Islam, still they did have some success in this field by enforcing Islamic rules and regulations in the daily life of Muslims. At least they made Bengali Muslims alert and conscious about the true nature of their religion and showed them how far they had deviated from the pristine Islamic path. Such guidance was extremely helpful and timely for those Muslims of Bengal at the time who did not have much access to knowledge and education, whose social position and prestige was at an all-time low and whose economic and political power had been submerged in a competitive and hostile environment. Expressing themselves through religious movements, the Muslims of Bengal signalled to others in high places of the country that they were very much alive in Bengal.

Modernist Adaptation

From the experience of the spontaneous and indigenous early Islamic revivalist movements described above, more practical, modern and progressive movements took shape. These were ultimately influenced by Western culture and civilisation, which emerged first in Bengal and later in other parts of India. In this context, the Mutiny of 1857 was the great watershed for the development of Islam in India and Bengal. To be sure, both Hindus and Muslims participated in the Mutiny, but Muslims played the predominant part in it and, as far as the Muslims were concerned, the Mutiny was the culmination of Muslim revivalist armed opposition to British rule. The Muslim *ulema* declared India as *Darul Harb* when the Mutiny started, and the Wahhabi leaders joined the sepoy mutiny en bloc.[20]

The British considered the Muslims to have been the predominant force in the Mutiny and singled out the Muslims for retribution when it was over. Hundreds of noble Muslim families were crushed. The Muslims of Bengal had first experienced the British policy of elimination (until 1857) and later bore the brunt of unsympathetic and harsh attitudes of the British Raj all over India. Wrong done to the Muslims by the British in the post-Mutiny years have been detailed by W.W. Hunter in his celebrated work *the Indian Musalmans* published in 1871. Hunter showed how "the Muhammadans have suffered most severely under the British rule".[21] He concluded:

> A hundred and seventy years ago it was almost impossible for a well-born Musalman in Bengal to become poor; at present it is almost impossible for him to continue to be rich.[22]

Learning from the hard school of suffering, the Muslim eventually realised the futility of resisting the British by depending simply on a spirit of protest and *jihad*. The British rulers had the advantage of modern science and organisation. The Muslims would have to accommodate themselves to British rule and to take Western education to save themselves from total ruination. They "felt the need for a new kind of leadership—a leadership of adjustment—to find a *modus vivendi* with the British rulers and their resurgent Hindu compatriots".[23]

Modernist Islam in Bengal: Nawab Abdul Latif (1828–1893)

The pioneers of the Islamic modernist movement in Bengal were Nawab Abdul Latif and Syed Ameer Ali. In contrast to the leaders of the Faraidi and Tariqah-i-Muhammadya (Wahhabi) movements, who were born in obscure families, Nawab Abdul Latif and Syed Ameer Ali came from noble and aristocratic families. The base of support for the modernist movement was also different from that of the earlier movements. Where the Wahhabi and Faraidi movements had drawn support from the peasants and other rural lower classes, the modernist movements were supported by middle- and upper-class Muslims.

Calcutta, the centre of British economic and cultural radiation, took the lead in this matter, originally through the leadership of Nawab Abdul Latif, who founded the Muhammadan Literary Society in 1863. This was the first formal Muslim organisation in the whole of India to express modernist hopes and aspirations, demands and grievances, of Muslim Bengal in particular and Muslims in all other parts of India as well. Sayyid Ahmad Khan (1817–1898), the famous advocate of Western learning and founder of the Muhammadan Anglo-Oriental College at Aligarh modelled after Oxford and Cambridge, was greatly influenced by the pioneering activities of Nawab Abdul Latif.

By 1863, when the Muhammadan Literary Society was formed, Bengali Muslims were already the objects of extreme distrust and suspicion on the part of the British government. They were blamed for bringing about the Sepoy Mutiny, even though Bengal had been quiet during that time. But there was no doubt that the propaganda of the Wahhabi leaders, as well as the teachings of the relatively educated and conscious sections of the *ulema* had fomented some kind of hatred against the infidel British, and especially against their language, among Bengali Muslims. This hatred was also directed against Hindu neighbours with whom the Muslims had lived for centuries.[24] In this atmosphere bringing about reconciliation between the Muslims and the British Raj was not an easy task.

Bengali Muslims at the time did not have a strong middle class to lead the community. Nor did the Muslim upper and aristocratic classes have the capacity to provide leadership to their own class, or to the Muslim peasantry. The Muslim upper classes were too tormented by their recent loss of political and economic power to the British. Besides, the aristocratic classes had always remained aloof from the ordinary Muslim peasantry, looking upon them with contempt. Nawab Abdul Latif, observing the pitiable condition of the Bengal Muslims and realising the fact "that British rule in India was too powerful to be resisted and too useful to be ignored", came out to rescue that sinking nation. Because of his determination and conviction he ultimately became successful in persuading both the rulers and the ruled to change their attitudes towards one another. To handle such an emotional, difficult and delicate situation he proceeded slowly, tactfully, but very firmly.

The Muhammadan Literary Society was the central point from which all of Nawab Abdul Latif's other activities were to emanate. The aim of this society was to introduce Islamic thought and values into modern consciousness. Exploration of Western learning and science was undertaken gradually, with the main emphasis initially on learning the English language. English education was possible, first, only if Bengali Muslims could be persuaded to give up their prejudice and apathy towards the English language—indeed, only if one could create genuine interest in learning the language. A major goal of Nawab Abdul Latif, therefore, was to persuade the British Indian government to provide educational opportunities.

A second aim of the Muhammadan Literary Society was to create opportunities for the Muslims to communicate with the best representatives of English and Hindu societies, for the cultivation of social and intellectual intercourse. The goal of the society was to serve as "a consultative body for advising the government on all occasions wherein Muhammadan interests may be concerned".[25] The principal activities of the society included addresses, discussions, lectures, meetings, discourses on various subjects, and an annual conference that was held at Calcutta Town Hall.

Nawab Abdul Latif understood the minds of Bengalis and the environment of Bengal. He did not want to hurt the feelings of Bengali Muslims by sudden and radical changes in the education system. What he wanted was to spread English education and science along with knowledge of Persian and Arabic. Such a development, he was convinced, could give Bengali Muslims the benefit of modern knowledge and a share in the process of government; at the same time, it would also enable them to "preserve their cultural heritage".[26] If a man with English knowledge alone was not respected by contemporary Bengali Muslim society, the English-educated man with knowledge of Arabic and Persian might be both respected and more effective in that society.

Based on the above reasoning, Nawab Abdul Latif advocated the continuation of the traditional *madrassa* education. The reason for retaining *madrassa* education was that only petty businessmen and petty service holders used to send their sons to English schools. If *madrassa* education had been stopped entirely there might have been an adverse reaction from among the important segment of common Muslims. Abdul Latif did advocate the revision and modification of the curricula of the *madrassas*, and sought improvements in the standards of Arabic learning, but he did not call for the abolition of traditional Islamic schools.

As a practical step towards English learning, English language and literature had been introduced to Hastings' Calcutta *madrassa*, and in new schools and colleges in Bengal and other parts of India, but Abdul Latif eventually persuaded the Government of India to spend more money for the spread of education in Bengal among rural Muslims. For example, the Muslim Fund money that was being spent for Hughli College, where most of the students were Hindus, was diverted in such a way as to be spent only for Muslim students as a result of Nawab Abdul Latif's efforts.

From its inception the pro-British and non-political Muhammadan Literary Society gained the confidence of the government, which treated it as the representative body of the educated Muslims of Bengal. On questions of Islamic law, and on other matters concerning the interests of the Muslims, members of the society were asked to give advice to the government. The society was also supported by the European community in Calcutta on a private basis, and by the few well-to-do Muslims still existing in Bengal.

The society's objectives were particularly beneficial to upper- and middle-class Muslims of Bengal in particular, and to Muslims in other part of India. Benefits to lower-class Muslims from the movement were rather small and indirect, for three reasons. First, it was not possible for rural Muslims to travel to Calcutta to attend discussions and conferences. Second, the peasantry did not know what was happening in Calcutta. Their ignorance and lack of consciousness in this matter was abysmal. And, finally, there was a language barrier between urban and rural Bengali Muslims. The society's activities—lectures, discussions, conferences, etc.—were conducted in Persian, Arabic or English, which the masses could not understand. The society did have some impact, however, on the petty government servants and businessmen, whose outward contacts were much more liberal in religious outlook than those of peasants. Government servants and small businessmen were interested in giving English education to their sons, as were the middle and upper classes. It was accurately reported, therefore, that the society's meetings "were very numerously attended by all respectable members of the community". These two classes thus benefited most in moulding their religious outlook in response to the needs of modern society under the leadership of Nawab Abdul Latif.

The Muhammadan Literary Society not only "gave a new tone to

Muhammadan thought and feeling" in Bengal, it also benefited Muslims in other parts of India. The Abstracts of the Proceedings of the society report that "more than 500 Muslims from all parts of India joined this society as ordinary members". Those people eventually formed the nucleus of a strong, educated Muslim middle class, which came to fruition at the turn of the century when it first began to qualify for government jobs and political positions. With the death of Nawab Abdul Latif in 1893, the Muhammadan Literary Society lost its initial vigour and enthusiasm; but the changes that he brought about in the minds of Bengali Muslims continued to produce significant results through the years. It might be pointed out that Abdul Latif's work was accomplished in a practical way, avoiding complex theological explanations without excluding them.[27]

Progressive Islam: Syed Ameer Ali

While Abdul Latif was a practical man of action, Syed Ameer Ali, like Sir Sayyid Ahmad Khan was both an intellectual and a capable organiser. Sayyid Ahmad argued that Islam did not have any contradiction with progress; Ameer Ali said that Islam was that progress.[28] According to Ameer Ali, "Islam is par excellence the religion of civilisation". He spent much of his life describing the civilising force of Islam over Muslim nations during the days of the Prophet Muhammad, the Four Caliphs and Abbasid rule. Islamic civilisation, Syed Ameer Ali pointed out, had tremendous influence over all of the countries conquered by Muslim heroes in all parts of the world. In the fields of literature, art, agriculture, science and technology, the rule of law, and democracy, Islam had a brilliant past. Syed Ameer Ali proudly cited the names of world-famous universities—Baghdad, Cairo, Cordoba, Kufa, and Basrah—as centres of learning. He also cited pioneering scientific discoveries, especially in the fields of mathematics, geography, chemistry and astronomy, by Muslim scholars. In Syed Ameer Ali's view, Europe was indebted to Islam, directly or indirectly, for progress in scientific discovery, learning, culture and civilisation.[29]

Ameer Ali emphasised the glorious past of Islam in an attempt to bring about a moral and political revival among the Muslims. Like preceding Muslim thinkers, he also understood the value of organisation as an instrument for moral awakening and political mobilisation. Thus Ameer Ali, in contrast to Sayyid Ahmad and Abdul Latif, sought formation of political association as well as educational and academic training. He formed the Central Mohammadan Association, with an eye on those newly-emerging middle-class Muslims whose political consciousness was imperative for the future development of the Muslim nation.[30]

Modernist Islamic Writings in Bengali

A key element in the spread of Islamic modernism in Bengal areas has been the growth of enormous Islamic modernist writings in the Bengali language since the beginning of the twentieth century, which has been virtually ignored by the Western analysts of subcontinental Islam, like W.C. Smith, H.A.R. Gibb and L.S. May. Although, as we have seen above, Bengal was the main theatre of the activities of Nawab Abdul Latif and Syed Ameer Ali, these two early modernisers of Islam in Bengal came from Urdu-speaking upper classes and belonged to the cultural milieu developed by the Urdu-speaking, Western-educated Muslim of Central and North-western India, led intellectually first by Sayyid Ahmad Khan. While the Muslims in British India lagged behind the Hindus in taking up Western education, the Muslims of Bengal were even later than their counterparts in Central and North-western India in Westernising themselves. As a "new middle class" (lawyers, college- and school-teachers, doctors, government service holders, university and college students, and the like) began to grow among the Bengali Muslims in the early twentieth century, modernist Islamic ideas began to flourish in Bengali writings.[31]

The pioneer in the field of Islamic scholarship in the Bengali language was Mohammad Akram Khan (1868–1968), usually dubbed Sayyid Ahmad Khan of Bengal. Like Sayyid Ahmad Khan, Akram Khan had a long literary, journalistic, scholarly and organisational career, spreading from 1905 (when he first published his translation of *al-Fatiha*—the first chapter of the Koran—and its Exegesis) until his death in 1968. Unlike Sayyid Ahmad Khan, Akram Khan came from a rural lower-middle-class family (he was born in a village in the 24 Pargana district of West Bengal). Although educated in *madrassa*, (orthodox Islamic religious institute), Akram Khan developed a scientific, rational outlook and a keen analytical mind. Akram khan wrote two monumental works in Bengali. The first one, *Mustafa Charit* (Character of Mohammad) first published probably in 1926, was an 871-page biography of the Prophet Mohammad.[32] Akram Khan's second important work was *Tafsirul Koran* (Exegesis of the Koran), in five volumes. The first two volumes were published in 1930,[33] and the five completed volumes were published in 1959.[34] In these two works Akram Khan interpreted the Prophet Mohammad's life and the Koran in the light of modern science and liberal ideas. Akram Khan repudiated the orthodox interpretation of events like the *Miraj* (the ascent of the Prophet Mohammad into heaven), the opening of the breast of the Prophet Mohammad, and the immaculate conception of Jesus. He also argued that descriptions of hell and heaven, and of angels and other non-human creatures in the Koran were all symbolic.[35] Successive newspapers and magazines founded and edited by Akram Khan—*Weekly Mohammadi* (1910), *Daily Sevak* (1922), *Monthly Mohammadi* (1927), and *Daily Azad* (1936)—all propagated the modernist view in Islam among educated Bengalis in the vernacular—a role comparable to that played by *Tahdhibul Akhlaq* ("Reform of character", a monthly paper edited and published by Sayyid Ahmad Khan) and other publications by Sayyid Ahmad Khan among the Urdu-speaking people in Central and North-western India.[36]

In the vein of Sayyid Ahmad Khan, Akram Khan made a clarion call to Muslims—"Back to the Koran".

In the Koran Allah advised the Muslims to resort to *adl*. *Adl* means to put everything in its proper place. To place a particular thing below its proper station is the opposite of *adl*. The opposite of *adl* is injustice and Allah repeatedly states in the Koran that an unjust person or nation is bound to perish. . . . If we observe the condition of the Muslims we find that their national life is filled with injustice. . . . The Muslims are not practising *adl* with respect to the Koran. They have not placed the Koran in its proper place. They have rather brought down the Koran from the highest place and put the Hadith (Tradition of the Prophet) and *fiqh* (jurisprudence) above the Koran. . . . Put the Koran at its proper place and Allah will place you in your proper place.[37]

Why should the Muslims go "back to the Koran"? Akram Khan explains in his article, "The Islamic Ideal", in the very first issue of his monthly *Mohammadi* (1927):

It is the special mission of Islam that it guides man step by step to the ideals of higher and higher progress and ultimately brings his meeting with God: "Ye shall surely travel/ From stage to stage" (LXXIV:19); "Thou man!/Verily thou art ever/Toiling on towards thy Lord/Painfully toiling—but thou/Shall meet Him" (LXXXIV:6). For this reason, while the Islamic ideal does not deny the present, it does not end in the present. It urges man for innumerable new creations. The Islamic ideal will remain effective for all time to come to direct to successful completion the continuous striving of man enjoined in the Koran.[38]

Akram Khan continuously emphasised the "principle of movement" in Islam:

What is Islam is not stationary, what is stagnant is not Islam. Islam welcomes all creative innovations. Islam never lacked nor ever will lack in providing solutions to any problem in the world, because its gate of ijtehad remains open at all times.[39]

Some of the contemporaries of Akram Khan, like Yakub Ali Choudhury (1880–1940), Mohammad Lutfor Rahman (1889–1936), and Mohammad Wajed Ali (1896–1954) in elegant, stirring and poetic language analysed the Prophet Mohammad as the highest fulfilment of human life on earth, and his uniqueness among the prophets as servant and guide for mankind as a whole without referring to the miraculous events attributed to the Prophet by the traditionalist, orthodox or popular writers.[40] Mohammad Barkatullah (1898–1974) eulogised the free and independent thinking developed by *Mutazilites* (Withdrawers) in Basrah and Baghdad in the eighth century, and described in beautiful poetic prose the great Muslim achievements in philosophy, science and literature in the ninth to twelfth centuries, especially in Persia and Spain, which resulted from the development of the independent spirit of the *Mutazilites*.[41] S. Wajed Ali (1890–1951) and Principal Ibrahim Khan (1894–1978), wrote in racy and appealing fashion about Bengali Islam's great relevance for man's worldly as well as his spiritual development.[42] These powerful writings in Bengali produced a sense of pride among the vernacular-educated Bengali Muslims, removed their inferiority complex *vis-a-vis* the Hindus and Christians, and developed in them a positive outlook on life as Syed Ameer Ali's work did for the earlier generation of English-educated upper classes of Bengal and Central India.[43]

Possibly the most important Bengali-speaking Islamic modernist thinker after Akram Khan was Abul Hashim (1905–1974). Unlike Akram Khan,

Abul Hashim chose to write his most important work in English. Abul Hashim's, *The Creed of Islam, or The Revolutionary Character of Kalima*, was first published in 1950.[44] In this book, Abul Hashim presented Islam as an ideology providing directions for the solution of social, political and economic problems faced by man in building an ideal socio-political-economic order in lucid, succinct and elegant style. He writes,

> The pragmatic and the operative aspect of the Holy Quran is divided into two parts—duty to God and duty to man, called in Arabic "Huq-ul-lah" and "Huq-ul-ibad". Duty to God is private and duty to man is the public and social part of the teachings of the Holy Quran. The novelty of the Holy Quran is that it makes performance of duty to God void and invalid when duty to man is ignored or is not duly performed. The Holy Quran puts it like this, "Do you see the one who belies religion? Such is the one who is inimical to the orphans and encourages not the feeding of the indigent. So woe to the prayer performers who are neglectful of prayers, those who make a show and refuse neighbourly needs" (S. CVII:V.1–7). This is the greatest tragedy of man that this human aspect of Islam is now completely forgotten. This is why we do not find anywhere in the world of today a typical Muslim society although there are so many so-called Muslim states and nations in the world.[45]

What is the "public and social part of teaching" of the Holy Koran? Abul Hashim argues that the very first Principle of Islam (Kalima)—"There is no deity but God and Mohammed is His Prophet"—is a radical and revolutionary doctrine. It liberates the human mind from the servitude of polytheistic gods and spirits, and also from the bondage of pride and vanity of man that goes with atheism, agnosticism and nihilism. According to the Koran, man is inferior only to God but he is superior to everything that is in the earth and universe. Thus the Koran states,

> And He had made subservient to you the night and the day and the sun and the moon and the stars are made subservient by His commandment, most surely there are signs in this for a people who ponder (XVI:12),

and again,

> Do you see that Allah has made what is in the heavens and what is in the earth subservient to you and made complete to you His favour outwardly and inwardly? (XXXI:20).[46]

The Kalima thus brings about an intellectual revolution by making man "free and sublime". Man, following the Koranic injunction to "ponder", "think" and "understand", continuously seeks newer and newer frontiers of knowledge to protect, sustain and nourish the earth and the universe on the pattern of God Himself.[47]

The Kalima by establishing "the fatherhood of God and brotherhood of man", demolishes all distinctions between human beings based on race, colour, sex, and the like. The only distinction that the Koran makes among human beings is the distinction between the virtuous and the vicious. Thus the Koran proclaims,

> O ye men! Verily We have created you from a man and a woman and We have made you groups and tribes to identify you, verily the best of you before God are thus who are most virtuous among you (XLIX:13).

Could there be a more real sense of brotherhood than the one enjoined by the Koran?[48]

As for the political revolution, the Koran enjoins that the rulership is the vice-gerency of God, and only the persons having Godly attributes—"the knowledge of the ultimately good"—would be selected as rulers who will be entitled to obedience as long as they obey God and the Prophet.[49]

According to Abul Hashim, the economic system enjoined by Islam is different from both capitalism and socialism. He argues,

> God of the Kalima, the Nourisher of the universe, is the absolute owner of material wealth of the earth. The Kalima liquidated pretensions of man to ownership of wealth— private or public, individualistic or collective. "For to God belongeth the dominion of the heavens and the earth, and all that is between" (S. v:V.19), is the clear verdict of the Holy Quran in this matter. Man is entitled to possession and use of wealth and that too in his capacity as the caliph or vice-gerent of God on earth for his own nourishment, consistently with the nourishment not merely of the rest of humanity but of the rest of the creation.[50]

For Abul Hashim the Golden Age of man has yet to come, and only an Islamic revolution can bring it about. A group of fairly competent Western-educated Bangladeshi scholars who are mainly university and college professors, and are associated with Islamic Foundation, Bangladesh, of which Abul Hashim was the first Director (in 1960 when it was the Islamic Academy, Dacca, Pakistan), have continued till now the tradition of radical interpretation of Islam initiated by Abul Hashim.[51]

Continuing Strengths of Orthodox Revivalism and Adapted Islamic Tradition

However, as we shall see below in Chapter III, the Islamic modernist movement in Bangladesh areas could transform only a very small section of the Bangladeshi Muslims to date. Orthodox Islamic revivalism continues to compete with medieval adapted Islamic tradition, which still seems to command the allegiance of nearly half of the Muslim population of Bangladesh.[52]

It is the *madrassa* (higher schools for orthodox religious education) system of education which has probably helped most to keep the orthodox revivalist movement alive in Bangladesh areas. Although the syllabi of the different levels and streams of *madrassa* education had been "modernised" in Pakistan and Bangladesh periods by inserting in them smatterings of mathematics and social, physical and biological sciences, the learning of the Arabic language and literature, and the scholastic, literalist and fundamentalist exegesis of the Koran, Hadith and *al-fiqh* (Islamic jurisprudence) still dominate the course contents of the *madrassas*.[53] The *madrassa*-educated people provide the teachers for the course on *Islamyat* (Islamic religious studies), which has been a compulsory subject for all Muslim students in primary and secondary schools throughout Pakistan and Bangladesh periods. They also provide *imams* (persons who lead prayer in the mosques) for the major mosques in Bangladesh,[54] and teachers for private *madrassas* and *maktabs* (primary level schools for religious education) attached to most of these mosques. The people with orthodox Islamic education from *madrassas* usually man the numerous religious organisations, like *Tablig-Jamaat* (Preachers' Association), *Islam Prochar Samity* (Association for Preaching Islam), the *Koranic School Society*, and *Bangladesh Masjid* Mission (Bangladesh Mosque Mission), engaged in preaching and propagating orthodox Islam. The *madrassa*-educated scholars have produced in the modern Bengali language a vast literature on orthodox Islam with profuse citations from the Koran in Arabic, and their translations and exegesis in Bengali, this literature is the twentieth-century substitute for the *puthi* literature[55] which catered to the religious hunger of Bengali Muslims in earlier centuries.

The medieval "popular" or "syncretistic" tradition of Islam seems to be sustained by the institutions of *pirs* (religious leaders with miraculous powers) and *mazars* (tombs of the dead *pirs*). People regularly visit *khanqahs* (convents of the living *pirs*) and *mazars* to invoke intercession of the *pirs* for the acceptance of their prayers to God, and to offer votive prayers and donations. Besides, the *khanqahs* and *mazars* have become centres for annual assemblies for the death or birth anniversaries of the *pirs* where mass prayers are held and sermons are preached. The *mullahs* (the rural priestly class, usually with lower-level *madrassa* education), who earn part of their living by acting as shamans and by selling amulets and other charms, provide the border-line between the orthodox and popular Islamic traditions in Bangladesh.[56]

Furthermore, a family in Bangladesh, in both formal and informal ways, is playing a significant role in Islamic socialisation. As will be seen in Chapter IX, large numbers of children in rural areas, and a majority of the children in urban areas, are receiving early Islamic education (learning of the Koran, Hadith, Namaz, Roza and other Islamic principles) from their parents and other relatives.

NOTES

1   See Chapter I above, pp. 27–8.
2   A.R. Mallick, *British Policy and the Muslims in Bengal (1757–1856)* (Dacca: Bangla Academy, 1977), pp. 3–4.
3   M. Iqbal, quoted in *ibid.*, p. 30.
4   See *ibid.*, pp. 3–30: M.A. Rahim *et al.*, *Bangladesher Itihash* (History of Bengal) (Dacca: Nowroj Kitabistan, 1977), pp. 367–8; M.A. Rahim, *Social and Cultural History of Bengal*, Vol. II (Karachi: Pakistan Historical Society, 1967), pp. 381–9; M.U.A. Khan, *History of Faraidi Movements in Bengal* (Dhaka: Islamic Foundation, second edition, 1984), pp. 89–106; R. Ahmed, *The Bengal Muslims 1871–1906: A Quest for identity* (Delhi: Oxford University Press, 1981), pp. 53–5.
5   For the details of Faraidi leaders, see Mallick, *op. cit.*, pp. 66–78, 82.
6   For the reform programme of Shariatullah, see A.I. Shaikh, *Pir Dudu Miyan* (in Bengali) (Dacca: Islamic Foundation, 1980, published to celebrate the commencement of 1400 al-Hijra), pp. 7–9.
7   Mallick, *op. cit.*, p. 79.
8   *Ibid.*, pp. 80–91.
9   M.U.A. Khan, *op. cit.*, pp. 285–6.
10 Mallick, *op. cit.*, p. 86.
11 M.U.A. Khan, *op. cit.*, pp. 272–84; Shaikh, *op. cit.*, pp. 10–11.
12 Mallick, *op. cit.*, p. 86.
13 M.A. Rahim, *The Muslim Society and Politics in Bengal* (Dacca: University of Dacca, 1978), p. 80.

14 For a detailed discussion of the reform movements launched by Shah Waliullah and Shah Abdul Aziz, see H. Malik, *Muslim Nationalism in India and Pakistan* (Washington, D.C.: Public Affairs Press, 1963), pp. 123–53.

15 M.T. Titus, *Islam in India and Pakistan* (Madras, The Christian Literature Society, first published, 1930, revised and reprinted, 1959), p. 189

16 W.W. Hunter, *The Indian Musalmans* (Dacca: Banalipi Mudrayon, Bangladesh edition, 1975), pp. 49–50.

17 Mallick, *op. cit.*, p. 116.

18 *Ibid.*, p. 162. For more on Bengal's role in the *jihad* movement, see Rahim, *op. cit.*, pp. 86–93.

19 Titus, *op. cit.*, pp. 194–5.

20 Abdullah, *Sir Sayyid Ahmad Khar Dharmio O Samajik Chintadhara* (Religious and Social Thought of Sir Sayyid Ahmad) (Dhaka, Islamic Foundation, 1982), p. 379.

21 Hunter, *op. cit.*, p. 141.

22 *Loc. cit.*

23 A. Ahmed, *Studies in Islamic Culture in the Indian Environment* (Oxford: Clarendon Press, 1964), p. 55.

24 Nawab A. Latif, *A Short Account of My Public Life* (Calcutta: Newman, Dalhousie Square, 1885), p. 29.

25 Enamul Haq (ed.), *Nawab Bahadur Abdul Latif,* his writings and related documents (Dacca: Samudra Prakashani, 1968), p. 168.

26 *Loc. cit.*

27 For a detailed account of the role of Nawab Abdul Latif and the Muhammadan Literary Society, see S. Ahmed, *The Muslim Community in Bengal, 1884–1912* (Dhaka: Oxford University Press, 1974), pp. 165–76.

28 W.C. Smith, *Modern Islam in India* (London: Gollancz, 2nd edition, 1946), p. 49.

29 For an excellent discussion on Ameer Ali's ideas, see *ibid.*, pp. 49–55.

30 For more on Ameer Ali's association, see L.S. May, *The Evolution of Indo-Muslim Thought after 1857* (Lahore: Sh. Muhammad Ashraf, 1970), pp. 111–4.

31 The depth and extent of scholarship on Islam in the Bengali language is indicated by the fact that by the middle of the twentieth century Bengali had become the language with the second largest number of translations of the Koran in the whole world. Urdu is the language with the highest number of translations of the Koran—about 99 in 1950. In the same year, the Bengali translations of the Koran numbered about 80. Persian occupies third place with 52 translations of the Koran. For the list of languages and the number of translations of the Koran in each of them, see M.M. Rahman, *Bangla Vashai Koran Charcha* (Culture/Study of the Holy Koran in the Bengali Language) (Dhaka: Islamic Foundation, Bangladesh, 1986), pp. 6–7. The first complete translation of the Koran in Bengali was done by a Brahmo scholar, Bhai Girish Chandra Sen, and was published in 1886. See *ibid.*, p. 42.

32 The first edition of *Mustafa Charit,* published by Mohammadi Press, Calcutta (a copy of which is available in the Rare Copy Section of the Library of the University of Dhaka), does not mention the date of publication. The Library seal on the second cover page of the book shows the accession date as 26 January 1927.

33 Published by Mohammadi Publishing Company, Calcutta.

34 Published by Mohammad Badrul Anam Khan and Mohammad Kamrul Anam Khan, 27-B Dacceshwari Road, Dacca.

35 Rahman, *op. cit.*, pp. 126–44.

36 See "Maulana Akram Khan", in M. Abdullah, *Muslim Jagorone Koekjon Kabi—Shahityik* (Some Poets and Litterateurs in the Muslim Reawakening) (Dacca Islamic Foundation, Bangladesh, 1980), pp. 384–423.

37 "Back to the Koran", *Mohammadi,* Vol. 2, No. 9, 1929; reprinted in A. Jafar (ed.), *Maulana Akram Khan* (in Bengali) (Dacca: Islamic Foundation, Bangladesh, 1986), pp. 419–20. The English rendering of the Bengali passage of Akram Khan has been done by the present writer.

38 *Mohammadi,* Vol. 1, No. 1, 1927, reprinted in *ibid.*, p. 394. The English translation of the Bengali paragraph of Akram Khan has been done by the present writer.

39 Quoted in Abdullah, *op. cit.*, p. 407. Akram Khan's Bengali passage has been translated into English by the present writer.

40 See Y.A. Choudhury, *Manab Mukut* (The Crown of Men) (Calcutta: Nowroj Library, 1926); M.L. Rahman, *Manab Jiban* (Man's Life) (Calcutta: Mohammadi Book Agency, 1936); M.W. Ali, *Moroo Bhashkar* (The Desert Sun) (Calcutta: Bulbul House, 1941).

41 See M. Barkatullah, *Paraysya Prativa* (The Talents of Persia) (Calcutta: Bengal Press, 1924).

42 See S.W. Ali, *Jibaner Shilpa* (The Art of Life) (Calcutta: Gulista Publishing House, 1941); I. Khan, *Islamer Marmakatha* (The Essence of Islam) delivered as a speech at the meeting held in remembrance of Raja Ram Mohan Ray in Tangail in 1934.

43 The "new middle-class" character of these writers was evident from their professional backgrounds. Yakub Ali Choudhury, Mohammad Lutfor Rahman and Mohammad Wajed Ali were respectively high-school teacher, homeopathic doctor, and journalist. Mohammad Barkatullah started his career as a Deputy Magistrate, while S. Wajed Ali alternately practised law and held the job of the Presidency Magistrate in Calcutta. Ibrahim Khan was a college professor. The important works of these writers mentioned in Footnotes 40, 41 and 42, as well as *Mustafa Charit* and *Tafsirul Koran* by Akram Khan, have undergone numerous reprints, and are even widely read today by the educated Muslims in Bangladesh.

44 The book was published by B.M. Umar for Umar Brothers, 26–1 Madan Mohan Basak Road, Dacca. A Bengali translation of the book by B.M. Umar was published in 1968 by Umar Brothers, Dacca. Another translation of the book by Moslem Choudhury was published by Islamic Foundation Bangladesh, Dacca, in 1981. The Islamic Foundation, Bangladesh, brought a reprint of the translation by Moslem Choudhury in 1987.

45 A. Hashim, *The Creed of Islam or the Revolutionary Character of Kalima* (Dacca: Islamic Foundation, Bangladesh, 3rd edition, 1980), p. 34.

46 *Ibid.*, p. 57.

47 *Ibid.*, pp. 70–1.

48 *Ibid.*, pp. 79–90.

49 *Ibid.*, pp. 104–5.

50 *Ibid.*, p. 116.

51 See, for examples, M. Azraf, *Jiban Samashyar Samadhane Islam* (Problems of Life and Their Solutions as put forward by Islam) (Dacca: Islamic Foundation, Bangladesh, 1985); S. Ali, *Jiban Nirabachchinna* (Life is Uninterrupted) (Dacca: Islamic Foundation, Bangladesh, 1980); H. Zaman, *Samaj, Sangskriti, Sahitya* (Society, Culture, and Literature) (Dacca: Islamic Cultural Centre, 1980); A. Ghafur, *Shwashwata Nabi* (The Eternal Prophet) (Dacca: Islamic Cultural Centre, 1980); A. Kashem, *Bigghan, Samaj, Dharma* (Science, Society and Religion) (Dacca: Islamic Foundation, Bangladesh, 1987).

52 See Chapter III, below, pp. 62–3.

53 For the syllabi of different levels and streams of *madrassa* education in Bangladesh, see A.K.M.A. Ali, *The History of Traditional Islamic Education in Bangladesh* (Dacca: Islamic Foundation, Bangladesh, 1983), pp. 208–13. There are now about 3,312 government and affiliated *madrassas* (secondary level and above) under the Bangladesh Madrassa Education Board. The total number of teachers and students of these *madrassas* are 30,988 and 619,000 respectively. See *Statistical Yearbook of Bangladesh, 1986* (Dacca: Bangladesh Bureau of Statistics, 1986), p. 810.

54 The total number of mosques in Bangladesh is 131,641. See *ibid.*, p. 811.

55 The word *puthi* literally means a book or manuscript. It refers generally to all ancient and medieval Bengali works. In the nineteenth century the term came to be associated with a class of literature created by semi-literate Muslims in a mixture of Bengali, Arabic, Persian and Urdu.

56 For discussions on the institutions and organisations fostering orthodox and popular traditions of Islam in Bangladesh, see Professor Ghulam Azam, *Bangladeshe Islamic Andolon* (Islamic Movement in Bangladesh) (Dacca: Islamic Publication, 1978), pp. 11–22; K.M. Mohsin, "Trends in Bangladesh Islam", in R. Ahmed (ed.), *Islam in Bangladesh: Society, Culture and Politics* (Dacca: Bangladesh Itihas Samiti, 1983), pp. 227–49; T. Maniruzzaman, "Bangladesh Politics: Secular and Islamic Trends", in *ibid.*, pp. 184–219.

CHAPTER III

RELIGIOUS BELIEFS IN BANGLADESH ISLAM

The core of any religion is its system of beliefs about the relationship between man and the Supernatural Power, between the created and the Creator, between the mortals and the Immortals. Belief systems explain the meaning of life in the present world and in the world hereafter. A belief system defines the relationship between man and his surroundings. It clarifies the place of man in the world and in the whole universe. In short, it helps man to understand himself and his total environment and thus helps reduce his tensions to manageable limits. Since this is the basic function of all mono-theistic religions, particularly a monotheistic religion like Islam, the belief-system is the central part of the religious arch.

What is the nature of the system of beliefs in Bangladesh Islam? The general contours of religious beliefs in contemporary Bangladesh are clearly indicated by our discussions in Chapters I and II. Bangladesh Islam after centuries of evolution has today three clear types of religious beliefs—modern, orthodox and popular. Modernist Islam tries to give a rational interpretation of the Koran and Hadith. It seeks to differentiate between the fundamental aspects of Islam which are meant for all men for all time and ancillary parts of Islam which were dictated by the time and place of its birth. It urges the adoption of the essentials and rejection of the accidentals of Islam. Modern-ists emphasise the dynamic, scientific and progressive nature of Islam. They do not reject the rituals enjoined as compulsory in Islam, but argue for imbibing the spirit behind as well as the performance of those rituals. Modernist Islam envisages a narrowly personal and specific role of religion in life, and stresses self-determination rather than divine will in the affairs of man.

The orthodox, puritan and literal Islam enjoins total and literal accep-tance of the Koran and the Hadith. It stands for rigid adherence to the canonical laws of Islam and strict observance of compulsory religious injunc-tions—praying five times a day, fasting for one month in a year, annual alms-giving to the poor and pilgrimage to Mecca. While the modernist Muslim would emphasise rationalism and individual judgment in interpret-ing the Koran and the Hadith, the orthodox Muslim would rely more heavily on the scholastic literature and commentaries developed by the literal theolo-gians in the Middle Ages in Arabic, Persian and Urdu for their interpretation of all religious questions. Again, unlike a modernist Muslim, an orthodox Muslim would accept Islam as a complete code of life and believe in determination of all events by God's will.

Both the modernist and orthodox Muslim would not, however, make any compromise on the core ideal of Islam—monotheism. Each of them take literally the Islamic Confession of Faith—"There is no god but God and Mohammad is His Prophet"—and reject any practice and belief suggesting polytheism as totally unIslamic. In contrast to the pure monotheism of modern and orthodox beliefs, the third type of Islamic belief in Bangladesh, variously called "popular", "folk" or "syncretistic", has polytheistic and animistic dimensions. A popular Muslim would formally subscribe to the Confessional Statement about unity of God and finality of Mohammad's Prophethood. But he would in practice acknowledge the sharing of super-natural power of God by the *Pirs*, sacred places, Hindu gods and local deities and spirits by observing rituals and practices meant for cajoling or gratifying these near-Godly forces. The populist Muslim would resort to these idola-trous and polytheistic rituals and practices to avoid danger and misfortune, to cure illness or to increase the prospect of their success in mundane affairs, and the like.

While the existing literature on subcontinental and Bengali Islam delin-eates the three types of religious beliefs mentioned above, it can hardly indicate the extent and depth of the spread of each of these beliefs among the Bangladesh Muslim population. What percentage of the Muslims of Bangla-desh subscribes to the modernist Islamic beliefs? How successful were the efforts of the puritanic, revivalist movements of the nineteenth century in weaning the Muslims of Bangladesh areas from the "great syncretistic tradition" of medieval Bengal Islam? How large is the orthodox segment of the Bangladesh Muslim population today? How accurate is the suggestion of Rafiuddin Ahmed and Asim Roy—the two eminent recent scholars of Bengal Islam—that popular Islam still has sway over a significant section of the Muslim population of the Bangladesh areas?[1]

One of the objectives of our survey was at least a rough quantitative determination of the extent of the spread of modernist, orthodox and popular Islamic religious beliefs among the Bangladesh Muslims. In order to identify the religious beliefs of each of our respondents, we developed a six-item scale of religious beliefs. This scale is based in part on a similar scale developed by Karl D. Jackson in his study, *Traditional Authority, Islam and Rebellion: A Study of Indonesian Political Behavior*.[2] The items used to develop the scale of religious beliefs, the questions asked to the respondents under each item, the process of categorising the answers expressing modern, orthodox and popular beliefs, and the method of coding the answers under each question and item, the distribution of total scores for tabulating the three types of religious beliefs and, finally, the findings resulting from our survey, are discussed in the pages that follow.

Mazar

The first item that we attempted to scale for measuring the religious beliefs of Bengali Muslims concerns perceptions of the *Mazar*, the tomb of a religious divine which is regarded as a sacred place. Contemporary orthodox Muslims in Bangladesh would consider visits to the *Mazar*, or the attribution of supernatural powers to a dead "saint", as a major sin—*shirk* (meaning to attribute partnership with God)—since such practice or belief violates tenets of Islam that demand the unity of all Godly powers. An orthodox Muslim might go to the *Mazar* (the so-called rite of *Ziarat*) in order to pray to Allah for the salvation of the dead, but would not attempt to seek the help of the dead "divine" by invoking magical or sacred powers. Within Bangladesh, however, some populist Muslims still attribute supernatural powers to dead "saints" and solicit their magical or sacred powers as means to attain particular objectives.

Two questions were asked in our survey that were designed to tap the dimensions of our respondents' attitudes towards *Mazar*. The questions were as follows:[3]

Question No.	*Question*
R7A/U18	Why do people go to the *Mazar?*
R8/U19	Do you go to the *Mazar?*

If a respondent answered "No" or "Never" to the second of these questions, that person was classified as modern in so far as this survey item was concerned, on the assumption that the person had given up, or had never engaged in a practice suggesting polytheism. Those respondents who said that they did go to the *Mazar* and mentioned prayer (i.e., "To pray for the dead", "To seek the blessings of Allah", or "Just to pray") as reasons for people's going to the *Mazar*, were classified as orthodox. Finally, those who went to the *Mazar* and mentioned reasons like "To pray to the saint", "To make votive prayers", or "To make offerings to the dead", for people's going to the *Mazar* were classified as popular Muslims. We coded modern answer as 1, orthodox answer as 2, and popular answer as 3.

Accident or Fate

The second criterion that was used to classify respondents in our survey relates to perceptions of *accident and fate*. The question asked to determine such perceptions was the following:

> R9/U8: If you have an accident, who would
> you most likely hold responsible:
> (a) the wrath of God;
> (b) fate;
> (c) the result of past sins;
> (d) just an accident.

Those who answered "Just an accident" were classified as modern. Those who were disposed to view accidents as the wrath of God or the result of sin were categorised as orthodox. Respondents attributing accidents to fate have been classified as popular Muslims. We again coded modern answers as 1, orthodox answers as 2, and popular answers as 3.

Monotheism

We tried to test the monotheistic beliefs of our respondents from three angles—their attitudes towards spirits, unity of Godhead, and *Pirs* (religious divines). The scholars emphasising the syncretistic nature of Bengal Islam usually refer to some Bengali Muslims' proclivity to believe in spirits like ghosts, female ghosts, and demons. The Koran, however, mentions one kind of spirits called *jinn*. While the modernist Muslims would interpret *jinn* as a particular group of uncivilised men, the orthodox Muslims who take the Koran literally, do believe in the *jinn* as a living, non-bodily creature.[4] The question regarding spirits in our survey was as follows:

R10/U9: Do you believe in the influence of *jinn*/ghosts/female ghosts/demons?

The respondents who did not believe in any of these spirits were classified as "modern" and given the weight 1. The interviewees who indicated their beliefs in *jinn* were categorised as orthodox and coded as 2. The respondents who believed in ghosts/female ghosts/demons were grouped as popular and given the score 3.

With regards to the unity of Godhead, we asked our respondents the following question:

R12/U11: I will read to you two other sayings of wise men. In the light of your own experience of life, which one of these sayings is closer to you?
a) Aside from believing in God and giving praise to Him, man should take care in his dealings not to offend the spirits in his environment.
b) God is the one and the only, and outside man and angels, there are no spirits who should be worshipped.

The respondents who chose the first alternative were classified as popular and given the weight 3. The respondents who selected the second were classified as either modern or orthodox, and each of these respondents was given the score 1.

Regarding the respondents' attitudes towards the *Pir* (religious divine), we asked the following two questions:

R19/U20: Are you a disciple of a *Pir*? Yes/No.
R19a/U20a: If yes, why did you become a disciple of a *Pir*?

The modernist Muslim believing in direct communication between God and man would reject the system of *Pir* as a sacrilege and as a manifestation of attributing partnership to Allah (*shirk*). Orthodox Muslims would not attribute any supernatural power to the *Pir*, but would seek knowledge and spiritual guidance from the latter because of his high religious learning. A popular Muslim would attribute miraculous power to the *Pir*.

Thus all respondents who were not disciples of *Pirs* were categorised as modern and given the weight of 1. Those respondents who were disciples of a *Pir* and mentioned religious reasons for becoming so ("To reach Allah through guidance of a *Pir*", "To be on the path of Allah", "To seek spiritual knowledge" and the like) were grouped as orthodox and given weight 2. The respondents whose reasons for becoming the disciples of *Pirs* indicated their belief in the supernatural powers of the latter (the amulet given by the *Pir* cures illness, *Pirs*' intercession to help succeed in life, *Pirs*' help to avert misfortune, and the like) were classified as popular, and were given the weight of 3.

Adding the scores in the sub-items under monotheism, modern, orthodox and popular beliefs were given the weights of 3, 5 and 9 respectively. Since religious beliefs form a continuum we used the following distribution of scores for tabulating the three kinds of religious beliefs under this general item:

    3–4 = Modern
    5–6 = Orthodox
    7–9 = Popular

This scoring is slightly biased to modern beliefs because of the distribution of points for the question No. R12/U11(b), where both modern and orthodox were given the score 1.

Determinism

Our next item for measuring religious belief was determinism—the question about controlling forces affecting man's destiny. To tap differences on this dimension, respondents were asked to choose between four statements.

R11/U10:   I shall read to you four sayings of wise men. With which do you agree?
                                 a) Man's fate is dependent only on his work.
                                 b) Whatever happens in life is due to the will of Allah.
                                 c) Man's fate is determined by both his own work and the will of Allah.
                                 d) Man's life is determined only by his fate.

The respondents who chose the first or third alternatives were coded as modern with weight 1. This is because these respondents did not believe in the divine determination of all aspects of life. They, on the other hand, believed either in man's exclusive control over his destiny, or in the interaction of man and God as the determining factor of man's fate. Those who agreed with the second alternative, "God alone determines the course of life", were classified as orthodox and given weight 2. The respondents who attributed life's twist and turns to fate were grouped as popular and given score 3.

In Bangladesh the question of determinism is usually expressed in terms of *tadbir* and *takdir* whose literal translations are "planning" and "fate" respectively. The term, *tadbir*, however is used to mean a variety of perceptions. *Tadbir* may mean endeavor at self-development, self-help or hard work for achieving life's goals. It may mean efforts at scrupulous observance of religious duties and dependence on Allah. It may mean cajoling or gratifying powerful people for securing favours. To determine our respondents' attitudes towards *tadbir* and *takdir*, we asked the following questions:

R36/U38:   Do you believe in *tadbir* and *takbir? Tadbir/takdir.*
R37/U39:   What do you mean by *tadbir?*
  a) *Tadbir* means to work on the basis of one's own endeavour and capacity. Yes/No.
  b) *Tadbir* means to please powerful people to achieve something. Yes/No.
  c) Please given an example of *tadbir.*

We classified all respondents expressing belief in *takdir* or in *tadbir*, meaning pleasing people for achieving ends as popular, and gave the weight 3. We categorised the respondents who believed in *tadbir*, and interpreted it as hard work for self-fulfilment as modern, with weight 1. The respondents who believed in *tadbir* and explained it as scrupulous performance of religious duties and dependence on God, were classified as orthodox with weight 2.

By adding the weights allocated to the answers of the two sub-items, we have scores of 2, 4 and 6 for modern, orthodox and popular beliefs under the general item of determinism. In tabulating the answers, respondents scoring totals 2–3, 4–5 and 6 under this general item were classified as modern, orthodox and popular respectively.

Change in Islam

As we have seen in Chapter II,[5] and as we have stated at the beginning of this chapter, one of the important points of difference between modernist and orthodox Muslims relates to the question of change and modification of the Islamic injunctions. The modernists would keep the fundamentals of Islam intact, but would reject or modify the Islamic prescriptions which, according to them, were dictated by the special circumstances and time of Islam's birth. The orthodox Muslim, on the other hand, would consider all Islamic canonical laws as immutable and any attempt at their alteration as sacrilege. We read five statements to the respondents in our survey with clear choice to agree or disagree with each of them to indicate whether the respondents showed consistency in accepting change in Islam or not. We argued that those respondents who consistently opt for change are modernist, and those who showed steadfast opposition to change were orthodox. We also argued that the popular Muslims with their beliefs in *Pirs*, sacred places, local deities and spirits, and pragmatic way of dealing with life's problems, would not be steady in expressing support either for change or non-change. Our question on this item, thus, was as follows:

R27/U30: i) Indicate whether you agree to disagree with the following statements:
  a) Bangladesh should be administered according to the *Shariat* (Islamic religious laws). Agree/Disagree.
  b) Bangladesh should be administered according to the laws currently prevailing. Agree/Disagree.
  c) Punishments according to *Shariat* (like one hundred stripes for adultery, the cutting off of hands for theft) are irrelevant in our age. Agree/Disagree.
  d) As Islam was revealed about 1,400 years ago, some of its injunctions need to be changed in the context of the present age. Agree/Disagree.
  e) Injunctions of *Shariat* should prevail in the sphere of religion, but the state should be run according to the laws enacted by the legislature. Agree/Disagree.

We have given the weight of 1 to a modern answer, and weight 2 to an orthodox answer. We distribute modern/orthodox in the following way:

Question No.	Answer	Weight
30(a)	Yes	2
	No	1
30(b)	Yes	2
	No	1
30(c)	Yes	1
	No	2
30(d)	Yes	1
	No	2
30(e)	Yes	1
	No	2

Respondents scoring 5–6 have been called "modern". Those scoring 9–10 and 7–8 have been called "orthodox" and "popular" respectively.

Attitudes towards Hindus and anti-Islamic Views

The last time that we used to measure the religious beliefs of our respondents was their attitudes towards Hindus and anti-Islamic views. The modernist Muslims present Islam as a tolerant and liberal religion and highlight the Koranic verses like, "There is no compulsion in religion" (II:256), and "To you [those who reject faith] be your way, and to me mine" (CIX:6). They also argue that the Islamic *jihad* (religious war) is defensive war.[6] The orthodox Muslims, however, give more emphasis to the Koranic verses urging the believers to fight "in God's cause" or against "those who believe not in God or the Last Day" (IX:20, 29; IV:74, 76, 84; II:190–3), and the Koran's repeated promise that the believer who fights in God's cause will have "the highest rank in the sight of God" and will be greatly rewarded "whether he is slain or gets victory" (IX:20; III; IV:74). The modernist Muslim, therefore, has a liberal and tolerant attitude towards non-Muslims. The orthodox Muslim, on the other hand, tends to be intolerant towards non-Muslims, particularly the idolatrous and historically inimical Hindus. The popular, like the modern Muslim, is generally tolerant of Hindus. But they are so for reasons of tradition, custom and convenience, not on the liberal grounds used by the modernist. Similarly, a modern Muslim would try to behave rationally in the face of anti-Islamic opinion and postures and meet these on an intellectual plane, while on orthodox Muslim would tend to oppose anti-Islamic views and stances in a fanatical way. Again, the popular Muslim is likely to respond fatalistically in this regard. Of course, both modern and orthodox Muslims would shun *pujas* (the ceremonial worship of gods and goddesses by the Hindus), although the popular Muslims might not be particularly careful in avoiding these.

Thus, under this item, we asked the following questions:

R17/U18:	Do you go to Hindu *pujas*?
R17c/U18b:	Do you think that the Hindus should stay in this country, or should go away?
R22/U23:	If anybody insults Allah/Rasul/Koran/Islam what will you do?

For the first question the respondents who answered "No" to the question were regarded as either modern or orthodox, and were given the score 1. Those answering "Yes" were grouped as popular, and were given score 3.

For the second question, we have categorised the following and similar answers wherein the respondents provide a rationale for allowing Hindus to stay as modern: (1) "need to stay"; (2) "Better to stay"; (3) "God created Hindus"; (4) "Hindus are advanced in trade", (5) "Ours is a secular state". Answers which indicated that Hindus should leave Bangladesh were classified as orthodox, e.g., (1) "Better for the Hindus to go"; (2) "We should drive them away", (3) "It is the land of Muslims so that the Hindus should go". Finally, respondents who would merely tolerate Hindus in Bangladesh (with answers like, "There is no harm for Hindus to stay"; "Muslims stay in India so Hindus should stay in Bangladesh"; "Hindus should stay if they do not do any harm") were classified popular. Modern, orthodox and popular answers were given the weights 1, 2, and 3 respectively.

With regards to the question concerning insults to Allah, Rasul, the Koran and Islam, all answers indicating the use of persuasive techniques ("I shall persuade him or her not to do so"; "I shall warn"; "I shall protest"; "I shall protest with others", and the like) were regarded as modern. Answers showing extreme positions—"I shall declare *jihad*"; "I shall sacrifice my life for Islam"; "I shall eliminate him"; "He should die"; "Nobody would dare say that"—were taken as orthodox. Answers that were fatalistic in nature—such as, "I shall do nothing"; "I am unable to do anything"; "I have no opinion"—were classified as popular. Again, modern, orthodox and popular answers were coded as 1, 2, and 3 respectively.

Respondents scoring totals of 3–4, 5–6 and 7–9 under this general item were classified as modern, orthodox and popular respectively.

We changed all scores in all the six items to one for modern, two for orthodox and three for popular. Since religious beliefs form a continuum we used the following distribution of scores in tabulating the three kinds of religious beliefs:

6– 9 = Modern
10–13 = Orthodox
14–18 = Popular

By applying this scale to all respondents, we got the following tables.

We do not claim absolute correctness of the questions that we designed and used to tap the dimensions of religious beliefs of the respondents in our survey, nor do we claim perfection of procedures of scoring that we have followed in the construction of scale of religious beliefs. However, we argue that Tables 3.1 (Rural) and 3.1 (Urban), developed on the basis of the analysis in this chapter, give at least a rough idea of the extent of the spread of modern, orthodox and popular beliefs amongst Bangladesh Islam.

Table 3.1 (Rural) shows that only 1.2 per cent of our rural sample can be classified as modern, while 50.6 per cent is orthodox and 48.2 per cent popular. According to Table 3.1 (Urban), 12 per cent of our urban sample is modern, 62.1 per cent orthodox, and 25.9 popular.

The figures are revealing. First, these figures clearly indicate that the modernist movement in Bangladesh Islam, which began in the late nineteenth century and continued till now, could transform only a tiny minority of Bangladesh Muslims. Secondly, the puritanical revivalist movement that was started by the fundamentalist *ulema* in the early nineteenth century, and was carried on by them in various forms up to the present time, has been only partially successful in "purifying" Islam in Bangladesh. The orthodox Muslims in Bangladesh seem to constitute just the bare majority of the Muslim population of Bangladesh. Asim Roy's analysis of the erosion of "the Islamic syncretistic tradition in Bengal" is only partially correct.[7] The syncretistic

TABLE 3.1: Rural

Distribution of Religious Beliefs

Category	Frequency	Percentage
Modern	41	1.2
Orthodox	1752	50.6
Popular	1668	48.2
Total	3461	100.0

TABLE 3.1: Urban

Distribution of Religious Beliefs

Category	Frequency	Percentage
Modern	251	12.0
Orthodox	1295	62.1
Popular	540	25.9
Total	2086	100.0

performer does not seem to have lost both his stage and audience even in Bangladesh today. Popular Islam seems to command the allegiance of nearly half of the Muslims of present-day Bangladesh.

A rough idea of the distribution of modern, orthodox and popular Islamic religious beliefs among the Bangladesh Muslims is only one result of our discussion in this chapter. A more important result is the development of the categories of the religious beliefs themselves, because the use of the categories of the religious beliefs developed here to correlate other factors in our sample, should make it possible to gain a better understanding of some of the dynamics at work in modern Bangladesh as regards religious convictions and their impact on society. The first question that arises in this connection is: Can one explain the existence of the three types of religious beliefs in present-day Bangladesh sociologically? It is to this question that the next chapter is addressed.

NOTES

1 Rafiuddin Ahmed argues that "The reformist (of the 19th century) succeeded in 'converting' only a fraction of the total Muslim population to their point of view; the vast majority remained steadfastly opposed to any new dogma, and faithful to the traditional system . . .". "The practices condemned as heretical by the fundamentalist reformers a hundred years ago were found persisting at every level of Bengali Muslim Society as late as the 1960s." R. Ahmed. *The Bengal Muslims 1871–1906: A Quest for Identity* (Delhi: Oxford University Press, 1981), pp. 70, 71. Asim Roy similarly writes, " . . . sundry sources, coming down well into the present century, attest to the persistence of traditional beliefs and practices among Bengali Muslims", A. Roy, *The Islamic Syncretistic Tradition in Bengal* (Princeton: Princeton University Press, 1983), p. 251.

2 K.D. Jackson, *Traditional Authority, Islam and Rebellion: A Study of Indonesian Political Behavior* (Berkeley: University of California Press, 1980), pp. 88–91, 339–49.

3 We put R and U as the abbreviations of Rural and Urban respectively. The questions used in the rural and urban areas are the same, with the exception of those on demographic variables. The difference in the questions on demographic factors and in the ordering of questions to rouse easy and spontaneous replies from the rural and urban respondents have caused different numbering of identical questions in the rural and urban questionnaires.

4 See M.M. Rahman, *Bangla Vashai Koran Charcha* (Study of the Holy Koran in the Bengali Language) (Dacca: Islamic Foundation, Bangladesh, 1986), p. 144. Jinn is mentioned in the following verses of the Koran: VII:12; II:119; XVIII:50; XXXVIII:76; XLVI:29; LI:56; LXXII:1; CXIV:5–6.

5 See Chapter II, above, pp. 46–50.

6 See, for example, A. Hashim, *The Creed of Islam or the Revolutionary Character of Kalima* (Dacca: Islamic Foundation, Bangladesh, 3rd edition, 1980), pp. 112–4.

7 See Roy, *op. cit.*, p. xviii.

CHAPTER IV

SOCIAL BASES OF ISLAMIC RELIGIOUS BELIEFS

In the preceding chapter we have seen that 1.2, 50.6 and 48.2 per cent of our rural sample and 12, 62.1 and 25.9 per cent of our urban sample belong respectively to modernist, orthodox and popular categories of Islamic religious beliefs. But who are these *dramatis personae*? Who is the modernist Islamist? Who is the orthodox Muslim? Who subscribes to popular Islamic beliefs? How do these adherents of different types of religious beliefs compare with one another? Does each category of believers constitute a distinctive social type? How are the different religious beliefs related to social variables—urbanisation, rurality, education, occupation, landownership and yearly income? Do religious beliefs have corresponding constellations of social correlates? Can we, in short, explain the differences in the religious beliefs in Bangladesh Islam in terms of their varying social bases? After having identified the types of religious beliefs and the extent of their spread, we now want to discover in this chapter the social conditions which nurture and foster, if not determine, these religious beliefs.

In order to understand the relationship between the social variables and the different types of religious beliefs, we have cross-tabulated the relevant data collected in our survey and carried out Chi-square (X^2) test and residual analysis for each of the pertinent contingency tables.

The X^2 test is widely used by social scientists to examine the relationship between two qualitative variables. The test is performed under the assumption that there is no association between the variables concerned. A high value of X^2 shows the presence of association between the variables and a low value shows absence of association.

Every X^2 for a cross-table has some degrees of freedom (df). The number of rows minus one multiplied by the number of columns minus one gives the degrees of freedom. For every value of X^2 and its df of a cross-table, there is a P (Probability)-value obtained from the Chi-square distribution. If this P-value is greater than 0.05 for the table, it is inferred that there is no association between the variables concerned. When the P-value is less than 0.01, it is concluded that the variables have highly significant association with each other. If the P-value lies between 0.01 and 0.05, then the association is said to be simply significant.[1]

While a significant overall Chi-square test for an r × c contingency table (where r is the number of rows and c is the number of columns) points out non-independence of the two variables, it "provides no information as to whether non-independence occurs throughout or in a specific part of the table".[2] We have thus made additional comparisons for each cell within a table for identifying categories responsible for a significant Chi-square value by the method of analysis of residuals. When the adjusted residual of a particular cell is greater than 1.96, the association between the two categories

TABLE 4.1: Rural-Urban

Scale of Religious Beliefs by Rural-Urban Categories

Rural-Urban Categories	Religious Belief			
	Modern	Orthodox	Popular	Row Total
Rural Area	41	1752	1668	3461
	1.19	50.62	48.19	62.0
	14.04	57.49	75.54	
	−17.38	−8.26	17.41	
Urban Area	251	1295	540	2086
	12.03	62.08	25.88	38.0
	85.95	42.50	24.45	
	17.64	8.33	−21.07	
Col. Total	292	3047	2208	5547
	5.3	54.9	39.8	100

$X^2 = 484.867$ with 2 d.f., $P < 0.00001$

involved in the cell is significant at the 5 per cent level. When the adjusted residual is greater than 2.57, the association is significant at the 1 per cent level.[3]

Rural-Urban Differential and Religious Beliefs

Let us begin our examination of the relationship between social variables and religious beliefs delineated in our survey by looking first at the relationship between rural-urban categories and religious beliefs. Table 4.1 (Rural and Urban) examines the relationship between the two variables. (In each cell of Table 4.1 (Rural and Urban) the first number is the cell frequency, the second number is the horizontal percentage, the third number is the vertical percentage, and the fourth number is the adjusted residual. This pattern of arrangement of figures in each cell has been followed in all subsequent contingency tables.)

As Table 4.1 (Rural and Urban) shows, the value of the X^2 for the table is highly significant. This means that rural and urban categories have a very high association with scales of religious beliefs. A look at the adjusted residual of each cell of the table shows that the rural area is much more conducive to popular religious beliefs than to orthodox and modern religious beliefs, while the urban area tends to foster modern and orthodox beliefs more than popular religious beliefs.

Education and Religious Beliefs

The second social variable having an association with the religious beliefs that we have delineated is education. Tables 4.2 (Rural) and 4.2 (Urban) examine the relationship.

Both Table 4.2 (Rural) and 4.2 (Urban) clearly point to the influence of education on religious beliefs. As Table 4.2 (Rural) shows, in the rural areas illiteracy has higher association with popular belief than with modern and orthodox beliefs. On the other hand, middle (Classes VI-X) and upper levels (Intermediate and above) of education have greater association with modern and orthodox beliefs than with the popular belief and primary level (Classes I-V) education does not seem to have an discriminating effect on religious beliefs.

Table 4.2 (Urban) shows that the association between the level of education and religious beliefs is even stronger in the urban area than in the rural region. The value of X^2 for Table 4.2 (Urban) is several times larger than that for Table 4.2 (Rural), both tables having the same degrees of freedom. Of course, there is a vast quantitative difference between data on education in the two tables 4.2 (Rural) and 4.2 (Urban). While 54.78 per cent of the rural sample has no education, the corresponding figure in the urban sample is only 5.94. Again, as few as 4.77 per cent of the rural respondents have higher education (intermediate and above), while the percentage in the

TABLE 4.2: Rural

Scale of Religious Beliefs by Education in Rural Area

Education		Religious Belief		Row Total
	Modern	Orthodox	Popular	
No education	15	905	976	1896
	0.79	47.73	51.48	54.78
	36.59	51.66	58.51	
	−2.35	−3.74	4.25	
Class I-V	7	410	360	777
	0.90	52.77	46.33	22.45
	17.07	23.40	21.58	
	−0.83	1.35	−1.17	
Class VI-X	13	325	257	595
	2.18	54.62	43.19	17.19
	31.71	18.55	15.41	
	2.47	2.14	−2.68	
Intermediate and Above	6	95	64	165
	3.64	57.58	38.78	4.77
	14.64	5.42	3.84	
	2.98	1.83	−2.47	
Not stated	0	17	11	28
	0	60.71	39.29	0.81
	0	0.97	0.66	
	−0.58	1.07	−0.94	
Col. Total	41	1752	1668	3461
	1.18	50.62	48.20	100.00

$X^2 = 35.966$ with 8 d.f., P < 0.001

TABLE 4.2: Urban

Scale of Religious Beliefs by Education in Urban Area

Education	Modern	Religious Belief Orthodox	Popular	Row Total
No education	2	33	89	124
	1.61	26.61	71.77	5.94
	0.80	2.55	16.48	
	−3.67	−8.39	12.02	
Class I-V	0.0	48	48	96
	0.0	50.00	40.00	
	0.0	3.21	8.89	4.60
	−3.71	−2.49	5.52	
Class VI-X	50	413	203	666
	7.51	62.01	30.48	
	19.92	31.89	37.59	31.93
	−4.35	−0.04	3.28	
Intermediate and Above	198	793	200	1191
	16.62	66.58	16.80	
	78.88	61.24	37.04	57.09
	7.43	4.88	−10.93	
Not stated	1	8	0.0	9
	11.11	88.89	0.0	
	0.40	0.61	0.0	0.44
	−0.08	1.66	−1.77	
Col. Total	251	1295	540	2086
	12.03	62.08	25.89	

$X^2 = 255.501$ with 8 d.f., $P < 0.00001$

urban sample is as high as 57.09. Despite this huge numerical difference in data, as indicated by the values of adjusted residuals in the relevant cells of the two tables, the pattern of association between these two levels of education and the religious beliefs found in the rural table is reinforced by the urban table. "No education" tends to be more highly associated with popular religious belief, and higher education seems to have greater connection with modern and orthodox beliefs in the urban sample than in the rural sample. The contrasting patterns in the two Tables 4.2 (Rural) and 4.2 (Urban) are at primary and middle levels of education. In the rural sample, primary education does not show any significant association with scale of religious belief. In the urban areas, on the other hand, primary-level education seems to have a higher degree of association with popular belief than with the other two forms of beliefs. Again, while in the rural areas middle-level education seems to be more associated with modern and orthodox beliefs, in the urban areas this level of education seems to have greater association with popular belief.

TABLE 4.3: Rural

Scale of Religious Beliefs by Occupation in Rural Area

Occupation	Modern	Religious Belief Orthodox	Popular	Row Total
Agriculture	9 0.75 21.95 −1.71	642 53.64 36.64 2.57	546 45.61 32.73 −2.20	1197 34.6
Trade	5 2.12 12.19 1.37	110 46.61 6.28 −1.27	121 51.27 7.25 0.98	236 6.8
Professionals (teacher, service-holder, doctor, lawyer)	6 2.66 14.63 3.08	87 38.67 4.96 1.05	66 58.66 7.91 −1.72	159 6.5
Housewives	14 0.96 34.15 −1.05	682 46.65 38.93 −3.99	766 52.39 45.92 4.22	1462 42.2
Students	3 1.32 7.32 0.19	138 60.79 7.88 3.17	86 37.89 5.16 −3.21	227 6.6
Unemployed and Others	4 2.23 9.76 1.32	93 51.95 5.31 0.28	83 46.36 4.98 −0.57	180 5.17
Col. Total	41 2.2	1752 50.6	1668 48.2	3461 100.00

$X^2 = 41.704$ with 10 d.f., P < 0.001

Rural Occupation and Religious Beliefs

The association between religious beliefs and occupation is in order for investigation. Let us look first at Table 4.3 (Rural) (Scale of Religious Beliefs by Occupation in Rural Area).

As Table 4.3 (Rural) shows, there is significant correlation between occupation and religious beliefs. The adjusted residuals of the cells in the table indicate a clear pattern. Agriculture is seen as more associated with orthodox belief than with any other belief. Housewives show greater association with popular belief and students with orthodox belief. By contrast, professionals seem to have a higher degree of association with modern religious belief than with orthodox and popular beliefs.

Landownership and Religious Beliefs

Any discussion on occupation and religious beliefs in Bangladesh would be incomplete without an examination of the relationship between categories of landownership and types of religious beliefs. Bangladesh is "the most rural of the world's largest agricultural economies" with 86 per cent of Bangladeshi people living in rural areas.[4] We have seen in Table 4.3 (Rural) above that 34.6 per cent of the rural people have agriculture as their occupation. This figure, however, does not give the full picture of rural dependence on agriculture. First, we have shown "Housewife" as a separate category of occupation. In rural Bangladesh the wives of cultivators are, in fact, also engaged in agriculture. Although village housewives observe purdah (seclusion of women from public view) and do not go to work in the fields, they usually feed and take care of cattle used for ploughing as well as dairy cattle. They also maintain small flocks of poultry—rearing a few chickens, geese, ducks and pigeons for eggs and meat. During the harvest seasons, while the harvesting and threshing of rice and other foodgrain crops is done by men, the drying of the rice and other foodgrains is done by the women. During the rainy season, when there is no adequate sunshine, drying has to be done by artificial heat, and the women have to work day and night for that. Besides, as modern husking mills are still rare in rural Bangladesh, and as husking in those mills is costly for most villagers, village housewives have to spend much time in the manual husking of rice and other foodgrains. Village housewives are thus full partners of men in agricultural production in Bangladesh, although their work is done within the house.

Since housewives constitute 92 per cent of total female respondents,[5] and since 34.6 per cent of the respondents in our survey have agriculture as occupation, at least $\left(\dfrac{34.6 \times 92}{100}\right)$ = 31.8 per cent of housewives are also agriculturist by occupation. Thus our survey shows that a total of 34.6 + 31.8 = 66.4 per cent of the rural population are directly employed on the land.[6] As students in Bangladesh are almost all dependent on their parents $\left(\dfrac{6.6 \times 34.6}{100}\right)$ = 2.9 per cent more of our respondents are dependent on agriculture. Besides, as even a casual observer of Bangladesh rural areas can easily notice, village teachers, doctors and traders are partly dependent on land as their sources of income. Thus land is the single most important wealth in the rural areas.

As the study by F. Tomasson Jannuzi and James T. Peach shows, the middle and larger farmers who constitute less than 15 per cent of the people, own almost 51 per cent of the land.[7] For their survival, the landless, the functionally landless people and small farmers develop dependent client-patron relationships with these larger farmers. Land is thus not only the most important economic wealth, it is also a symbol of status and social power.[8] The socio-economic development of Bangladesh depends much on the attitudes, values and beliefs of the middle and large farming groups of Bangladesh.

TABLE 4.4: Rural

Scale of Religious Beliefs by Land Owned (other than Homestead Land)

| Land owned[10] (in acres) | Religious Belief | | | |
	Modern	Orthodox	Popular	Row Total
00–0.5	8	440	524	972
	0.82	45.26	53.90	28.1
	19.51	25.11	31.14	
	−1.22	−3.90	4.19	
0.51–2.00	5	374	382	761
	0.65	49.14	50.00	22.00
	12.19	21.34	22.90	
	1.51	−0.91	1.25	
2.01–4.00	2	240	189	431
	0.46	55.68	43.85	12.5
	4.87	13.69	11.33	
	1.47	0.15	1.91	
4.01–8.00	5	214	164	383
	1.30	55.87	42.82	11.06
	12.19	12.21	9.83	
	0.24	2.16	−2.22	
Over 8.00	6	125	88	219
	2.74	57.07	40.18	6.32
	14.63	7.13	5.27	
	2.20	1.97	−2.45	
Not Stated	15	359	321	695
	2.15	51.65	46.18	20.1
	36.58	20.49	19.24	
	2.65	0.60	−1.19	
Col. Total	41	1752	1668	3461
	1.2	50.6	48.2	100.00

$X^2 = 41.62$ with 10 d.f., $P < 0.001$

The political relevance of these landed groups is also highly significant. About 71 per cent of the members of the 1970 legislative assembly and 75 per cent of those in the 1973 assembly belonged to the upper farming classes. Each of these members owned over 6.5 acres.[9] These landed groups also provided the vast majority of members of the 1979 assembly. Successive military regimes of Bangladesh since 1975 have vigorously tried to court the support of this group.

How does landownership relate to religious beliefs? Table 4.4 (Rural) provides some clues.

The X^2 test of Table 4.4 (Rural) shows a highly significant association between categories of landownership and types of religious beliefs. A look at the adjusted residuals of the individual cells indicates that the lowest level of

TABLE 4.5: Urban

Scale of Religious Beliefs by Occupation in Urban Area

Occupation	Modern	Religious Belief Orthodox	Popular	Row Total
Business and Industry	38 12.79 15.14 0.43	192 64.65 14.83 0.98	67 22.56 12.41 −1.41	297 14.2
Professionals (lawyers, doctors, teachers, service-holders)	62 14.97 24.80 2.05	253 61.11 19.53 −0.45	99 23.91 18.30 −1.02	414 19.85
Housewives	43 5.98 17.1 −6.16	427 59.39 33.0 −1.83	249 34.63 46.1 6.61	719 34.5
Students	101 16.78 40.2 4.24	394 65.45 30.4 2.01	107 17.77 19.8 −5.38	602 28.9
Unemployed and Others	7 20.42 2.8 0.21	29 54.47 2.3 −1.28	18 25.2 3.14 1.26	54 2.58
Col. Total	251 12.0	1295 62.1	540 25.9	2086 100.00

$X^2 = 78.835$ with 8 d.f., $P < 0.001$

landownership (00–0.5 acre) is more significantly associated with popular beliefs than with modern and orthodox beliefs. As the level of land owned increases from 00–0.5 acre through 2.01–4.00 acres, association between landownership and popular belief seems to decrease from highly significant to a non-significant level. The association of upper middle-level landownership (4.01–8.0 acres) with orthodox belief is comparatively higher than its association with modern and popular beliefs. Upper-level landownership (over 8 acres) seems to have greater association with modern and orthodox beliefs rather than with popular belief.

Urban Occupations and Religious Beliefs

Let us now look at Table 4.5 (Urban) to see how urban occupations are related to different scales of religious beliefs.

The pattern of relationship between occupation and scale of religious beliefs in the urban sample displayed in Table 4.5 (Urban) is almost the same as that of the rural sample shown in Table 4.3 (Rural) above. Professionals in the urban area seem to have greater association with modern beliefs than with orthodox or popular beliefs, paralleling the pattern in the rural area. Urban housewives, like their sisters in the rural area, seem to be more associated with popular beliefs rather than modern and orthodox beliefs, and urban trade and industry like rural trade do not seem to have any particularly significant association with any of the religious beliefs. Only in the relationship between students and religious beliefs does the urban sample differ from the rural one. While in the rural areas students seem to have a significant relationship with orthodox, they seem to have a similar relationship with both modern and orthodox beliefs in the urban area. This difference is possibly explained by the fact that the urban sample contains proportionately more students with higher education than the rural sample. Thus higher education again seems to prove to be a correlate of modern belief.

Yearly Income and Religious Beliefs

One of the most distinctive aspects of the Bangladesh economy is the vast inequality of the distribution of wealth between the urban and rural areas.[11] Thus the categories of yearly income that emerged from our survey for measuring association between levels of income and religious beliefs are one to four or five times larger in the urban areas than in the rural areas. The relationship between yearly income and religious beliefs is shown in Tables 4.6 (Rural) and 4.6 (Urban).

Both Table 4.6 (Rural) and 4.6 (Urban) show that yearly income has strong associations with religious beliefs. In both the rural and urban areas lower-level income groups (up to 2,500 and 2,501–5,000 in rural areas, and up to 10,000 and 10,001–20,000 in urban areas) are more highly associated with popular belief than with orthodox and religious beliefs, although poverty is a stronger predictor of popular belief in the urban area. While lower-middle level income groups in the rural area (5,001–7,500 through 7,501–12,000) do not seem to have a particularly close association with any of the religious beliefs, the upper-middle level (12,001–18,000) and the highest level (18,001 and above) income groups seem to have a more significant association with orthodox belief than with modern or popular beliefs. The urban middle-level income groups show a greater degree of variation with regards to their association with religious beliefs than the rural middle level income groups. While the urban lower-middle income group (20,001–30,000) does not particularly associate with any one type of religious belief, the middle-middle level urban income group (30,001–50,000) is more significantly associated with orthodox belief than with modern or popular beliefs. In contrast to the rural pattern, the urban upper-middle (50,001–100,000) and highest income groups (100,001 and above) are more highly associated with modern religious belief than with orthodox or popular beliefs.

TABLE 4.6: Rural

Scale of Religious Beliefs by Yearly Income in Rural Area

Yearly Income in Taka	Modern	Religious Belief Orthodox	Popular	Row Total
Up to 2,500	5	175	209	389
	1.28	44.98	53.72	11.2
	12.19	9.98	12.52	
	0.19	−2.35	2.31	
2,501–5,000	5	255	335	595
	0.84	42.86	56.30	17.2
	12.19	14.55	20.08	
	−0.85	−4.16	4.34	
5,001–7,500	9	391	355	755
	1.19	51.78	47.01	21.8
	22.0	22.32	21.3	
	0.02	0.72	−0.73	
7,501–12,000	8	357	309	674
	1.19	53.96	45.85	19.5
	19.5	20.4	18.5	
	0.006	1.35	−1.35	
12,001–18,000	7	264	213	484
	1.4	54.5	44.0	14.0
	17.1	15.1	12.8	
	0.57	1.86	−1.98	
18,001 and above	7	310	247	564
	1.32	54.0	44.7	16.3
	17.1	17.7	14.8	
	0.13	2.25	−2.28	
Col. Total	41	1752	1668	3461
	1.2	50.6	48.2	100.00

$X^2 = 30.559$ with 10 df   P<0.001

Sex, Age and Religious Beliefs

With regard to demographic factors, we have examined the relationship of religious beliefs with two variables—sex and age. The relationship between sex and religious belief is examined first in Tables 4.7 (Rural) and 4.7 (Urban).

Tables 4.7 (Rural) and 4.7 (Urban) show that in both the urban and rural areas the female sex is more closely associated with popular than with modern and orthodox beliefs. But here the social factors rather than sex *per se* could be the determining element. In Bangladesh the extent of the spread of modern education is much less among females than among the male section of the population.[12] As we have seen above, 92 per cent of our female respondents work as housewives. The vast majority of women in Bangladesh also

TABLE 4.6: Urban

Scale of Religious Beliefs by Yearly Income in Urban Area

Yearly Income in Taka	Modern	Religious Belief Orthodox	Popular	Row Total
Up to 10,000	5 3.35 2.0 −3.07	64 48.6 5.0 −3.63	66 47.6 12.2 6.30	135 6.5
10,001–20,000	41 13.2 16.4 0.84	144 46.7 11.1 −5.72	119 39.9 22.0 5.70	304 14.4
20,001–30,000	9 4.6 3.6 −3.38	131 66.5 10.1 1.34	57 28.9 10.6 1.02	197 9.4
30,001–50,000	73 10.7 29.0 −0.67	431 68.2 33.3 2.98	141 21.1 26.0 −2.80	645 31.1
50,001–100,000	65 14.9 25.9 2.09	282 64.8 21.8 1.32	88 20.2 16.3 −3.02	435 20.9
100,001 and above	58 15.7 23.1 2.37	243 65.7 18.8 1.57	69 18.6 12.8 −3.5	370 17.7
Col. Total	251 12.0	1295 62.1	540 25.9	2086 100.00

X^2 = 110.235 with 10 df   P<0.0001

depend on the income of their husbands or parents. As most women in Bangladesh remain confined within their homes because of the prevalence of purdah system, even women in the urban area remain largely outside the modernising effects of urbanisation. As non-urbanisation, illiteracy, low income and household work go together with popular belief as well as the female sex, the particularly significant association between the female sex and popular belief might be the effect of social variables rather than of gender.

The relationship between age and religious beliefs is examined in Tables 4.8 (Rural) and 4.8 (Urban). Table 4.8 (Rural) shows that different age groups and religious beliefs are independent of each other. That is, there is no association between age groups and religious beliefs in the rural areas. Table 4.8 (Urban), however, shows that in the urban area the age group 16–25 has a more significant association with orthodox than with modern or popular

TABLE 4.7: Rural

Scale of Religious Beliefs by Sex in Rural Area

Sex	Modern	Religious Belief Orthodox	Popular	Row Total
Male	26	1005	836	1867
	1.39	53.82	44.77	53.94
	63.41	57.36	50.11	
	1.22	4.08	−4.35	
Female	15	747	832	1594
	0.94	46.86	52.20	46.06
	36.58	42.64	49.9	
	−1.22	−4.08	4.35	
Col. Total	41	1752	1668	3461
	1.2	50.6	48.2	100.00

X^2 = 19.541 with 2 d.f., P<0.0001

TABLE 4.7: Urban

Scale of Religious Beliefs by Sex in Urban Area

Sex	Modern	Religious Belief Orthodox	Popular	Row Total
Male	154	640	246	1040
	14.81	61.54	23.65	49.86
	61.35	49.42	45.55	
	3.88	−0.50	−2.32	
Female	97	655	294	1046
	9.27	62.62	28.1	
	38.64	50.58	54.44	
	−3.88	0.50	2.32	
Col. Total	251	1295	540	2086
	12.0	62.1	25.9	100.00

X^2 = 18.312 with 2 d.f., P<0.001

religious belief, and the age group 36 and above has a higher association with popular belief than with modern and orthodox beliefs.

Conclusion

To conclude our analysis of data presented in the various tables given above in this chapter, we find distinct and striking patterns of relationships between the social variables and religious beliefs. We find that each of three types of Islamic religious beliefs—modern, orthodox and popular—has a corresponding constellation of social correlates:

a) Illiteracy, poverty and low income seem to be more highly associated with

TABLE 4.8: Rural

Scale of Religious Beliefs by Age in Rural Area

| Age | | Religious Belief | | |
	Modern	Orthodox	Popular	Row Total
16–25	21	729	652	1402
	1.50	52.0	46.50	40.2
	51.22	41.61	39.09	
26–35	10	440	399	849
	1.2	51.83	47.0	24.53
	24.39	25.1	23.92	
36–50	7	335	335	677
	1.03	49.48	49.48	19.56
	17.07	19.12	20.08	
51 and above	3	248	282	533
	0.56	47.53	52.90	15.40
	7.32	14.16	16.91	
Col. Total	41	1752	1668	3461
	1.18	50.62	48.19	100.00

$X^2 = 9.508$ with 6 d.f., P>.10.

As the X^2 test does not show significant association between the variables, analysis of residuals for the Table has not been done.

TABLE 4.8: Urban

Scale of Religious Beliefs by Age in Urban Area

| Age | | Religious Belief | | |
	Modern	Orthodox	Popular	Row Total
16–25	128	642	196	966
	13.25	66.46	20.30	46.30
	51.00	49.58	36.30	
	1.58	3.82	−5.42	
26–35	65	324	137	526
	12.36	61.6	26.05	25.22
	25.9	25.02	25.4	
	0.26	−0.26	0.09	
36–50	38	201	106	345
	11.00	58.30	30.72	16.5
	15.01	15.52	19.63	
	−0.63	−1.60	2.24	
51 and above	20	128	101	249
	8.03	51.41	40.6	11.93
	7.97	9.88	18.70	
	−2.06	−3.69	5.63	
Col. Total	251	1295	540	2086
	12.03	62.08	25.9	100.00

$X^2 = 48.761$ with 6 df   P<0.001

popular religious belief than with modern and orthodox beliefs in both urban and rural areas.

b) In the urban area higher education, professional occupations and a high yearly income seem to be clear predictors of modern Islamic belief.

c) High/middle-level education and middle-level income in the urban area seem to have a higher degree of association with the orthodox rather than modern and popular beliefs.

d) In the rural area the middle level of education and the upper and middle levels of landownership and incomes seem to be associated more with orthodox belief than with modern and popular beliefs.

Thus there seem to be distinct "social carriers" of Islamic religious beliefs in Bangladesh.

The relationship of significance between variables even at the very high level does not prove causal relationships between them, nor can it indicate the direction of the causal process. The historical process of change of Islam in Bangladesh areas, however, gives us the clue to understanding the direction of the causal relationship between social variables and religious beliefs in contemporary Islam in Bangladesh. As we have seen in Chapter II above, change in Islam in Bangladesh areas started as social conditions began to change with the introduction of the forces of modernisation under British rule. Our data in this chapter indicate that the direction of change has continued to date. Thus we can argue that high levels of urbanisation, modern education and modern professional occupations have continued to "modernise" Islam. Partially modernised social conditions seem to produce orthodox belief. Low or the absence of modernisation is keeping popular beliefs alive among the still large traditional sections of Bangladesh Muslims.

We can possibly extend our analysis yet further. If we conceptualise class on the basis of levels of education, income and occupation,[13] we can say that the urban upper classes tend to produce modern beliefs. The urban middle classes and the rural upper and middle classes foster orthodox religious belief. The lower classes in both urban and rural areas nurture popular beliefs. Thus the conclusion we reach is more Marxian than Weberian: social conditions tend to determine Islamic religious beliefs in Bangladesh.

NOTES

1 For a discussion on the nature and function of the Chi-square test, see H.M. Blalock, Jr., *Social Statistics* (New York: McGraw Hill, second edtion 1980), pp. 275–314; B.S. Everitt, *The Analysis of Contingency Tables* (London: Chapman and Hall, reprinted 1980), pp. 1–66.

2 *Ibid.*, p. 41.

3 For a discussion on the nature and function of the analysis of residuals, see S.J. Haberman, "The Analysis of Residuals in Cross-classified Tables", *Biometrics*, 29 March 1973, pp. 205–20. The analysis of residuals has been particularly advocated by Everitt for "isolating sources of association in r × c tables". See Everitt, *op.cit.*, pp. 46–8, 66.

4 See *Statistical Pocket Book of Bangladesh 1986* (Dhaka: Bangladesh Bureau of Statistics, Statistics Division, Ministry of Planning, 2 December 1986), p. 173.

5 Housewives constitute 42.2 per cent of respondents, and all women constitute 46.1 per cent of the respondents. So the housewives constitute $\left(\dfrac{42.2 \times 100}{46.01}\right)$ = 92 per cent of the total female respondents.

6   Significantly, the percentage of rural people employed in agriculture shown by our survey almost corresponds to the figure of 66.5 per cent of rural people engaged in cultivation in rural Bangladesh by the Bureau of Statistics, Government of Bangladesh, for the year 1983–84. See Table 4.15: "Per cent distribution of employed population 10 years and above by major industry: national, urban and rural residence 1983–84", *ibid.*, p. 188.

7   Jannuzi and Peach find the following distribution of land owned (other than homestead land) in rural Bangladesh:

Land Owned (in acres)	Owners as Percentage of Rural Population	Percentage of Land Owned
0–0.5	40.92 ⎫ 70.32	20.35
0.51–2.0	29.40 ⎭	
2.01–4.0	15.01	24.15
4.01–8.0	9.65	25.09
Over 8.0	5.02	25.59

The above figures are derived from Table D.11, "Size Distribution of Land owned other than Homestead Land in Bangladesh", and Table D.111, "Landless in Rural Bangladesh", in F. Tomasson Jannuzi and James T. Peach, *Report on the Hierarchy of Interests of Land in Bangladesh, based on the 1977 Land Occupation Survey of Rural Bangladesh* (Washington, D.C.: United States Agency for International Development, September 1977), pp. xxi, xxii.

8   See Shapan Adnan and Hussain Zillur Rahman, "Peasant Classes and Land Mobility: Structural Reproduction and Change in Rural Bangladesh", *Studies in Rural History* (Dacca: Bangladesh Itihas Samiti, 1979), pp. 106–11.

9   See Rounaq Jahan, "Members of Parliament in Bangladesh", *Legislative Studies Quarterly*, Vol. I, August 1976, pp. 339–61.

10 If the percentage of "not stated" is proportionately distributed among the percentages of people owning different categories of land in Table 5.4 (Rural), the following distribution of land in rural Bangladesh is obtained:

Land Owned (in acres)	Owners of Percentages of Rural Population
0–0.5	35.12 ⎫ 62.62
0.51–2.0	27.50 ⎭
2.01–4.0	15.61
4.01–8.0	13.83
Over 8.0	7.89

These figures roughly correspond to the figures of the Januzzi and Peach survey mentioned in Note 7 above.

11 See Chapter 13, "The Future of Bangladesh", in Talukder Maniruzzaman, *Group Interests and Political Changes: Studies of Pakistan and Bangladesh* (New Delhi: South Asian Publishers, 1982), pp. 229–32; W. de Vylder, "Urban Bias in Development: Bangladesh", *Journal of Social Studies*, No. 4, July 1979, pp. 1–14.

12 In Bangladesh 96.7 per cent of the female population aged ten years and over are illiterate. The corresponding figure for the male population is 72 per cent. See *Statistical Yearbook of Bangladesh 1986*, p. 841.

13 For the conceptualisation of class on the basis of occupation, income and education, see J. Blondel, *Voters, Parties and Leaders: The Social Fabric of British Politics* (Baltimore: Penguin Books, reprinted 1967), pp. 32–41.

CHAPTER V

ISLAMIC RELIGIOUS PRACTICE IN BANGLADESH AND ITS SOCIAL BASES

K.B. Sayeed, a perceptive analyst of social and political change in the former united Pakistan, wrote in 1963: "The questions which have not yet been answered satisfactorily are: what kind of Muslim is a rural East Bengali? How strictly or sincerely does he practise his faith?"[1] For the last two-and-a-half decades, Sayeed's questions remained unanswered. We tried to understand the religious beliefs of the Muslims of Bangladesh (former East Bengal) in Chapters III and IV. In this chapter we shall first try to identify the extent and depth of Islamic religious practices in Bangladesh. Secondly, we shall try to understand how far the levels of observance of religious practices can be explained in terms of social and demographic variables as we have done in interpreting the different types of religious beliefs. Thirdly, we shall make an attempt to examine how far levels of observance of religious practice are related to the kinds of religious beliefs that we have analysed.

Islamic Religious Practices

Compared to a religion like Hinduism, Islam enjoins simpler and fewer religious practices. While Hindus have grand religious ceremonies "thirteen times in twelve months", Muslims have only two major religious festivals during the whole year. Islam enjoins only five religious practices as obligatory. These "five pillars" of Islam are as follows:

1. *Iman* (faith): The most important element in the religious practice of Islam is faith in Allah as the one and only God. The other four pillars of Islam noted below are "branches (i.e., secondary offshoots) of the beliefs 'in the heart'".[2] A man remains a Muslim as long as he believes in *Tawhid* (oneness of God) even if he does not carry out the "branch duties".[3]
2. *Namaz* (prayer): Every adult Muslim has to pray five times a day.
3. *Roza* (fasting): Fasting (total abstention from drinking and eating from dawn till sunset) is prescribed for the whole month of *Ramadan* in every year.
4. *Zakat* (welfare tax): It is obligatory on every Muslim to donate a certain percentage of his accumulated wealth towards the welfare of the poorer section of the community every year.
5. *Hajj* (pilgrimage): One pilgrimage to Mecca is obligatory for every Muslim who can afford not only the travel from his home to Mecca and back, but can also provide for his family during his absence.[4]

Measuring Levels of Observance of Religious Practice

To ascertain the degree of religious practice observed by Bangladesh Muslims, we put a number of questions to our respondents.

Under the item faith, we asked the following question:

R12/U11: I shall mention to you two sayings of wise men. In the light of your own experience of life, which one of these sayings is closer to you?

1. Aside from believing in God and giving praise to Him, man should take care in his dealings not to offend the spirits in his environment.

2. God is the one and only one, and outside of man and angels, there are no spirits which should be worshipped.

Those respondents agreeing with the second statement were placed in the category of high religious practice and given score 1, and those respondents subscribing to the first were grouped under the category of low religious practice, and scored 3.

Under the second item, *namaz*, our question was:

R13(C)/U12(C): Do you say your prayers five times a day?

Regular/irregular/don't say prayers.

The respondents reporting performance of five-a-day prayers were classed under high religious practice and coded 1. The interviewees stating irregular performance of prayers were categorised under medium religious practice and coded 2, and the respondents stating that they did not pray at all were classified under low religious practice and coded 3.

With regards to the third item, *roza*, we asked the following question:

R14/U13: Do you keep fast?

Fast all of them/do some fasting/don't fast.

The answers falling under "fast all of them" were regarded as high religious practice and coded 1. Answers falling under "Do some fasting" were taken as medium religious practice and coded 2. Answers coming under "Don't fast" were taken as low religious practice and coded 3.

On *zakat* we asked the following:

R15/U14: Do you pay *zakat*?

Yes/no ability, but would pay if I had/no.

Answers falling under any one of the first two options were taken as high religious practice with 1 as code, and answers coming under "No" were classed as low religious practice having 3 as code.

Regarding *hajj*, the following question was asked:

R16/U15: Have you performed *hajj*?

Have performed/have desire to perform/no ability, but have desire to perform/don't desire to perform.

Answers falling under any one of the first three options were regarded as high religious practice with score 1, and answers falling under "Don't desire to perform" were taken as low and scored 3.

Adding the scores on all the five items, the total score for each respondent ranged from 5 to 15. We used the following distribution of scores in tabulating high, medium and low levels of religious practice:

  5– 6 = high
  7–10 = medium
  11–15 = low

By applying this scale to all respondents, we got the following tables:

TABLE 5.1: Rural

Distribution of Religious Practice

Category	Frequency	Percentage
High religious practice	1779	51.4
Medium religious practice	1656	47.8
Low religious practice	26	0.8
Total	3461	100.0

TABLE 5.1: Urban

Distribution of Religious Practice

Category	Frequency	Percentage
High religious practice	1035	49.6
Medium religious practice	975	46.8
Low religious practice	76	3.6
Total	2086	100.0

We have stated in Chapter III that we do not claim perfection in the questions and procedure of scoring that we used in the construction of the scale of religious beliefs.[5] We also do not claim sophistication for the questions and method of scoring that we have used in this chapter to measure the levels of observance of religious practice. We argue here again that Tables 5.1 (Rural) and 5.1 (Urban) based on our index, give at least a rough idea of the levels of observance of Islamic religious practice in Bangladesh today.

The figures in Tables 5.1 (Rural) and 5.1 (Urban) show the extensive observance of Islamic religious practice in contemporary Bangladesh. Only about 1 per cent of our rural sample and about 4 per cent of our urban sample belongs to the category of low religious practice. While 47.8 per cent of our rural sample belongs to the category of medium religious practice, 51.4 per cent can be classified under the category of high religious practice. In the urban sample the high and medium levels of religious practice achieve scores of 49.6 and 46.8 per cent respectively. Thus about half of both the rural and urban samples have more than a casual interest in religion. The other halves of both the samples are high religious practitioners.[6]

Rural-Urban Categories and Religious Practice

After having roughly estimated the extent and levels of observance of obligatory Islamic religious practices among the rural and urban respondents of our survey, we can now proceed to examine whether various levels of observance of religious practices can be analysed in terms of social and demographic variables. Let us look first at the relationship between rural-urban categories and religious practice. Table 5.2 (Rural and Urban) examines this relationship.

The X^2 test of Table 5.2 (Rural and Urban) shows significant association between rural and urban categories and religious practice. The adjusted residuals of the cells of the table, however, reveal that high and medium levels of religious practice are not significantly associated with either rural or urban areas. The level of significant association occurs only between the urban area and low religious practice, that is to say, the urban area tends to be more significantly associated with low religious practice than with high and medium levels of religious observance.

Education and Religious Practice

How is education related to religious practice? Tables 5.3 (Rural) and 5.3 (Urban) examine the relationship between education and religious practice.

It is usually held that illiterate Muslims in Bangladesh are punctilious in observance of religious practices and that educated Bangladeshis "become either indifferent or lax in the observance of the rituals".[7] Our Tables indicate that the above view about relationship between education and religious practice is too simplistic. As the X^2 test of Table 5.3 (Rural) shows, levels of education do not seem to make any difference in the degrees of observance of religious practices in the rural area where about 55 per cent of our respon-

TABLE 5.2: Rural-Urban

Religious Practice by Rural-Urban Categories

Rural-Urban Categories	High Religious Practices	Medium Religious Practices	Low Religious Practices	Row Total
Rural Area	1779 51.40 63.21 1.27	1656 47.85 62.94 0.8	26 0.75 25.49 −7.76	3461 62.4
Urban Area	1035 49.61 36.78 −1.28	975 46.74 37.05 −0.79	76 3.64 74.5 10.01	2086 37.6
Column total	2814 50.73	2631 47.43	102 1.84	5547 100.0

$X^2 = 58.284$ with 2 df, P<0.005

dents are illiterate and only 4.8 per cent of them have higher levels (intermediate and above) of education.

However, we find a different picture of the relationship between education and religious practice in our urban sample in which 94 per cent of our respondents are literate, and where 57 per cent of our interviewees have higher education (intermediate and above). The X^2 test of Table 5.3 (Urban) shows a significant association between education and religious practice, and a distinct pattern of relationship between levels of education and degrees of religious practice emerges if we look at the adjusted residuals of the cells of the Table. Illiteracy seems to be associated with high religious practice. The degree of association between primary-level education and high religious practice seems to be even stronger. The level of association between high religious practice and education begins to decrease with middle-level education, although association between the two variables seems still strong at that level of education. At the level of high education (intermediate and above) education seems to have more significant association with medium and low levels of religious practice, particularly with the latter.

TABLE 5.3: Rural

Religious Practice by Education in Rural Areas

Education	High Religious Practice	Medium Religious Practice	Low Religious Practice	Row Total
No education	940	939	17	1896
	49.6	49.5	0.9	54.8
	52.8	56.7	65.4	
Class I–V	418	357	2	777
	53.8	46.0	0.2	22.4
	23.5	21.6	7.7	
Class VI–X	321	270	4	595
	54.0	45.3	0.7	17.2
	18.4	16.3	15.4	
Intermediate and above	81	81	3	165
	49.1	49.1	1.8	4.8
	4.6	4.9	11.5	
Not stated	19	9	0	28
	67.9	32.1	0	0.8
	1.1	0.5	0	
Column Total	1779	1656	26	3461
	51.4	47.8	0.8	100.0

$X^2 = 14.265$ with 8 df, P>0.05

As X^2 test does not show significant association between the variables, analysis of residuals for the table has not been done.

TABLE 5.3: Urban

Religious Practice by Education in Urban Areas

Education	High Religious Practice	Medium Religious Practice	Low Religious Practice	Row Total
No education	84	39	1	124
	67.7	31.4	0.8	5.9
	8.1	4.0	1.3	
	4.16	−3.51	−1.73	
Class I–V	69	27	0.0	96
	71.9	28.1	0.0	4.7
	6.7	2.8	0.0	
	4.46	−3.74	−1.95	
Class VI–X	362	299	5	666
	54.8	44.9	0.8	31.9
	35.0	30.7	6.6	
	2.96	−1.15	−4.82	
Intermediate and above	518	603	70	1191
	43.49	50.62	5.9	57.0
	50.0	61.8	92.1	
	−6.45	4.1	6.28	
Not stated	2	7	0	9
	22.2	77.8	0	0.4
	0.2	0.7	0	
	−1.64	1.87	−0.58	
Column total	1035	975	76	2086
	49.6	46.7	3.6	100.0

$X^2 = 88.861$ with 8 df, P<0.001

Occupation and Religious Practice

The third social variable with which we want to examine the relationship of religious practice is occupation. Our Tables 5.4 (Rural) and 5.4 (Urban) given below, in this regard show significant association between occupation and religious practice.

Table 5.4 (Rural) shows that the agriculturists in the rural area seem to be associated more with the medium level of religious practice than with high or low levels. The village traders are also likely to be oriented more towards medium rather than high or low level of religious conformity. The rural professionals (teachers, service-holders and doctors) whose professional education and training are of a much lower order than those of their counterparts in the urban area, tend to have more association with high-level rather than medium or low levels of religious practice. Rural housewives are more likely to have association with high religious practice than with medium and low degrees of religious observance. Rural students do not seem to be associated

TABLE 5.4: Rural

Religious Practice by Occupation in Rural Areas

Occupation	High Religious Practice	Medium Religious Practice	Low Religious Practice	Row Total
Agriculture	519	667	11	1197
	43.4	55.7	0.9	34.6
	29.2	40.3	42.3	
	−6.88	6.74	0.83	
Trade	92	142	2	236
	39.0	60.2	0.8	6.8
	5.2	8.6	7.7	
	−3.95	3.92	0.17	
Professionals	94	65	0	159
(teachers,	59.1	40.9	0	4.6
service-holders,	5.3	3.9	0	
doctors)	1.99	−1.8	−1.12	
Housewives	901	552	9	1462
	61.6	37.8	0.6	42.2
	50.6	33.3	34.6	
	10.29	−10.16	−0.79	
Students	109	117	1	227
	48.0	51.5	0.4	6.6
	6.1	7.1	3.8	
	−1.05	1.15	−0.56	
Unemployed and	64	113	3	180
others	35.6	62.8	1.7	5.2
	3.6	6.8	11.5	
	−4.36	4.11	1.46	
Column total	1179	1656	26	3461
	51.4	47.8	0.8	100.0

X^2 = 132.126 with 10 df, P<.001

particularly with any level of religious practice.

As Table 5.4 (Urban) shows, in contrast to the pioneers of capitalist revolution in the West, the business and industrial group in Bangladesh does not seem to have any particular association with high religious practice. The new urban professionals (lawyers, doctors, teachers and civil servants), the usual leaders of the modernisation process in the Third World, seem to have more association with low rather than high or medium levels of religious observance. In contrast to rural students, urban students seem to have more association with medium religious practice. Lastly, like their sisters in the rural area, the urban housewives seem to be more significantly associated with high rather than medium or low levels of religious practice.

TABLE 5.4: Urban

Religious Practice by Occupation in Urban Area

Occupation	High Religious Practice	Medium Religious Practice	Low Religious Practice	Row Total
Business and industry	138 46.5 13.3 −1.17	146 49.12 15.0 0.90	13 4.4 17.1 0.72	297 14.2
Professionals (lawyers, doctors, teachers, service-holders)	193 46.6 18.6 −1.36	193 46.6 19.8 −0.05	28 6.8 36.8 3.78	414 19.8
Students	203 33.7 19.6 −9.24	374 62.1 38.4 8.97	25 4.2 32.9 0.79	602 28.9
Housewives	480 66.8 46.4 11.35	232 32.3 23.8 −9.6	7 1.0 9.2 −4.71	719 34.5
Unemployed and others	21 38.9 2.0 −1.59	30 55.6 3.0 1.31	3 5.6 4.0 0.75	54 2.6
Column total	1035 49.6	975 46.7	70 3.6	2086 100.0

X^2 = 166.361 with 8 df, P<.001

Yearly income and Religious Practice

Does yearly income make any difference to religious practice? Tables 5.5 (Rural) and 5.5 (Urban) provide some answers to the question.

The X^2 test for Table 5.5 (Rural) shows an association between income and religious practice in the rural area. The Table also shows that this association takes place between high levels of rural income (35,001–50,000, 50,001 and above) and high religious practice, i.e., high levels of rural income tend to associate more with high rather than medium or low levels of religious practice.

As the X^2 test for Table 5.5 (Urban) indicates, an association between income and religious practice occurs in the urban area too. Table 5.5 (Urban) shows that in contrast to the rural pattern, the urban highest income group seems to be associated more with low rather than high or medium levels of religious practice. However, the most interesting finding here is that the lower middle-income group (20,001–30,000) tends to be associated more with high rather than medium and low levels of religious observance. We have found in Table 5.3 (Urban) above that urban primary and middle levels of education also tend to have a more significant association with high rather than medium or low levels of religious practice. Since lower-middle income and primary and middle-level education seem to be the correlates of the urban lower-middle classes, we can argue that members of the lower-middle class of the metropolitan areas of Bangladesh seem to be high observers of religious practices. This is in line with a common theme in the literature on religion and social change in the Muslim countries that the recently educated urban lower-middle classes under the stress of their competition with the more established middle and upper classes seek security in high religious conformity.[8]

Demographic Variables and Religious Practice

As we have done with regard to religious beliefs, we have examined the relationship between religious practice with two demographic variables—age and sex. Let us look at Tables 5.6 (Rural) and 5.6 (Urban).

The Tables show that females in both the urban and rural areas tend to have a more significant association with high levels of religious practice than with medium and low levels of it. While in the rural area males seem to be more medium rather than high and low religious performers, in the urban area they tend to belong more to the medium and low rather than high categories of religious practitioners.

As shown below in Tables 5.7 (Rural) and 5.7 (Urban), different age groups seem to be associated with different levels of religious observances. In both the rural and urban areas, respondents belonging to the 16–25 age group tend to be more middle level religious performers than do members of other age groups. The age group 26–35 does not seem to have particular association with any one level of religious observance. The respondents over 36 seem to be more high- rather than medium- and low-level performers of obligatory religious practices.

Summation and Conclusion

To sum up our discussion so far in this chapter, we find that urban environment, higher education and high income (in the urban area) and modern professions tend to be associated more with low religious practice rather than with the high or or medium levels of religious practice. We have seen in Chapter IV above that these are the social variables which also tend to foster modern religious belief.[9] Certain social settings like the agricultural profession and male sex are more likely to correlate with medium level than with high or low levels of religious practice. As we have found in the

TABLE 5.5: Rural

Religious Practice by Yearly Income in Rural Area

Yearly Income (in taka)	High Religious Practice	Medium Religious Practice	Low Religious Practice	Row Total
Up to 2,500	195	190	4	389
	50.1	48.8	1.0	11.2
	11.0	11.5	15.4	
	−0.53	0.41	0.65	
2,501–5,000	291	302	2	595
	48.9	50.8	0.3	17.2
	16.4	18.2	7.7	
	−1.33	1.56	−1.28	
5,001–7,500	375	374	6	755
	49.7	49.5	0.8	21.8
	21.1	22.6	23.1	
	−1.07	1.05	0.15	
7,501–12,000	358	311	5	674
	53.1	46.1	0.7	19.5
	10.1	18.8	19.2	
	0.99	−0.98	−0.03	
12,001–18,000	244	237	3	484
	50.41	48.9	0.62	14.0
	13.7	14.3	11.5	
	−0.46	0.53	−0.36	
18,001–25,000	128	126	5	259
	49.4	48.6	1.9	7.5
	7.2	7.6	19.2	
	−0.66	0.26	2.28	
25,001–35,000	73	58	0	131
	55.7	44.3	0	3.8
	4.1	3.5	0	
	1.009	−0.83	−1.01	
35,001–50,000	77	38	0	115
	67.0	33.0	0	3.3
	4.3	2.3	0	
	3.39	−3.23	−0.94	
50,001 and above	38	20	1	59
	64.4	33.9	1.7	1.7
	2.1	1.2	3.8	
	2.01	−2.16	0.84	
Column total	1779	1656	26	3461
	51.4	47.8	0.8	100.0

X^2 = 29.195 with 16 df, P<0.05

TABLE 5.5: Urban

Religious Practice by Yearly Income in Urban Area

Yearly Income (in taka)	High Religious Practice	Medium Religious Practice	Low Religious Practice	Row Total
Up to 10,000	66	68	1	135
	48.9	50.4	0.7	6.5
	6.4	7.0	1.3	
	−0.17	0.87	−1.86	
10,001–20,000	141	153	10	304
	46.4	50.3	3.3	14.6
	13.6	15.7	13.2	
	−1.22	1.35	−0.35	
20,001–30,000	119	75	3	197
	60.4	38.1	1.5	9.4
	11.5	7.7	3.9	
	3.18	−2.56	−1.66	
30,001–50,000	340	290	15	645
	52.7	45.0	2.3	31.0
	32.9	29.7	19.7	
	1.89	−1.08	−2.14	
50,001–100,000	212	205	18	435
	48.7	47.1	4.1	20.9
	20.5	21.0	23.7	
	−0.41	0.18	0.61	
100,001 and above	157	184	29	370
	42.4	49.7	7.8	17.7
	15.2	18.9	38.2	
	−3.04	1.27	4.74	
Column total	1035	975	76	2086
	49.6	46.7	3.6	100.0

X^2 = 42.876 with 10 df, P<0.001

preceding chapter these same social settings tend to produce orthodox religious beliefs.[10] Illiteracy (in the urban area), the profession of housewife and female sex seem to have a more significant association with high religious practice than with the two other levels of religious observance. We have seen in Chapter IV that these variables associate more with popular religious belief than with modern or orthodox belief.[11] We have argued in the chapter on religious beliefs that it is social conditions like non-urbanisation, illiteracy, low income and household work which produce popular belief among womenfolk, particularly among housewives.[12] With regard to age, we find that the age groups 16–25 and 35 and above, seem to be more associated with medium and high levels of religious practice respectively. Here again we have

TABLE 5.6: Rural

Religious Practice by Sex in Rural Area

Sex	High Religious Practice	Medium Religious Practice	Low Religious Practice	Row Total
Male	816	1036	15	1867
	43.7	55.5	8.8	53.9
	45.9	62.6	57.7	
	−9.80	9.74	0.38	
Female	963	620	11	1594
	60.4	38.9	0.7	46.1
	54.1	37.4	42.3	
	9.80	−9.74	−0.38	
Col. Total	1779	1656	26	3461
	51.4	47.8	0.8	100.0

$X^2 = 96.330$ with 2 d.f., P<0.001

TABLE 5.6: Urban

Religious Practice by Sex in Urban Area

Sex	High Religious Practice	Medium Religious Practice	Low Religious Practice	Row Total
Male	415	561	64	1040
	40.0	53.9	6.1	49.8
	40.1	57.4	84.2	
	−8.84	6.57	6.10	
Female	620	414	12	1046
	59.3	39.6	1.1	50.1
	59.9	42.5	15.8	
	8.84	−6.57	−6.10	
Col. Total	1035	975	76	2086
	49.6	46.7	3.6	100.0

$X^2 = 98.329$ with 2 d.f., P<0.0001

seen in the preceding chapter[13] that the age groups 16–25 and 35 and above are likely to be more associated with orthodox and popular religious beliefs respectively. Thus we find that different social environments that tend to produce modern, orthodox and popular religious beliefs, also seem to be associated with low, medium and high levels of religious practice respectively.

This conclusion is corroborated when we examine the relationship between religious belief and religious practice. Let us look closely at Tables 5.8 (Rural) and 5.8 (Urban).

The X^2 test of Table 5.8 (Rural) shows a highly significant association between religious belief and religious practice, and adjusted residuals in the cells of the Table show the patterns of association. Thus we find that in the

TABLE 5.7: Rural

Religious Practice by Age in Rural Area

Age	High Religious Practice	Medium Religious Practice	Low Religious Practice	Row Total
16–25	595	792	15	1402
	42.4	56.5	1.1	40.5
	33.4	47.8	57.7	
	–8.7	8.39	1.79	
26–35	424	419	6	849
	49.9	49.4	0.7	24.5
	23.8	25.3	23.1	
	–0.97	1.01	–0.17	
36–50	399	274	4	677
	58.9	40.5	0.6	19.6
	22.4	16.5	15.4	
	4.37	–4.28	–0.53	
51 and above	361	171	1	533
	67.7	32.1	0.2	15.4
	20.3	10.3	3.8	
	8.2	–7.92	–1.63	
Column total	1779	1656	26	3461
	51.4	47.8	0.8	100.0

X^2 = 119.46 with 6 df, P<0.001

rural area modern religious belief tends to be associated more with medium and low levels of religious practice, and that association between modern belief and low religious practice seems to be even more significant than the association between modern belief and medium religious practice. Orthodox religious belief is found to be associated more with medium level rather than high and low levels of religious practice. Popular belief seems to have a higher degree of association with high religious practice rather than with medium and low levels of religious practice. A careful scrutiny of Table 5.8 (Rural) reveals that the patterns of relationship between different types of religious beliefs and levels of religious practice found in the rural area seem to exist with stronger force in the urban area.

As in the concluding section of the preceding chapter[14] we are faced here again with the difficult problem of finding the direction of causal relations. We find that particular social settings as well as their corresponding religious beliefs are associated with different levels of religious practice. Is the level of religious practice caused by religious belief or by the social environment associated with the religious belief? We have argued in the chapter on religious beliefs that religious beliefs themselves seem to derive from particular social settings, and we can possibly argue that social conditions rather than religious beliefs are prior to religious practice.

TABLE 5.7: Urban

Religious Practice by Age in Urban Area

Age	High Religious Practice	Medium Religious Practice	Low Religious Practice	Row Total
16–25	381	549	35	965
	39.5	56.9	3.6	46.3
	36.8	56.3	46.1	
	–8.58	8.62	–0.03	
26–35	245	265	16	526
	46.6	50.4	3.0	25.2
	23.7	27.2	21.1	
	–1.61	1.93	–0.85	
36–50	228	101	16	345
	66.1	29.3	4.6	16.5
	22.0	10.4	21.1	
	6.69	–7.11	1.07	
51 and above	181	60	9	250
	72.4	24.0	3.6	12.0
	17.5	6.2	11.8	
	7.67	–7.68	–0.03	
Column total	1035	975	76	2086
	49.6	46.7	3.6	100.0

$X^2 = 140.372$ with 6 df, $P<0.001$

TABLE 5.8: Rural

Religious Practice by Religious Belief in Rural Areas

Religious Belief	Religious Practice			Row Total
	High Practice	Medium Practice	Low Practice	
Modern	12	27	2	41
	24.3	65.9	4.9	1.2
	0.7	1.6	7.7	
	–2.85	2.32	3.07	
Orthodox	860	881	11	1752
	49.1	50.3	0.6	50.6
	48.3	53.2	42.3	
	–2.75	2.9	–0.85	
Popular	907	748	13	1668
	54.4	44.8	0.8	48.2
	51.0	45.2	50.0	
	3.37	–3.41	0.18	
Column total	1779	1656	26	3461
	51.4	47.8	0.8	100.0

$X^2 = 26.372$ with 4 df, $P < 0.00001$

TABLE 5.8: Urban

Religious Practice by Religious Belief in Urban Areas

Religious Belief	Religious Practice			
	High Practice	Medium Practice	Low Practice	Row Total
Modern	74	147	30	251
	29.5	58.6	12.0	12.0
	7.1	15.1	39.5	
	−6.80	4.0	7.49	
Orthodox	608	647	40	1295
	46.9	50.0	3.1	62.1
	58.7	66.4	52.6	
	−3.11	3.77	−1.72	
Popular	353	181	6	540
	65.4	33.5	1.1	25.9
	34.1	18.6	7.9	
	8.5	−7.15	−3.64	
Column total	1035	975	76	2086
	49.6	46.7	3.6	100.0

$X^2 = 138.115$ with 4 df, $P < 0.00001$

NOTES

1 K.B. Sayeed, "Religion and Nation-building in Pakistan", *The Middle East Journal*, Vol. 17, No. 3, Summer 1963, p. 288.
2 R. Levy, *The Social Structure of Islam* (Cambridge: Cambridge University Press, reprinted 1979), p. 192.
3 For a discussion on the primary importance of *Iman* in Islamic religious practice, see *ibid.*, pp. 192–3; F. Rahman, *Islam* (Chicago: University of Chicago Press, second edition 1979), p. 35.
4 For extended discussions on prayer, fasting, welfare tax and pilgrimage, see Levy, *op.cit.*, pp. 154–62; Rahman, *op.cit.*, pp. 35–6.
5 See Chapter III above, p. 62.
6 Although modern, orthodox and popular are the common categories used by recent scholars on comparative Islam for the analysis of Islamic beliefs, I have not yet come across any national survey of the extent of the spread of the different types of Islamic beliefs of any Muslim country like the one we have done for Bangladesh. We have not thus been able to show how the extent of the spread of Islamic religious beliefs described in Chapter IV compares with that of any other Muslim country. There is, however, a survey of Punjab in Pakistan. See Lynda Malik, "Measuring Consensus in Pakistan", *Journal of South Asian and Middle Eastern Studies*, Vol. VI, No. 1, Fall 1982, pp. 33–47.
Lynda Malik used the following questions (see *ibid.*, p. 34) for her survey conducted in February-May 1980 for constructing her "index of religious conformity":
A. Have you ever recited the Qur'an?
B. Do you offer daily prayers?
C. Do you ever go to the mosque? (Asked of males only.)
D. Do you (does your wife) observe *purdah*?

Excepting the question on prayer, the questions used by Malik relate to non-obligatory Islamic practices. Still Malik's study gives some rough idea of the extent of religious practice in the Punjab. Malik has one Table (see *ibid.*, p. 35) for both urban and rural respondents, and provides the following frequencies of scores in the Conformity category:

Category	Frequency	Percentage
Low	283	22.62
Medium	583	46.60
High	300	23.98
Other	2	0.15
No answer	83	6.63
Total	1251	100.00

A comparison of Malik's figures with those of our Tables 5.1 (Rural) and 5.1 (Urban) clearly indicates that the level of observance of religious practice is much higher in Bangladesh than in the Punjab in Pakistan.

7   Sayeed, *op.cit.*, p. 289.
8   Thus Jansen reports, "The lower middle classes—one of the characteristic products of urbanization—are among the most devout, not to say fanatical, elements of Islamic society. The clerks and the small shopkeepers are the most fervent supporters of the fundamentalist and reform movements in the partially urbanized societies of Indonesia, Pakistan, Egypt, Iran and Turkey". See G.H. Jansen, *Militant Islam* (New York: Harper and Row, 1979), p. 46. Malik writes about the pattern in the Punjab in Pakistan: "The phenomenon of the members of the middle class, who are striving to rise into upper levels (but have not quite made it) being the highest conformers is familiar to observers of comparative stratification systems". See Malik, *op.cit.*, p. 37. See also K.B. Sayeed, *The Political System of Pakistan* (Boston: Houghton Mifflin, 1967), pp. 218–9; L.E. Creevey, "Religion and Modernization in Senegal", in J. Esposito (ed.), *Islam and Political Development: Religion and Sociopolitical Change* (Syracuse: Syracuse University Press, 1980), pp. 218–9.
9   See Chapter IV, pp. 76–8.
10   *Ibid.*, pp. 69–70, 74–6.
11   *Ibid.*, pp. 76–8.
12   *Ibid.*, pp. 74–7.
13   *Ibid.*, pp. 75–7.
14   *Ibid.*, p. 78.

CHAPTER VI

ISLAM AND MUSLIM-HINDU RELATIONS IN BANGLADESH

The discussion of Islam in Bangladesh can hardly be complete without a reference to Hindu-Muslim relations. Religious cleavage provided the main dynamics of politics in the India-Pakistan-Bangladesh subcontinent in the first half of the twentieth century. The partition in 1947 came in the wake of large-scale Hindu-Muslim riots. The partition of Pakistan in 1971 was accompanied by an ideological revolution in former East Pakistan (now Bangladesh) which upheld secularism as against the Islamic ideology of Pakistan.[1] Secularism was not however defined in the Western sense of the term—freedom of the human spirit from the tyranny of all religious doctrines. Secularism was defined by leaders of independent Bangladesh as a condition in which "all religions practiced. . . . are entitled to equal freedom and protection". Secularism meant absence of government or political control over religion. It was a negative and non-discriminatory secularism.[2] Islam came to be associated with the constitution of Bangladesh after the collapse of the regime of Sheikh Mujibur Rahman. However, as we shall see in Chapter X, the Islamic provisions added to the constitution were of a symbolic nature and did not have much substantial content.

There had been a long-term trend of a gradual decline in the number of Hindus in Bangladesh areas through migration to neighbouring areas from the beginning of this century. The largest migration, of course, took place immediately before and after the partition in 1947. The dwindling of the Hindus continued. According to the 1951 Census, the Hindus constituted 22 per cent of the population.[3] The 1961 Census put the figure at 18.4.[4] Now in the 1980s Hindus constitute 12.1 per cent of the population of Bangladesh with the Muslims having an overwhelming majority of 86.6 per cent.[5] (While the Hindus constitute 12.19 per cent of the population in the rural areas, they constitute 11.8 per cent of the urban population.[6] In the Dhaka Metropolitan Area, from which our sample is drawn, the Hindus constitute 5.8 per cent of the population.)[7] About 61 per cent of our rural and 18 per cent of urban respondents report the presence of Hindus in their *paras* (immediate neighbourhoods). How do Islam and Hinduism relate to each other in contemporary Bangladesh?

Muslim-Hindu Religious Connections

From the Muslim religious point of view the most important question of Islam-Hinduism relations is whether the Muslims attend the *pujas* of the Hindus. Attending the *pujas* is a grievous sin because idolatry violates the concept of the unity of Allah (God), the fundamental doctrine in Islam.

As Tables 6.1 (Rural) and 6.1 (Urban), given below, show, only 14.6 per

TABLE 6.1: Rural

Attendance at Hindu *pujas*

Category	Frequency	Percentage
Yes	507	14.6
No	2946	85.1
Not stated	8	0.2
Total	3461	100.0

TABLE 6.1: Urban

Attendance at Hindu *pujas*

Category	Frequency	Percentage
Yes	382	18.3
No	1698	81.4
Not stated	6	0.3
Total	2086	100.0

cent of our rural respondents and only 18.3 per cent of the urban respondents attend the Hindu *pujas*.

Muslim-Hindu Non-religious Connections

If there is not much religious connection between Hindus and Muslims, what are the social and economic connections between the two communities? We shall now try to understand whether our respondents have friendship, business connections or any other type of economic relations with the Hindus. Respondents are categorised in the following tables.

Tables 6.2 (Rural) and 6.2 (Urban) show the depth of Muslim-Hindu relations in Bangladesh. About 20 per cent of rural Muslims report friendship with Hindus, although Hindus constitute only 12.19 per cent of the rural population. The level of Muslim-Hindu friendship is striking as the Hindus in the rural area are mostly low-caste ones engaged in activities like hair-cutting, shoe-repairing, washing, and pottery. The figures in Table 6.2 (urban) are all the more striking. About 47 per cent of our urban respondents state that they have friendships with Hindus when only about 6 per cent of the population of Dhaka are Hindus. The urban percentages indicate the extent of non-communal attitudes developed in the city of Dhaka. Of course, the economic dominance that the Hindu upper classes exercised over the Muslims of the Bangladesh area from the middle of the eighteenth through to the first half of the twentieth century has been eroded by the political and social changes from the 1940s to the present time. Possibly reflecting this development, Tables 6.3 (Rural) through to 6.4 (Urban) show that there are not many

TABLE 6.2: Rural

Friendship with Hindus

Category	Frequency	Percentage
Yes	689	19.9
No	2422	70.0
Not stated	350	10.1
Total	3461	100.0

TABLE 6.2: Urban

Friendship with Hindus

Category	Frequency	Percentage
Yes	989	47.4
No	1094	52.4
Not stated	3	0.1
Total	2086	100.0

TABLE 6.3: Rural

Business Connections with Hindus

Category	Frequency	Percentage
Yes	131	3.8
No	2935	85.7
Not stated	365	10.5
Total	3461	100.0

TABLE 6.3: Urban

Business Connections with Hindus

Category	Frequency	Percentage
Yes	223	10.7
No	1860	89.2
Not stated	3	0.1
Total	2086	100.0

TABLE 6.4: Rural

Other Connections with Hindus

Category	Frequency	Percentage
Yes	65	1.9
No	3028	87.5
Not stated	368	10.6
Total	3461	100.0

TABLE 6.4: Urban

Other Connections with Hindus

Category	Frequency	Percentage
Yes	85	4.1
No	1998	95.8
Not stated	3	0.1
Total	2086	100.0

business or other economic connections between Muslims and Hindus in Bangladesh, although the level of such connections is comparatively higher in urban areas than in rural regions.

To understand the degree of Muslim hostility towards the Hindus, we asked our respondents the following question:

R18(C)/U17(C):   Do you think that there is need for the Hindus to stay in this country, or should they migrate to any other place?

The frequency Tables below give us some idea about how the Muslims view Hindu presence in Bangladesh.

As the Tables show, 79 per cent of our urban respondents and 60 per cent of rural Muslims are tolerant of the Hindu presence. The answers to Question R18(C) and U17(C) revealed the secular attitude that the majority of Muslims in Bangladesh have towards their Hindu compatriots. A few representative answers are quoted below:

It is better to have co-operation among the various sections of the people.
There cannot be peace in the country unless thirty-six nations (*jati*) live together.
If the Hindus go they should go of their own will.
They [the Hindus] should live in their own way.
There cannot be peace if twelve nations (*jati*) do not live together.
I have no objections if the Hindus stay.
There is need for their [the Hindus'] staying in this country, because our Muslim brethren live in the land of Hindus.

TABLE 6.5: Rural

Need for Hindus to stay

Category	Frequency	Percentage
Need to stay	2079	60.0
Better to go	888	25.7
Others	101	2.9
Not stated	393	11.4
Total	3461	100.0

TABLE 6.5: Urban

Need for Hindus to stay

Category	Frequency	Percentage
Need to stay	1662	79.7
Better to go	330	15.8
Others	43	2.0
Not stated	51	2.5
Total	2086	100.0

Pirs, Hindu Gods and Goddesses

It is a common theme in the history of Bengali culture that Islam in the Bangladesh area lost its pristine form and absorbed many elements of the Hindu religion. It was particularly true in the Middle Ages when the Bengali Muslim literature often referred to Hindu gods and goddesses. Some of the saints common to both Muslims and Hindus were *Khijir Pir* (the guardian spirit of seas and rivers), *Panch Pir* (invoked when danger threatened), and *Badar Pir* (sharing with *Khijir* the domination of water).[8] Are these saints still known to the Muslims of Bangladesh today?

As Tables 6.6 (Rural) and 6.6 (Urban) show *Khijir Pir* is quite well known in both rural and urban areas with about 45 per cent of the respondents in the village areas and about 52 per cent of urban respondents recognising his name. Both *Panch Pir* and *Badar Pir* (Tables 6.7 and 6.8 (Rural and Urban)) are much less known in both rural and urban areas. The reason for the popularity of *Khijir Pir* is possibly that the massive erosion of land by the rivers of Bangladesh renders thousands of people homeless and landless every year, and the legend of *Khijir* continues to thrive.

It is claimed by historians of the Bangladesh area that besides these legendary saints there were certain gods and goddesses common to both lower-class Muslims and Hindus as late as the nineteenth century. These deities include *Dharmathakur* (the god dispensing even-handed justice), *Satya*

TABLE 6.6: Rural

Have you heard the name of *Khijir Pir?*

Category	Frequency	Percentage
Yes	1539	44.5
No	1876	54.2
Not stated	46	1.3
Total	3461	100.0

TABLE 6.6: Urban

Have you heard the name of *Khijir Pir?*

Category	Frequency	Percentage
Yes	1076	51.6
No	989	47.4
Not stated	21	1.0
Total	2086	100.0

TABLE 6.7: Rural

Have You Heard the Name of *Panch Pir?*

Category	Frequency	Percentage
Yes	924	26.7
No	2487	71.9
Not stated	50	1.4
Total	3461	100.0

TABLE 6.7: Urban

Have You Heard the Name of *Panch Pir?*

Category	Frequency	Percentage
Yes	850	40.7
No	1216	58.3
Not stated	20	1.0
Total	2086	100.0

TABLE 6.8: Rural

Have You Heard the Name of *Badar Pir*?

Category	Frequency	Percentage
Yes	801	23.1
No	2609	75.4
Not stated	51	1.5
Total	3461	100.0

TABLE 6.8: Urban

Have You Heard the Name of *Badar Pir*?

Category	Frequency	Percentage
Yes	733	35.1
No	1332	63.9
Not stated	21	1.0
Total	2086	100.0

Pir (a good-natured god ready to respond to small prayers), *Sitaladebi* (goddess of smallpox), *Olabibi* (goddess of cholera), and *Manashadebi* (goddess of snakes).[9] Are these gods and goddesses still known?

Tables 6.9, 6.10, 6.11, 6.12, and 6.13 (Rural and Urban) show that the names of gods and goddesses are better known in the urban areas than in the rural areas. This seems strange because the percentage of population who hold popular beliefs is much higher in the rural areas (48.2) than in the urban areas (25.9).

As shown in Tables 6.14 (Rural) and 6.14 (Urban) below, there are two main channels through which the legends about the *pirs*, gods and goddesses spread from people to people—popular tales and books and *puthis*. Percentages of people subscribing to popular stories are the same in both urban and rural areas. Because of the higher percentage of literacy among urban people, the urban respondents are, however, more widely acquainted with the legends described in popular literature and historical studies. This explains the wider spread of the names of the Hindu saints, gods and goddesses among the urban people.

Knowledge of legends alone does not signify the legendary figures' religious relevance for the respondents. If the respondent invokes blessings of the Hindu *pirs* and deities and attributes supernatural power to them, the respondent concerned commits *shirk* (partnership with Allah), a grievous sin in Islam. We therefore probed deeper in the minds of the respondents, and asked, "Do you offer votive donations in favour of these *pirs*?"

TABLE 6.9: Rural

Have You Heard the Name of *Dharmathakur?*

Category	Frequency	Percentage
Yes	292	8.4
No	3122	90.2
Not stated	47	1.4
Total	3461	100.0

TABLE 6.9: Urban

Have You Heard the Name of *Dharmathakur?*

Category	Frequency	Percentage
Yes	510	24.4
No	1574	75.5
Not stated	2	0.1
Total	2086	100.0

TABLE 6.10: Rural

Have You Heard the Name of *Satya Pir?*

Category	Frequency	Percentage
Yes	571	16.5
No	2843	82.1
Not stated	47	1.4
Total	3461	100.0

TABLE 6.10: Urban

Have You Heard the Name of *Satya Pir?*

Category	Frequency	Percentage
Yes	609	29.2
No	1475	70.7
Not stated	2	0.1
Total	2086	100.0

TABLE 6.11: Rural

Have You Heard the Name of *Manashadebi*?

Category	Frequency	Percentage
Yes	1047	30.3
No	2367	68.4
Not stated	47	1.4
Total	3461	100.0

TABLE 6.11: Urban

Have You Heard the Name of *Manashadebi*?

Category	Frequency	Percentage
Yes	1105	53.0
No	979	46.9
Not stated	2	0.1
Total	2086	100.0

TABLE 6.12: Rural

Have You Heard the Name of *Ola Bibi*?

Category	Frequency	Percentage
Yes	363	10.5
No	3051	88.2
Not stated	47	1.4
Total	3461	100.0

TABLE 6.12: Urban

Have You Heard the Name of *Ola Bibi*?

Category	Frequency	Percentage
Yes	712	34.1
No	1371	65.7
Not stated	3	0.1
Total	2086	100.0

TABLE 6.13: Rural

Have You Heard the Name of *Sitaladebi*?

Category	Frequency	Percentage
Yes	655	18.9
No	2757	79.7
Not stated	49	1.4
Total	3461	100.0

TABLE 6.13: Urban

Have You Heard the Name of *Sitaladebi*?

Category	Frequency	Percentage
Yes	777	37.2
No	1303	62.5
Not stated	6	0.3
Total	2086	100.0

TABLE 6.14: Rural

Under What Context Did You Hear the Names of *Pirs*, Gods and Goddesses?

Category	Frequency	Percentage
From popular tales	1219	35.2
From books and *puthis*	137	4.0
Others	83	2.4
Inapplicable	1892	54.7
Not stated	130	3.8
Total	3461	100.0

TABLE 6.14: Urban

Under What Context Did You Hear the Names of *Pirs*, Gods and Goddesses?

Category	Frequency	Percentage
From popular tales	735	35.2
From books and *puthis*	475	22.8
Others	29	1.4
Inapplicable	773	37.1
Not stated	74	3.5
Total	2086	100.0

TABLE 6.15: Rural

Do you offer votive donations in favour of these *pirs*?

Category	Frequency	Percentage
Yes	225	6.5
No	3236	93.5
Total	3461	100.0

TABLE 6.15: Urban

Do you offer votive donations in favour of these *pirs*?

Category	Frequency	Percentage
Yes	38	1.8
No	2048	98.2
Total	2086	100.0

Unless and until a Muslim offers votive donations to the supposed supernatural powers, he does not commit *shirk*. Tables 6.15 (Rural) and 6.15 (Urban) show that only a small percentage of rural people (6.5) actually make votive donations to Hindu *pirs*. The percentage of such people is even smaller in the urban areas. The Hindu *pirs*, gods and goddesses passed into legends a long time ago and now the legends themselves are fading away. Thus accretions from Hindu beliefs and practices do not seem to be a significant component of popular Islam in Bangladesh today. Popular Islam in contemporary Bangladesh centres mainly around the institutions of Muslim *pirs* and *mazars* which we included in the items that we used for the construction of the scale of religious beliefs.[10]

To sum up, on the evidence of the Tables given above in this Chapter, it seems quite safe to conclude that the vast majority of present-day Muslims in Bangladesh do not share any faith or god with the Hindus. On the one hand, 85 per cent of rural Muslims and 81 per cent of urban Muslims do not even watch the colourful Hindu *puja* festivities. On the other, the majority of Bangladesh Muslims are tolerant of the Hindu presence and give secular definition of Hindu citizenship. The Bangladesh Muslims seem to have developed an Islamic-cum-secular culture. This culture seems already to have had a positive effect in bridging the historical cleavage between Muslims and Hindus in Bangladesh. Thus there have not been any Muslim-Hindu riots in Bangladesh since it emerged as an independent state in December 1971. This development has taken place despite several attempts by the present military-backed government of General H. M. Ershad to provoke Muslim-Hindu conflicts in order to divert popular attention from its undemocratic and authoritarian character. Communal riots, on the other hand, have been on the increase of India,[11] and in Pakistan fanatic Islamic groups have forced the Government of Pakistan to declare Ahmadiyas—an heretical Muslim group—as a non-Muslim sect.[12]

NOTES

1 For more on this see Talukder Maniruzzaman, *The Bangladesh Revolution and its Aftermath* (Dacca: Bangladesh Books International, 1980), especially pp. 69–106.

2 It is interesting to note that the Bangladesh concept of secularism was identical with its Indian interpretation. See Talukder Maniruzzaman, "Bangladesh Politics: Secular and Islamic Trends", in S.R. Chakravarty and Virendra Narain (eds.), *Bangladesh*, Vol. I, *History and Culture* (New Delhi: South Asian Publishers, 1986), pp. 44–54.

3 Census of Pakistan, 1951, *Population According to Religion* (Table 6), *Census Bulletin No. 2* (Karachi: Government of Pakistan, Ministry of Interior, 1951), p. 1.

4 *Population Census of Pakistan, 1961, Bulletin No. 2* (Karachi: Ministry of Home and Kashmir Affairs, Home Affairs Division), p. 19.

5 *1986 Statistical Yearbook of Bangladesh* (Dhaka: Bangladesh Bureau of Statistics, Ministry of Planning, Government of People's Republic of Bangladesh, December 1986), p. 112.

6 The percentages of Hindu populations in the rural and urban areas are derived from Table 2.34, "Regionwise census population by religion 1974–81", in *ibid.*, p. 112, and "Percentage of urban population by religious groups", in *Bangladesh Population Census, 1981: Report on Urban Area* (Dhaka: Bangladesh Bureau of Statistics, November 1987), p. 1.

7 *Ibid.*, p. 24.

8 See above, Chapter II, pp. 34–5.

9 *Ibid.*, p. 34.

10 See above, Chapter IV, pp. 74–6. The centrality of saints and the tombs of dead saints is the common feature of popular Islam among Muslims all over the world. Studies on popular Islam in different Muslim countries abound. See for examples: E. Gellner, *Saints of the Atlas* (Chicago: University of Chicago Press, 1969); M. Gilsenan, *Saint and Sufi in Modern Egypt: An Essay in Sociology of Religion* (Oxford: Clarendon Press, 1973); R.M. Eaton, "The Profile of Popular Islam in the Pakistani Punjab", *Journal of South Asian and Middle Eastern Studies*, Vol. II, No. 1, Fall 1978, pp. 74–92; M. Gaborieau, "The Cult of Saints among the Muslims of Nepal and northern India", in S. Wilson (ed.), *Saints and their Cults: Studies in Religious Sociology, Folklore and History* (Cambridge: Cambridge University Press, reprinted 1985), pp. 291–308.

11 In India there had been at least 5,000 communal incidents since partition, with the lowest number (26) occurring in 1960, and the highest number (more than 350) in 1980. See M.F. Franda' "Fundamentalism, Nationalism and Secularism among the Indian Muslims", paper presented at the International Conference on "Islam, Communalism and Modern Nationalism", at Bellagio, Milan, Italy, held in April 1981, p. 52.

12 See G.H. Jansen, *Militant Islam* (New York: Harper and Row, 1979), p. 138; J.L. Esposito, *Islam and Politics* (Syracuse: Syracuse University Press, 1984), p. 163.

CHAPTER VII

ISLAM AND SOCIO-ECONOMIC DEVELOPMENT IN BANGLADESH

At the time of her birth in 1971, Bangladesh was variously dubbed an "international basket case", a "permanent disaster", or "simply an economic mistake".[1] After more than a decade and a half, a self-reliant Bangladesh still seems to be a distant prospect. With a territory of 55,598 square miles, Bangladesh had in 1981 a population of 90m,[2] with 1,617 people per square mile and 2,461 per arable square mile, making Bangladesh the world's most densely populated country. Yet according to official estimates, the Bangladesh population continues to grow at the rate of 2.4 per cent per year.

About 80 per cent of the people of Bangladesh are illiterate. Nearly 75 per cent of them live below the poverty line, with an annual per capita income of US$130. Agriculture produces nearly 55.5 per cent of the gross domestic product (GDP), while providing 77 per cent of jobs. But because primitive methods prevail in agriculture, yield per acre in Bangladesh is about one-fifth of that in advanced countries like Japan. The annual shortage of foodgrains runs between 1.8 and 2.3 million tons. Organised industry contributes 10 per cent to GDP and employs only 1.8 per cent of the total labour force. The annual trade deficits run at about US$1,000 million, which must be covered by foreign aid. Bangladesh is also dependent on outside sources for over 80 per cent of her annual development budgets. The figures about Bangladesh's underdevelopment can be multiplied. Our purpose here is to understand how social and economic change in Bangladesh today is related to the prevalent Islamic religious beliefs that we have delineated in Chapters III and IV above. We shall try to understand this relationship by examining how Islamic religious beliefs affect the work ethic of the Muslims of Bangladesh, their attitude towards family planning, and their readiness to adopt modern methods of production. In this connection we shall also try to examine how the religious beliefs influence the level of inter-personal trust among the Bangladesh Muslims as the prevalence of a high level of inter-personal trust in a society is regarded as a determinant of the ability of its members to co-operate in developmental activities. We shall also examine the relationship between education and the above four variables (work ethic, attitude towards family planning, inclination to adopt modern methods of production, and level of inter-personal trust) to see how education and religious beliefs compare with each other in affecting social and economic change in Bangladesh today.

Religion and Social Change: The Weberian Thesis

As we have stated in the preface,[3] any discussion on religion and social and economic development has to start with Max Weber, who, with "masterly ingenuity", developed the thesis that explanations of the differences between various groups of people in developing economic rationalism "must be sought in the permanent intrinsic character of their religious beliefs and not only in their temporary external historico-political situations".[4] He tried to prove his thesis by arguing that the capitalist revolution in the West would not have taken place without the Protestant Reformation. According to Max Weber, the capitalist development which required a spirit of dedication and commitment to work was the result of a distinct ethos, a work ethic, produced by Protestantism which became "a way of life" to all Protestants, particularly Calvinists and Puritans. This ethic was the creation of the Protestant doctrine of life as a calling—a set of duties and obligations whose excellent performance alone would enable a believer to be "elected" by God for eternal life. As Max Weber stated:

> The only way of living acceptably to God was not to surpass worldly morality in monastic asceticism, but solely through the fulfilment of the obligations imposed upon the individual by his position in the world. This is his calling.[5]

This idea of calling created a "mighty enthusiasm" among the Protestants who shunned every kind of self-indulgence, brought their life and work under rational control and predictability, worked ceaselessly for the glory of God, and thus brought about the capitalist revolution.

Unfortunately, Max Weber did not make a thorough study of the sociology of Islam comparable to his treatises on Confucianism and Taoism, Ancient Judaism, Hinduism and Buddhism.[6] In his scattered references to Islam he tended to regard Islam as a hedonistic religion, a polar opposite of ascetic puritanism. He mentioned Islam's attitudes towards women, luxuries and property as examples of Islam's accommodating ethic, and argued that as an Arab warrior class engaged in "the acquisition of booty" was the "social carrier" of Islam, the Islamic ethic had to emphasise these worldly pleasures, and the Islamic monotheistic message had to be fashioned in terms of military interests.[7]

It has been argued by some recent scholars on Islam that Max Weber was totally influenced by nineteenth-century writings on Islam which emphasised Mohammad's sexuality and his war with opponents of Islam as important factors in shaping the Koranic teachings. It has been pointed out by these scholars that emerging in the essentially urban environment of Mecca, Islam was tailored to commercialism and ascetism and that Islamic injunctions were designed more to constrain rather than accommodate Bedouin hedonism. Besides, it has also been argued that by ignoring the Koranic and other Muslim accounts of early Islam, Weber in effect ignored his own methodological principle of interpretative sociology—explaining an event from the perspectives of the actors' world view.[8]

However, Weber did not seem to argue that it was the warrior ethic which explained the lack of industrial revolution in the Islamic empires. In analysing the failure of Islamic societies to bring about capitalist development, Weber treated the role of values as secondary and dependent on Islamic social conditions. Weber argued that with prebendal feudalism and patrimonial bureaucracy, which were characteristic of the Abbasid, Mamluk and Ottoman dynasties, the prerequisites of capitalism—rational, formal law, autonomous cities, an independent burgher class and political stability— could not emerge in the Islamic empires.[9]

In any case, Weber's thesis on the Protestant ethic and the spirit of capitalism has itself been subjected to criticism. It has been argued that it was the economic movement and social changes effected by "the rising strata of the lower industrial middle classes", the "social carriers" of Weber's Protestant ethic, rather than their religious creed which might have produced the capitalist revolution. "Why insist", argued R.H. Tawney, "that causation can work in only one direction?.... Would it not be equally plausible, equally one-sided, to argue that the religious changes were themselves merely the result of economic movements?"[10] Besides, religious thought was not the only idealistic force affecting Europe in the sixteenth and seventeenth centuries. Political thought of the Renaissance did also play an effective role in defeating the forces of traditionalism which, according to Weber, were the opposite to the spirit of capitalism.[11]

As a student of social science I am disinclined to any mono-causal model of social change and to any kind of reductionism, whether cultural or economic. Thus the formulation of the issue between religion and social change by Winston Davis seems to me more relevant for our purpose here. Davis argues that those who investigate the problem of religious and social change should look at three questions: (a) does religion motivate social change?; (b) does religion fail to obstruct change?; (c) does religion promote a quiescent acceptance of social costs of development? Davis refers to question (a) as the question of religion's "positive enablement" of development. He calls the issues raised by questions (b) and (c) as religion's "negative enablement" of economic change. Davis argues that it is question (a) which interests Weber and Weberians most, but a complete accounting would include the issues raised by questions (b) and (c).[12] But even Davis fails to mention another relevant question: does religion hinder social and economic development?

We shall try to examine below the whole gamut of the questions involved in the issue between religious beliefs and economic change in Bangladesh. Do the prevalent Islamic religious beliefs in Bangladesh motivate social and economic change? Do these beliefs negatively help development by failing to obstruct change? Do these beliefs just impede social and economic development?

Work Ethic and Islamic Religious Beliefs

Let us, first, try to examine whether the Muslims of Bangladesh have a work ethic. This examination becomes particularly pertinent as the Bangladeshis have a general reputation of being averse to work, and this alleged trait of Bangladesh people is usually regarded as a factor in the slow process of socio-economic development in Bangladesh.[13] To ascertain their work ethic, we asked our respondents (R51/U54) whether they feel happy without

TABLE 7.1: Rural

Don't feel happy without any work

Don't feel happy without work	Frequency	Percentage
Yes	3268	94.4
No	155	4.5
Not stated	38	1.1
Total	3461	100.0

TABLE 7.1: Urban

Don't feel happy without any work

Don't feel happy without work	Frequency	Percentage
Yes	1958	93.9
No	114	5.4
Not stated	14	0.7
Total	2086	100.0

work. The answers to the question are given in Tables 7.1 (Rural) and 7.1 (Urban), above.

As Tables 7.1 (Rural) and 7.1 (Urban) show, about 94 per cent of respondents in both the urban and rural samples report that they do not feel happy without work. In the face of this very high percentage of the people saying that they do not feel happy without work, the general accusation about Bangladeshis as work-shirkers does not hold true. How is pleasure-in-work of Bangladeshis related to religious belief? Tables 7.2 (Rural) and 7.2 (Urban) examine the relationship.

Table 7.2 (Rural) shows that as far as the rural respondents are concerned, there is no association between pleasure-in-work and religious beliefs. Table 7.2 (Urban), however, shows significant association between the variables and that pleasure-in-work seems to have more significant association with modern Islamic religious belief than with either orthodox or popular beliefs.

Let us now try to explore the reason for finding pleasure in work. We asked our respondents what were the reasons for their finding pleasure in work (R51C/U54C). There were different kinds of answers which had certain common themes. Under the category of economic reason we included the following: "I can only have food if I work", "If I work I can buy more land", "If I work I can buy food and there is peace in the family", "If I work I can rear my children well", and the like.

We have categorised the answers like "Hard work leads to success and

TABLE 7.2: Rural

Pleasure-in-work by Scale of Religious Beliefs

Pleasure-in-work	Religious Beliefs			
	Modern	Orthodox	Popular	Row Total
Yes	40	1663	1565	3268
	1.2	50.9	47.9	94.4
	97.6	94.9	93.8	
No	1	77	77	155
	0.6	49.7	49.7	4.5
	2.4	4.4	4.6	
Not stated	0	12	26	38
	0.0	31.6	68.4	1.1
	0.0	0.7	1.6	
Total	41	1752	1668	3461
	1.2	50.6	48.1	100

$X^2 = 7.028$ with 4 df P>0.10

As the X^2 test does not show significant association between the variables, analysis of residuals for the Table has not been done.

TABLE 7.2: Urban

Pleasure-in-work by Scale of Religious Beliefs

Pleasure-in-work	Religious Beliefs			
	Modern	Orthodox	Popular	Row Total
Yes	245	1216	497	1958
	12.5	62.1	25.4	93.8
	97.6	93.9	92.0	
	2.63	0.08	−2.05	
No	6	73	35	114
	5.3	64.0	30.7	5.5
	2.4	5.6	6.5	
	−2.28	0.44	1.20	
Not stated	0	6	8	14
	0.0	42.9	57.1	0.7
	0.0	0.5	1.5	
	−1.38	−1.48	2.67	
Total	251	1295	540	2086
	12.0	62.1	25.9	100.00

$X^2 = 13.801$ with 4 df P<0.01

TABLE 7.3: Rural

Reasons for finding pleasure in work

Reasons	Frequency	Percentage
Economic reasons	1359	39.3
Achievement orientation	1413	40.8
Religious reason	55	1.6
Others	390	11.3
Not stated	244	7.0
Total	3461	100.0

TABLE 7.3: Urban

Reasons for finding pleasure in work

Reasons	Frequency	Percentage
Economic reasons	281	13.5
Achievement orientation	1434	68.7
Religious reason	6	0.3
Others	230	11.0
Not stated	135	6.5
Total	2086	100.0

success gives pleasure", "Work itself gives me pleasure", "If I work I achieve prosperity for my country", "If I work I achieve peace of mind", under the title "Achievement orientation". Under religious reason we have collected answers like, "I work because Allah will be pleased", "I work to obey the command of Allah", "I find pleasure in performing religious as well as worldly duties", "Allah gives us *rezek* (sustenance) only if we work". The results of these categorisations are given in the following Tables.

From the point of view of the Weberian thesis, the striking feature of Tables 7.3 (Rural) and 7.3 (Urban) is that almost all the respondents in our survey who find pleasure in work do not seem to derive their work ethic from their religious beliefs. Bangladeshi Muslims, both rural and urban, do not seem to consider themselves as "tools of God" in carrying out their this-worldly activities. The second aspect of the Tables is the high percentage of respondents reporting the need for achievement for their work ethic—about 69 per cent in the urban area, and 41 per cent in the rural area. The rural figure is particularly revealing as the rural Bangladeshis are usually thought of as placid, inactive and unambitious people, resigned to fatalism.

Religious belief is not the only idealistic force affecting social change in Bangladesh. Another intellectual force, Western education, is likely to play a positive role in bringing about attitudinal and motivational changes.[14] How

TABLE 7.4: Rural

Reasons for pleasure in work by education

| Reasons | Level of Education | | | | | |
	Illiterate	Class I–V	Class VI–X	Inter-mediate and above	Not Stated	Row Total
Economic reasons	860	311	160	24	4	1359
	63.3	22.9	11.8	1.8	0.3	39.3
	45.4	40.0	26.9	14.5	14.3	
	8.07	0.49	−6.79	−6.66	−2.71	
Achievement orientation	666	309	323	103	12	1413
	47.1	21.9	22.9	7.3	0.8	40.8
	35.1	39.8	54.3	62.4	42.9	
	−7.5	−0.63	7.34	5.78	0.21	
Religious reasons	27	16	10	1	1	55
	49.1	29.1	18.2	1.8	1.8	1.6
	1.4	2.1	1.7	0.6	3.6	
	−0.85	1.18	0.19	−1.03	0.84	
Others	201	92	67	22	8	390
	51.5	23.6	17.2	5.6	2.1	11.3
	10.6	11.8	11.3	13.3	28.6	
	−1.36	0.57	−0.01	0.85	2.9	
Not stated	142	49	35	15	3	244
	58.2	20.1	14.3	6.1	1.2	7.0
	7.5	6.3	5.9	9.1	10.7	
	1.11	−0.91	−1.22	1.04	0.76	
Column total	1896	777	595	165	28	3461
	54.8	22.5	17.2	4.8	0.8	100.0

$X^2 = 147.914$ with 6 df $P < 0.00001$

do levels of education relate to reasons for pleasure in work? Tables 7.4 (Rural) and 7.4 (Urban) provide some answers to the question.

The X^2 tests for both Table 7.4 (Rural) and 7.4 (Urban) indicate significant association between reasons for pleasure in work and levels of education. An examination of the adjusted residuals in the Tables seems to delineate a common pattern. In the rural area economic reasons for finding pleasure in work seem to have greater association with respondents having no education. On the other hand, respondents having middle (Class VI-X) and upper (intermediate and above) level education tend to have greater association with achievement orientation. In the urban area respondents having no education and respondents with primary and middle levels of education seem to have more significant association with economic reasons for their interest in work. By contrast, the urban respondents with high levels (intermediate and above) of education seem to be more associated with achievement orientation for success in life. Thus while illiterate rural people and illiterate and partly-educated urban people have to work just for living, the people with higher education in both urban and rural areas have an additional factor—

TABLE 7.4: Urban

Reasons for pleasure in work by education

Reasons	Level of Education				
	Illiterate	Class I–V	Class VI–X	Inter-mediate and above	Row Total
Economic	42	25	106	108	281
reasons	14.9	8.9	37.7	38.4	13.5
	33.9	26.0	15.9	9.0	
	6.86	3.69	2.22	−6.94	
Achievement	40	49	425	920	1434
orientation	2.8	3.4	29.6	64.2	68.7
	32.3	51.0	63.7	76.7	
	−9.03	−3.83	−3.39	9.14	
Religious	1	0	0	5	6
reasons	16.7	0.0	0.0	83.3	0.3
	0.8	0.0	0.0	0.4	
	1.11	−0.53	−1.68	1.28	
Others	15	10	91	114	230
	6.5	4.3	39.6	49.6	11.0
	12.1	10.4	13.6	9.5	
	0.39	−0.19	2.61	−2.57	
Not stated	26	12	45	52	135
	19.3	8.9	33.3	38.5	6.5
	21.0	12.5	6.7	4.3	
	6.76	2.45	0.34	−4.60	
Column total	124	96	667	1199	2086
	5.9	4.6	32.0	57.5	100.0

$X^2 = 177.207$ with 12 df P<0.001

the need for achievement to work for. Thus high education (intermediate and above) seems to be an important factor in producing a work ethic. We have just seen in Table 7.2 (Urban) above that modern Islamic religious belief seems to be associated more with work ethic in the urban area. We have found earlier in Chapter IV[15] that higher education is associated more with modern than either orthodox or popular beliefs. Thus association of modern belief with work ethic might be due to the correlation of modern belief with modern education.

Family Planning and Islamic Religious Beliefs

Possibly the key test of whether Islamic religious beliefs facilitate or obstruct change in Bangladesh would be to examine how these beliefs relate to the question of family planning in Bangladesh. From the point of view of religion, family planning is a controversial issue even in a highly secularised country like the United States where the Catholic church has been opposed to the use of many of the more efficient means of contraception, and where smaller size and lower fertility of Protestant families vis-a-vis Catholic families are regarded as factors in higher economic achievement of the Protestants in comparison with the Catholics.[16] In a country with virtually no resource excepting agricultural land and with the highest density of population in the world and an average family size of 5.7 persons, birth control is the first item for any recipe for individual and national development in Bangladesh, whether it is by a social scientist, economic planner or international aid organisation.[17]

Most vigorous opposition to family planning in Bangladesh on religious grounds comes from the orthodox *ulema* and the fundamentalist political organisation, Jamaat-e-Islami. The *ulema* and the fundamentalists argue that the Koran in a number of verses declares that it is Allah who provides sustenance to all creatures,[18] and that to control population through contraceptive measures for fear of lack of food and shelter is to express lack of faith in Allah, and thus to commit a grievous sin. Those who argue that Islam is not against birth control content that none of the verses mentioning Allah as the Sustainer forbids family planning. On the other hand, they refer to several Hadiths where the Prophet approved the practice of *azl* (coitus interruptus) for preventing conception on the grounds of health of the mother and child.[19]

To understand the attitude of our respondents towards family planning from the perspectives of their religious beliefs, we asked the following question:

R38/U40: Do you agree with the following statement: "Allah provides food and shelter for every man and woman, so we need not adopt a family planning programme?" Yes/No

The answers to the question are tabulated in Tables 7.5 (Rural) and 7.5 (Urban).

The X^2 test of Tables 7.5 (Rural) and 7.5 (Urban) show highly significant association between religious belief and that "Allah provides food and shelter so we need not adopt family planning". An examination of the adjusted residuals of the Tables shows a common pattern of relationship in both rural and urban areas. Respondents holding popular beliefs seem to agree more with the statement that "Allah provides food and shelter so we need not adopt family planning". As we expected, both rural and urban respondents subscribing to modern beliefs to be more in disagreement with the statement. Contrary to our expectation, we also find respondents holding orthodox beliefs in both rural and urban areas tending to disagree with the statement, i.e., with the interpretation of the Koran by the *ulema* and the fundamentalists on the issue of family planning.

As we shall see in Chapter VIII below, the Muslims of Bangladesh generally do not seem to consult the *ulema* for day-to-day mundane problems.[20] For the poor people in Bangladesh today family planning has become a necessity for sheer economic survival. Consequently, they seem more eager to listen to officials and volunteers advising family planning rather

TABLE 7.5: Rural

Allah provides food and shelter so we need not adopt family planning
by scale of religious beliefs

| Category | Religious Beliefs | | | |
	Modern	Orthodox	Popular	Row Total
Yes	11	815	957	1783
	0.6	45.7	53.7	51.5
	26.8	46.5	57.4	
	−3.14	−5.9	6.67	
No	30	883	638	1551
	1.9	56.9	41.1	44.8
	73.2	50.4	38.2	
	3.83	6.68	−7.04	
Not stated	0	54	73	127
	0.0	42.5	57.5	3.7
	0.0	3.1	4.4	
	−1.54	−2.62	3.32	
Column total	41	1752	1668	3461
	1.2	50.6	48.2	100.0

$X^2 = 65.473$ with 4 df P<0.00001

TABLE 7.5: Urban

Allah provides food and shelter so we need not adopt family planning
by scale of religious beliefs

| Category | Religious Beliefs | | | |
	Modern	Orthodox	Popular	Row Total
Yes	2	112	158	272
	0.7	41.2	58.1	13.0
	0.8	8.6	29.3	
	−6.06	−7.52	13.08	
No	249	1152	362	1763
	14.1	65.3	20.5	84.5
	99.2	89.0	67.0	
	6.88	5.61	−12.97	
Not stated	0	31	20	51
	0.0	60.8	39.2	2.4
	0.0	2.4	3.7	
	−6.61	0.27	2.28	
Column total	251	1295	540	2086
	12.0	62.1	25.9	100.0

$X^2 = 195.549$ with 4 df P<0.00001

than the *ulema* on the issue of birth control. In Bangladesh today there is no outstanding nationally respected *maulana*. The *ulema* in Bangladesh have not been well organised, and the fundamentalist organisation, Jamaat-i-Islami, is still a minor party in the country. Besides, the *ulema* and the people working in Jamaat-i-Islami are, to a great extent, alienated from the general populace of Bangladesh as many of them had supported the Pakistan army during the liberation war of 1971. All these factors possibly explain the lack of influence of the *ulema* and the fundamentalists on the programme of family planning, an issue of high religious susceptibility throughout the Muslim world.

How does education relate to the idea of dependence on Allah for food and shelter and non-acceptance of family planning? The relationship is examined in Tables 7.6 (Rural) and 7.6 (Urban).

The X^2 tests of Tables 7.6 (Rural) and 7.6 (Urban) show significant relationship between the idea of dependence on Allah and non-acceptance of family planning and levels of education. A look at the adjusted residuals in the cells of the two Tables indicates clear trends of relationship between the two variables. In the rural area illiteracy seems to be more significantly associated with the idea of dependence on Allah. Primary level of education also shows a lesser yet significant association with the idea of dependence on Allah. As the respondents attain the middle level of education, their disagreement with the idea of dependence on Allah tends to increase. The respondents with a high level of education tend to be associated more with non-acceptance of the idea of dependence on Allah and avoidance of family planning.

Table 7.6 (Urban) shows a similar trend of relationship between levels of association and the idea of reliance on Allah, except that while in the rural area disagreement with the idea seems to be associated with both middle and high levels of education, such disagreement in the urban area seems to be associated with only the high level of education.

The acceptance of an idea by a group of people does not always mean its implementation by them. How far do the adherents of different religious beliefs in our survey practise their ideas about family planning? To find out the level of practice of family planning by our respondents, we asked the following question:

R38(a)/U40(a): Do you adopt a family planning programme? Yes/No.

The answers are categorised in Tables 7.7 (Rural) and 7.7 (Urban).

Table 7.7 (Rural) shows that respondents adhering to modern and orthodox beliefs who, as we have seen above Table 7.5 (Rural) seem to disagree more with the statement that Allah gives food and shelter and so one need not resort to family planning, also tend more to adopt family planning. Table 7.7 (Rural) also shows that the respondents with popular beliefs who seem to put more reliance on Allah than on family planning, tend more not to adopt a family planning programme.

Table 7.7 (Urban) shows the pattern repeating itself in the urban area. The respondents holding modern beliefs seem to have near-significant association, and orthodox believers seem to have significant association with

TABLE 7.6: Rural

Allah provides food and shelter so we need not adopt family planning
By education

| Category | Education | | | | | |
	No Education	Class I–V	Class VI–X	Intermediate and Above	Not Stated	Row Total
Yes	1069	432	234	35	13	1783
	60.0	24.2	13.1	2.0	0.7	51.5
	54.4	55.6	39.3	21.2	46.4	
	6.35	2.05	−6.29	−7.74	−3.6	
No	770	323	321	122	15	1551
	49.6	20.8	20.7	7.9	1.0	44.8
	40.6	41.6	53.9	73.9	53.6	
	−5.42	−2.04	4.98	7.77	1.16	
Not stated	57	22	40	8	0	127
	44.9	17.3	31.5	6.3	0.0	3.7
	3.0	2.8	6.7	4.8	0.0	
	−2.18	−1.3	4.63	0.84	−1.048	
Column total	1896	777	595	165	28	3461
	54.8	22.5	17.2	4.8	0.8	100.0

$X^2 = 130.554$ with 8 df $P < 0.00001$

TABLE 7.6: Urban

Allah provides food and shelter so we need not adopt family planning
By education

| Category | Education | | | | |
	No Education	Class I–V	Class VI–X	Intermediate and Above	Row Total
Yes	62	39	92	79	272
	22.8	14.3	33.8	29.0	13.0
	50.0	40.6	13.8	6.6	
	12.7	8.57	1.21	−10.13	
No	61	55	545	1102	1763
	3.5	3.1	30.9	62.5	84.5
	49.2	57.3	81.7	91.9	
	−6.20	−4.21	−1.29	6.10	
Not stated	1	2	30	18	51
	2.0	3.9	58.8	35.3	2.4
	0.8	2.1	4.5	1.5	
	1.21	0.0	4.54	−3.18	
Column total	124	96	667	1199	2086
	5.9	4.6	32.0	57.5	100.0

$X^2 = 276.866$ with 6 df $P < 0.00001$

TABLE 7.7: Rural

Adoption of family planning
By scale of religious belief

Adoption of Family Planning		Religious Belief		
	Modern	Orthodox	Popular	Row Total
Yes	23	460	295	778
	3.0	59.1	37.9	22.5
	56.1	26.3	17.7	
	5.18	5.38	−6.51	
No	15	1138	1211	2364
	0.6	48.1	51.2	68.3
	36.6	56.0	72.6	
	−4.39	−4.28	−5.24	
Not needed	3	103	98	204
	1.5	50.5	48.0	5.9
	7.3	5.9	5.9	
	0.38	−0.03	−0.04	
Not stated	0	51	64	115
	0.0	44.3	55.7	3.3
	0.0	2.9	3.8	
	−1.19	−1.36	1.62	
Column total	41	1752	1668	3461
	1.2	50.6	48.2	100.0

X^2 = 65.932 with 6 df   P<0.00001

TABLE 7.7: Urban

Adoption of family planning
By scale of religious belief

Adoption of Family Planning		Religious Belief		
	Modern	Orthodox	Popular	Row Total
Yes	105	509	155	769
	13.7	66.2	20.2	36.9
	41.8	39.3	28.7	
	1.73	2.95	−4.56	
No	37	280	217	534
	6.9	52.4	40.6	25.6
	14.7	21.6	40.2	
	−4.2	−5.32	9.02	
Not needed	109	506	168	783
	13.9	64.6	21.5	37.5
	43.4	39.1	31.1	
	2.05	1.85	−3.58	
Column total	251	1295	540	2086
	12.0	62.1	25.9	100.0

X^2 = 87.044 with 4 df   P<0.00001

adoption of family planning. Popular belief again seems to be associated more with non-adoption of family planning.

How are the levels of education related to the adoption of family planning? Let the Tables speak for themselves.

As Table 7.8 (Rural) shows, in the rural area illiteracy seems to be associated more with non-adoption of family planning, but primary-level education does not seem to be significantly associated with either adoption or non-adoption of family planning. Middle and higher education, on the other hand, seems to be more significantly associated with adoption of family planning. As shown by Table 7.8 (Urban), the pattern of relationship is a little different in the urban area. Here illiteracy as well as primary and middle levels of education seem to be associated more with non-adoption of family planning. Higher level education, however, seems to have more significant association with adoption of family planning in the urban area too.

Scientific Methods of Production and Islamic Religious Beliefs

To have a further test of whether Islamic religious beliefs promote social change, we want to examine how these beliefs relate to the adoption of scientific methods of production. As development of the Bangladesh economy

TABLE 7.8: Rural

Adoption of family planning
By education

Adoption of Family Planning	Illiterate	Level of Education				
		Class I–V	Class VI–X	Intermediate and Above	Not Stated	Row Total
Yes	344	185	189	52	8	778
	44.2	23.8	24.3	6.7	1.0	22.5
	18.1	23.8	31.8	31.5	28.6	
	−6.72	1.00	5.96	2.84	0.77	
No	1421	529	324	76	14	2364
	60.1	22.4	13.7	3.2	0.6	68.3
	74.9	68.1	54.5	46.1	50.0	
	9.24	−0.15	−7.97	−6.29	−2.09	
Not needed	77	39	61	22	5	204
	37.7	19.1	29.9	10.8	2.5	5.9
	4.1	5.0	10.3	13.3	17.9	
	−5.03	−1.17	4.95	4.15	2.69	
Not stated	54	24	21	15	1	115
	47.0	20.9	18.3	13.0	0.9	3.3
	2.8	3.1	3.5	9.1	3.6	
	−1.71	−0.41	0.30	4.23	0.07	
Column total	1896	777	595	165	28	3461
	54.8	22.5	17.2	4.8	0.8	100.0

$X^2 = 159.332$ with 12 df $P < 0.00001$

TABLE 7.8: Urban

Adoption of family planning
By education

Adoption of Family Planning		Level of Education			
	Illiterate	Class I–V	Class VI–X	Intermediate and Above	Row Total
Yes	29	28	224	488	769
	3.8	3.6	29.1	63.5	36.9
	23.4	29.2	33.6	40.7	
	−3.2	−1.6	−2.12	4.22	
No	87	54	222	171	534
	16.3	10.1	41.6	32.0	25.6
	70.2	56.3	33.3	14.3	
	11.72	7.04	5.51	−13.79	
Not needed	8	14	221	540	783
	1.0	1.8	28.2	69.0	37.5
	6.5	14.6	33.1	45.0	
	−7.37	−4.75	−2.84	8.22	
Column total	124	96	667	1199	2086
	5.9	4.6	32.0	57.5	100.0

X^2 = 288.207 with 12 df   P<0.00001

hinges much on the modernisation of agriculture, and as adoption of irrigation and the use of manure and insecticides are crucial factors in improving agricultural production, we asked our rural respondents the following question:

R39(b): Do you agree with the following statement: "Without depending on nature we should adopt a modern irrigation system and use manure and insecticides"? Yes/No.

The answers are categorised in Table 7.9 (Rural).

The X^2 test and analysis of residuals of Table 7.9 (Rural) show that popular religious belief seems to be associated more with the adoption and use of manures and insecticides than either modern or orthodox beliefs. As we have indicated in Chapter III[21] the popular Muslims interested in the immediate success in mundane affairs tend to deal with the world in a pragmatic way. After having seen the quick results of the use of scientific methods of cultivation, the peasants holding popular Islamic beliefs might eagerly resort to these methods for quick material gains.

How do levels of education relate to the use of modern techniques of agricultural production in comparison with religious beliefs in the rural areas? Table 7.10 (Rural) provides some answers to this question.

The X^2 test for Table 7.10 (Rural) shows significant results, and a look at the adjusted residual in the Table indicates a clear trend of relationship between levels of education and the degree of adoption of modern means of production in agriculture. Thus illiteracy seems to be associated more with

TABLE 7.9: Rural

Should adopt modern irrigation system, etc.
By scale of religious beliefs

Adopt. Modern Irrigation	Modern	Religious Belief Orthodox	Popular	Row Total
Yes	34	1475	1508	3017
	1.1	48.9	50.0	87.2
	82.9	84.2	90.4	
	−0.81	−5.31	5.49	
No	6	224	123	353
	1.7	63.5	34.8	10.2
	14.6	12.8	7.4	
	0.94	5.08	−5.29	
Not stated	1	53	37	91
	1.1	58.2	40.7	2.6
	2.4	3.0	2.2	
	−0.07	1.47	−1.45	
Column total	41	1752	1668	3461
	1.2	50.6	48.2	100.0

$X^2 = 31.329$ with 4 df $P<0.0001$

TABLE 7.10: Rural

Should adopt modern irrigation system, etc.
By education

Adopt. Modern Irrigation	No Education	Class I–V	Level of Education Class VI–X	Intermediate and Above	Not Stated	Row Total
Yes	1614	670	548	159	26	3017
	53.5	22.2	18.2	5.3	0.9	87.2
	85.1	86.2	92.1	96.4	92.9	
	−3.95	−0.89	3.95	3.61	0.9	
No	227	84	38	4	0	353
	64.3	23.8	10.8	1.1	0.0	10.2
	12.0	10.8	6.4	2.4	0.0	
	3.79	0.63	−3.37	−3.38	−1.79	
Not stated	55	23	9	2	2	91
	60.4	25.3	9.9	2.2	2.2	2.6
	2.9	3.0	1.5	1.2	7.1	
	1.09	0.65	−1.87	−1.16	1.49	
Column total	1896	777	595	165	28	3461
	54.8	22.5	17.2	4.8	0.8	100.0

$X^2 = 38.703$ with 8 df $P<0.00001$

the non-adoption of modern techniques, but primary level education does not seem to have significant association with either the use or non-use of these techniques. Middle and higher levels of education then seem to be more significantly associated with the adoption of scientific methods of production.

Inter-personal Trust and Islamic Religious Beliefs

The last item that we want to discuss in this chapter is the relationship between the level of inter-personal trust among the Bangladesh Muslims, and Islamic religious beliefs. As we have argued in Chapter III above, there is increasing agreement among the developmental social scientists that development requires large-scale organisation and that large-scale organisation can be built only by the people who know the "art of associating together". The growth of "associational sentiment" in any nation requires a sense of social and civic co-operation and mutual trust among her people. It has been argued by many foreign observers that Bangladeshis are too factious, too distrustful and too suspicious of each other. They cannot, therefore, sort out their problems among themselves. The resulting breakdown of organisations block all developmental efforts.[22] How far is this thesis valid? What is the level of trust among the Bangladesh Muslims? How is the level of trust related to Islamic religious beliefs?

To measure the level of inter-personal faith among the Bangladeshis we have used the five-item scale of "faith in people" developed by Morris Rosenberg and applied by Gabriel A. Almond and Sidney Verba in their comparative study of political cultures in Germany, Italy, Mexico, Great Britain and the United States.[23] The five items in the scale are:

1. Some people say that most people can be trusted. Others say that you can't be too careful in your dealings with people. How do you feel about it?
2. Would you say that most people are more inclined to help others or more inclined to look out for themselves?
3. If you don't watch yourself, people will take advantage of you.
4. No one is going to care much what happens to you when you get right down to it.
5. Human nature is fundamentally co-operative.

To form a "faith in people" scale, respondents were given one point for responding that "Most people can be trusted", that "People are inclined to help others", for disagreeing with items 3 and 4, and for agreeing with item 5. Those who gave the opposite answer to those listed above were given a score of minus 1 for each of these answers. Equivocal answers, such as "It depends", or "Some people can be trusted and others not", were given a score of zero. The respondents were then classified into three groups, depending on their level of "faith in people". In the high group are those whose scores ranged from plus 2 to plus 5; in the middle are those who scores ranged from minus 2 to plus 1, and in the low groups are those whose scores ranged from minus 3 to minus 5.

TABLE 7.11:
Social Trust and Distrust by Rural Bangladesh, Urban Bangladesh, USA and UK

Percentage Who Agree That	Rural Bangladesh	Urban Bangladesh	USA	UK
Statements of distrust:				
No one is going to care much what happens to you.	35	19	38	45
If you don't watch yourself people will take advantage of you.	87	86	68	75
Statements of trust:				
Most people can be trusted.	14	9	55	49
Most people are more inclined to help others than to think of themselves first.	25	15	31	28
Human nature is fundamentally co-operative.	62	48	80	84

In the following table we have compared the answers of our respondents to each of the items in the scale with those collected by Almond and Verba in the USA and UK.

An examination of Table 7.11 shows the extent of mutual distrust. If we look first at the statements of trust under the label "Most people can be trusted", we find 14/9 per cent of our respondents agree with the statement. Percentages under that category as found by Almond and Verba are 55 and 49 in the USA and UK respectively. Under the statement, "Most people are more inclined to help others than to think of themselves first", 25/15 per cent of our interviewees agreed with the statement, along with 31 and 28 per cent of interviewees in the USA and UK respectively. The difference between the degree of trust among our respondents and those of Almond and Verba is more pronounced under the category, "Human nature is fundamentally co-operative". While 62/48 per cent of our respondents agree with the statement, the percentages of people agreeing with the statement are as high as 80 in the USA and 84 in the UK.

As for the statement of distrust under the category, "If you don't watch yourself people will take advantage of you", as many as 87/86 per cent of our respondents agreed, as against 68 per cent in the USA and 75 per cent in the UK. In only one statement, "No one is going to care much what happens to you", do the Bangladesh respondents fare slightly better than the respondents in the USA and UK. More people in Bangladesh than in the USA and UK feel that some people will help them in distress. But this may not indicate the prevalence of high trust among the Bangladeshis. As the social scientists working on developing nations have already noted, the process of modernis-ation puts severe strains and stresses on the people of the developing nations,

TABLE 7.12: Rural

Trust-Distrust

Category	Frequency	Percentage
High trust	155	4.5
Medium trust	2004	57.9
Low trust	1302	37.6
Total	3461	100.0

TABLE 7.12: Urban

Trust-Distrust

Category	Frequency	Percentage
High trust	55	2.6
Medium trust	1095	52.5
Low trust	936	44.9
Total	2086	100.0

and the people concerned seek refuge in the primordial loyalties—in kinship, family, clan and the like—for mental as well as physical security.[24] The Bangladeshi respondents are not likely to be different from the people of other developing countries.

By applying the scale of trust and distrust developed by Almond and Verba to our respondents, we get the following tables.

As Tables 7.12 (Rural) and 7.12 (Urban) show, the percentage of high trust is as low as 4.5 per cent of the responses in the rural area, and 2.6 per cent in the urban area. The percentages of low trust in the rural and urban areas are 37.6 and 44.9 respectively. Of course, the percentages of medium trust (57.9 in the rural area and 52.5 in the urban area) is quite high. But as we have seen above (pp. 255–6), the level of inter-personal trust is, in general, lower in Bangladesh compared to the USA and the UK.

The key question for our purpose here is how far this low level of trust in Bangladesh is associated with Islamic religious beliefs. The relationship between levels of trust and religious beliefs in Bangladesh is examined in Tables 7.13 (Rural) and 7.13 (Urban).

The X^2 of Table 7.13 (Rural) shows significant association between levels of trust and religious beliefs. The adjusted residuals in Table 7.13 (Rural) indicate that in the rural area high trust seems to have more significant association with popular beliefs, while medium trust seems to have a similar association with orthodox beliefs. Intriguingly, low trust seems to be significantly associated with both modern and popular beliefs. The X^2 test of

TABLE 7.13: Rural

Trust-Distrust
By scales of religious beliefs

Trust	Religious Belief			
	Modern	Orthodox	Popular	Row Total
High	0	67	88	155
	0.0	43.2	56.8	4.5
	0.0	3.82	5.28	
	−1.39	−1.88	2.18	
Medium	19	1058	907	1984
	1.0	53.3	45.7	57.3
	46.34	60.39	54.38	
	−1.43	3.68	−3.38	
Low	22	627	673	1322
	1.7	47.4	50.9	38.2
	53.66	35.79	40.35	
	2.04	−2.95	2.51	
Column total	41	1752	1668	3461
	1.2	50.6	48.2	100.0

$X^2 = 19.387$ with 4 df P < 0.001

TABLE 7.13: Urban

Trust-Distrust
By scales of religious beliefs

Trust	Religious Belief			
	Modern	Orthodox	Popular	Row Total
High	4	35	16	55
	7.3	63.6	29.1	2.6
	1.6	2.7	3.0	
Medium	130	671	294	1095
	11.9	61.3	26.8	52.5
	51.8	51.8	54.4	
Low	117	589	230	936
	12.5	62.9	24.6	44.6
	46.6	45.5	42.6	
Column total	251	1295	540	2086
	12.0	62.1	25.9	100.0

$X^2 = 2.706$ with 4 df P > 0.70. As X^2 test does not show significant association between the variables, analysis of residuals for the Table has not been done

Table 7.13 (Urban), however, shows that the variables in the Table are independent, that is, there does not seem to be any association between levels of inter-personal trust and Islamic religious beliefs in urban areas.

Conclusion

To sum up our discussion in this chapter, our survey disproves the usually held notion that Bangladeshi Muslims are prone to idleness and do not have a work ethic. About 94 per cent of our respondents in both rural and urban areas state that they do not feel happy without any work. Our probe into reasons for pleasure-in-work of the overwhelming majority of Bangladeshi Muslims reveals that about 41 per cent of rural respondents and about 69 per cent of our urban respondents find pleasure in work because they want to achieve success in life. Thus the slow process of social and economic change does not seem to be caused by lack of motivation and idleness on the part of the Bangladesh Muslim population.

With regard to the crucial question for our purpose here whether the work ethic of Bangladeshi Muslims is especially associated with any particular type of Islamic religious belief on the parallel of Max Weber's findings about work ethic being particularly associated with Protestant belief in the case of Christianity, our survey shows that as far as the rural area is concerned, none of the Islamic religious beliefs has any significant association with pleasure-in-work. We did, however, find pleasure-in-work more significantly associated with modern religious beliefs than with either orthodox or popular beliefs in the case of the urban sample. By comparison, high education seems to have strong association with achievement orientation in both the rural and urban areas.

An individual's attitude towards family planning is regarded as indicative of his overall belief about man's individual initiative in shaping his own destiny. In this regard our findings are quite striking. We find that it is not only the modern Islamic religious beliefs which seem to be associated with the belief and practice of family planning. The orthodox Islamic religious beliefs also seem to be associated with belief in as well as acceptance of a family planning programme. Popular religious beliefs, on the other hand, seem to be associated more with the use of scientific techniques producing immediate material results. Again, by comparison, higher education seems to be more associated with the adoption of family planning and the use of scientific techniques of production.

With regard to the problem of inter-personal trust, we do not find any common pattern of relationship between types of religious beliefs and levels of trust in both rural and urban samples. The Islamic religious belief might not explain the prevalence of the lower level of trust in Bangladesh.

As we have discussed above, while talking about the role of religion in development, Winston Davis makes a distinction between religion's positive and negative "enablement of development".[25] According to Davis, Confucianism and Shintoism in Japan performed negative enablement functions in Japan's development by not obstructing it.[26] The Islamic religious beliefs, it seems from our discussion in this chapter, could play a more positive role in social and economic development than Japanese Confucianism and Shintoism. The leaders of development in Bangladesh need not despair of their goal because of Islamic religious beliefs in their country. They would, of course, do better if they could bring about a wider spread of modern higher education in Bangladesh.

NOTES

1   As quoted in T. Maniruzzaman, "The Future of Bangladesh", in A.J. Wilson and D. Dalton (eds.), *The States of South Asia: Problems of National Integration* (London: C. Hurst, 1982), p. 265.
2   See *Statistical Year Book of Bangladesh, 1986* (Dacca: Bangladesh Bureau of Statistics, December 1986), p. 111. All demographic data of Bangladesh quoted in the first two paragraphs of this chapter are taken or derived from the above *Year Book*.
3   See Preface, above, p. xiv.
4   M. Weber, *The Protestant Ethic and the Spirit of Capitalism*, translated by Talcott Parsons (New York: Charles Scribner's Sons, 1958), p. 40.
5   *Ibid.*, p. 80.
6   See Max Weber, *The Religion of China: Confucianism and Taoism*, translated by H.H. Gerth (New York: Free Press, 1951); Max Weber, *Ancient Judaism*, translated and edited by Hans H. Gerth and Don Martindale (New York: Free Press, 1952); Max Weber, *The Religion of India: The Sociology of Hinduism and Buddhism*, translated by Hans H. Gerth and Don Martindale (New York: Free Press, 1958).
7   See B.S. Turner, *Weber and Islam: A Critical Study* (London: Routledge and Kegan Paul, 1974), pp. 12–14.
8   *Ibid.*, pp. 34–8.
9   *Ibid.*, pp. 20–1, 171–84. Modernist Islamic thinkers like Fazlur Rahman would argue that the idea of life as a calling is innate to classical Islam. As he writes, "Islam is surrender to the Will of God, i.e., the determination to implement, in the physical texture of the world, the command of God or the Moral Imperative. This implementation is 'service to God' ('ibada)". See F. Rahman, *Islam* (Chicago: The University of Chicago Press, second edition, 1979), p. 254. However, a discussion on whether classical Islam considers all this-worldly activities as religious duties, is beyond the scope of this study.
10 See "Foreword", by R.J. Tawney, in Weber, *The Protestant Ethic and the Spirit of Capitalism*.
11 *Ibid.*, p. 8.
12 See W. Davis, "Religion and Development: Weber and the East Asia Experience", in M. Weiner and S.P. Huntington (eds.), *Understanding Political Development* (Boston, Mass.: Little Brown, 1987), p. 226.
13 See, for example, C. Maloney, *Why does Bangladesh remain so Poor?* Part II, *Eight Answers*, *UFSI Reports* 1985, No. 34 (Indianapolis: Universities Field Staff International).
14 See J.S. Coleman, "Introduction: Education and Development", and F.X. Sutton, "Education and the Making of Modern Nations", in J.S. Coleman (ed.), *Education and Political Development* (Princeton: Princeton University Press, 1966), pp. 3–32, 51–74.
15 See Tables 4.2 (Rural) and 4.2 (Urban), in Chapter IV above, pp. 67–8.
16 See Chapter 5, "Religion and Family Life", in G. Lenski, *The Religious Factor: A Sociological Study of Religion's Impact on Politics, Economics, and Family Life* (West Port: Greenwood Press, reprinted 1977), especially pp. 212–9.
17 See, for examples, Maloney, *op.cit.*; J. Faaland and J.R. Parkinson, "A Development Perspective for Bangladesh", *Bangladesh Development Studies*, Vol. IV, No. I, January 1976, pp. 49–66; R. Revell, "Possible Futures of Bangladesh", *Asia*, No. 29, Spring 1973, pp. 34–54; M.F. Franda, *Bangladesh: The First Decade* (New Delhi: South Asian Publishers, 1982), pp. 141–61.
18 To quote a typical verse:
    How many are the creatures
    That carry not their own
    Sustenance? It is God
    Who feeds [both] them and you:
    For He hears and knows
    [All things]. XXIX:60.

For similar verses in the Koran, see XXIX:62; LI:22, 38; XXIV:38; XIII:26; XLII:19, 27; XX: 124; LXV:2-3.

19   For a discussion on the various opinions as to whether family planning is in conformity with Islam, see A. Khaleque, *Jano Shankha Bishphoron-O-Bangladesh* (Population Explosion and Bangladesh) (Dhaka: Adhunik Prokashani, 1981), especially pp. 85–101.

20   See Chapter VIII below, pp. 131–2.

21   See Chapter III above, pp. 54, 59, 60.

22   See, for example, M.F. Franda, "Moral Implications of Bangladesh", *Asia Supplement* I, Fall 1974, p. 94; Revell, *op.cit.*, p. 54; Maloney, *op.cit.*, p. 8.

23   See G.A. Almond and S. Verba, *The Civic Culture* (Boston, Mass.: Little, Brown, 1965), pp. 212–3.

24   See, for example, C. Geertz, "The Integrative Revolution: Primordial Sentiments and Civil Politics in the New States", in C. Geertz (ed.), *Old Societies and New States: The Quest for Modernity in Asia and Africa* (New Delhi: Amerind Publishing Co., 1971), pp. 105–57.

25   See p. 110.

26   See Davis, *op.cit.*, pp. 248–70.

CHAPTER VIII

ISLAM AND WOMEN IN BANGLADESH

Being myself a woman, as women constitute 48.5 per cent[1] of the total population of Bangladesh, and writing in the decade of "Women and Development", I could hardly be forgetful about Islam and women in Bangladesh. How do women help mould Islam? What is the impact of Islam on Bangladesh womenfolk? Is Islam a hindrance to development of the full potential of women? What is the extent of discrepancy in the professions and practice of Bengal Islam with regard to women's rights?

Kin as Advisers

Before we try to understand the role of Muslim women in the process of religious socialisation in Bangladesh, let us first have some idea to whom the adult Bangladeshi Muslims usually turn for advice when they face any problem in their day-to-day life. We asked our respondents the following question in this connection:

R.29/U.32: Do you consult anybody when you face any problem? The answers to the question are given in Tables 8.1 (Rural) and 8.1 (Urban) (below).

As we see in Tables 8.1 (Rural) and 8.1 (Urban), 67.9 per cent of our rural respondents and 100 per cent of our urban respondents (considering all multiple answers) report that they consult their parents and immediate relatives (brother, sister, uncle, son, daughter, husband, wife, in-laws) when they face any problem. The generally held view that the villagers usually look to the *mo͗tabars* (the rural traditional leaders) for help and advice in temporal matters is partially borne out by our survey. About one-fifth of our rural respondents seek advice from the traditional village leaders. In the urban area friends are found to be the second important group (after kinsmen) of advisers for our respondents. From the point of view of our present study the important finding here is that only 2.3 per cent of our rural respondents and 0.8 per cent of our urban respondents report that they consult *maulanas* (persons educated in orthodox Islamic education) for advice on day-to-day problems. It is usually argued that Islam provides a total world view for its adherents and that Islam enjoins a complete code of life for the Muslims.[2] Bangladeshi Muslims, however, do not seem to consult religiously educated people for their guidance in day-to-day temporal affairs.

Women and Socialisation in Islam

In Chapter II we discussed, in general, how Islam is being inculcated and sustained by Islamic writings, *madrassas*, *maktabs*, mosques, *pirs*, *mullahs*, other Islamic organisations, and the family. We have also tried to identify

TABLE 8.1: Rural

Do you consult anybody when you face any problem?

Category	Frequency	Percentage
Parents	1063	30.7
Near relatives	1287	37.2
(brother, sister, uncle, son,		
daughter, husband, wife, in laws)		
mo<tabar (neighbourhood leader)	724	20.9
Friends	242	7.0
Pray to Allah	38	1.1
Educated person	160	4.6
Maulana (person educated	78	2.3
in orthodox Islamic education)		
Others	207	6.0
Total	3799*	109.8**

* Number exceeds 3461 because of multiple answers
** Percentage exceeds 100 because of multiple answers

TABLE 8.1: Urban

Do you consult anybody when you face any problem?

Category	Frequency	Percentage
Parents	986	47.2
Near relatives	1142	54.7
(brother, sister, uncle, son,		
daughter, husband, wife, in laws)		
mo<tabar (neighbourhood leader)	45	2.2
Friends	594	28.2
Pray to Allah	76	3.6
Educated person	66	3.1
Maulana (person educated	17	0.8
in orthodox Islamic education)		
Others	88	4.2
Total	3014*	144.3**

* Number exceeds 2086 because of multiple answers
** Percentage exceeds 100 because of multiple answers

who are the main agents in fostering different types of religious beliefs—
modern, orthodox and popular. In this chapter one of our main concerns is
how women in particular are contributing to this Islamic socialisation process.

Inadvertently, we did not include the cross-tabulation of the answers
given in Tables 8.1 (Rural) and 8.1 (Urban) by sex while preparing the
programme for the computer, and we do not know what percentage of our

TABLE 8.2: Rural

At what age did you learn Namaz, Roza and other Islamic education?

Category	Frequency		Percentage	
0–5 years	67		1.9	
6–10	1719		49.7	
11–14	921	} 2640	26.6	} 76.3
15–24	476		13.8	
25+	68		2.0	
Don't remember	210		6.1	
Total	3461		100.0	

TABLE 8.2: Urban

At what age did you learn Namaz, Roza and other Islamic education?

Category	Frequency		Percentage	
0–5 years	164		7.9	
6–10	1375		65.9	
11–14	484	} 1859	23.2	} 88.9
15–24	47		2.3	
25+	4		0.2	
Don't remember	12		0.6	
Total	2086		100.0	

advisers belong to the female sex. Women's influence in society cannot, however, be measured only in terms of whether their advise is sought by others in their day-to-day problems. Napoleon is said to have stated that, "The hand that rocks the cradle rules the world". The perceptive soldier-leader was obviously referring to the subtle and effective role of women in the socialisation process of future citizens. What role do women in Bangladesh play in socialising the younger generation? How far do they train their children in Islamic religious practices? Let us first see at what age our respondents learn Namaz, Roza and other Islamic education.

As Tables 8.2 (Rural) and 8.2 (Urban) show, the 6–10 and 11–14 ages account for the Islamic education of 76 per cent of rural and 89 per cent of urban respondents. As Tables 8.3 (Rural) and 8.3 (Urban) show, these are the ages when the children are open to a number of influences: (a) mother, grandmother, and other surrounding women; (b) father; (c) *maktab* and *imam*, and (d) others.

As Tables 8.3 (Rural) and 8.3 (Urban) show, while 28.8 per cent of rural respondents report that they received their Islamic education from their mothers and other near female relatives, about 75 per cent of the urban interviewees got their religious education from their mothers and other near

TABLE 8.3: Rural

Sources of Islamic education for age groups 6–10 and 11–14 (R24A)

Category	Frequency		Percentage	
From mother	666		19.2	
Grandmother	155	} 997	4.5	} 28.8
Other women	176		5.1	
Father	510		14.7	
Maktab	1119		32.3	
Imam	1410	} 2529	40.7	} 73.0
Others	307		8.9	
Total	4343*		125.4**	

*   Total exceeds 3461 because of multiple answers
** Total exceeds 100 because of multiple answers

TABLE 8.3: Urban

Sources of Islamic education for age groups 6–10 and 11–14 (U25B)

Category	Frequency		Percentage	
From mother	1213		58.1	
Grandmother	303	} 1553	14.5	} 74.4
Other women	37		1.8	
Father	806		38.6	
Maktab	323		15.5	
Imam	781	} 1104	37.4	} 52.9
Others	180		8.6	
Total	3643*		174.5**	

*   Total exceeds 2086 because of multiple answers
** Total exceeds 100 because of multiple answers

women relatives. The female influence in the urban area is likely to be decisive as its impact is in the ratio of 75:53 *vis-a-vis* the *maktabs* (traditional primary level schools for religious instruction) and *imams* (orthodox religious leaders who lead prayer in the mosques).

What type of religious orientation is likely to be fostered by women among the impressionable children? One striking aspect of our findings in this study is the extensive prevalence of popular Islamic religious belief in Bangladesh to date despite orthodox revivalist and modern movements over long periods of time.[3] As we have found earlier, women seem to be more associated with popular religious beliefs than with either modern or orthodox beliefs.[4] One reason for this wide prevalence of popular religious belief could be that women play such a large role in imparting initial religious education to children in Bangladesh.

The religious orientation fostered by women could also be understood by the image of the women held as exemplars by the respondents. We asked our respondents, "Whom do you consider as an ideal woman—Begum Rokeya, Hazrat Rahma, Saint Rabi'a, Begum Shamsunnahar, Bibi Asiya"? (R.42/U.44b). Begum Rokeya had been the harbinger of modernist ideas among Muslim women in the Bangladesh area.[5] Begum Shamsunnahar Mahmud carried Rokeya's torch in former East Pakistan from 1950 to the 1960s.

Hazrat Rahma was the wife of Ayyub recognised by Islam as one of their 124,000 prophets, ending with the Prophet Mohammad. When the Prophet Ayyub was attacked with leprous diseases giving forth a foul smell unbearable to human beings, his kith and kin and his other three wives deserted him. However, the fourth wife, Rahma disproved Shakespeare's generalisation "Frailty thy name is woman!" long before he ever wrote it. She stayed with her husband during the whole period of his distress, and she did not even lose her patience when Prophet Ayyub, under the evil counsel of Satan, doubted her fidelity. Rahma was the very epitome of fidelity, patience and devotion.

Saint Rabi'a, born in Basra, Mesopotamia, in AD 800, was the symbol of woman's love for God. She remained so absorbed in worship all the time that she had no time to take her food. She practised extremities and penance, and "burnt herself through the light of Love of Allah".

Bibi Asiya had been the symbol of truth against falsehood. She was the queen of the pharaoh who declared himself as God and asked all his subjects to worship him. Asiya would not submit to any other god except the one and only God. She died under torture.

The preferences of our respondents regarding the ideal woman are given in Tables 8.4 (Rural) and 8.4 (Urban) (see below).

As the tables show, the admirers of Rokeya and Shamsunnahar constitute only about 11 per cent of the rural respondents, while those who consider these two women as ideals form 51 per cent of the urban people. Conversely only 42 per cent of the urban respondents, as against 67.4 per cent in the rural areas favour women whose legends have given them immortality as religious leaders.

TABLE 8.4: Rural

Whom do you consider as ideal women? (R42)

Category	Frequency		Percentage	
Begum Rokeya	360		10.4	
Begum Shamsunnahar Mahmud	16	} 376	0.5	} 10.9
Hazrat Rahma	1168		33.7	
Saint Rabi'a	517	} 2337	14.9	} 67.4
Bibi Asiya	652		18.8	
All of the above women	142		4.1	
Not stated	606		17.5	
Total	3461		100.0	

TABLE 8.4: Urban

Whom do you consider as ideal women? (U44b)

Category	Frequency		Percentage	
Begum Rokeya	1023		49.0	
Begum Shamsunnahar Mahmud	36	} 1059	1.7	} 50.7
Hazrat Rahma	251		12.0	
Saint Rabi'a	425	} 872	20.4	} 42.0
Bibi Asiya	196		9.4	
Not stated	155		7.4	
Total	2086		100.0	

How are these emancipator-cum-moderniser images of Rokeya and Nahar and the devotee images of Rahma, Rabi'a and Asiya, related to sex? Tables 8.5 (Rural) and 8.5 (Urban) give us some clues.

The X^2 test of Table 8.5 (Rural) shows significant association between sex and idealised womanhood in rural Bangladesh. While males seem to be associated more with moderniser and religious devotee types, females seem to have significant connection with answers which indicate preference for both the types simultaneously. Table 8.5 (Urban), on the other hand, shows that male and female respondents are almost equally divided in their preference

TABLE 8.5: Rural

Whom do you consider as ideal women?

Ideal Women	Male	Female	Row Total
Moderniser	232 61.7 12.4 3.19	144 38.2 9.0 −3.19	376 10.87
Religious devotee	1304 55.8 70.0 3.15	1033 44.2 68.8 −3.15	2337 67.52
Both types	62 43.66 3.32 −2.51	80 56.34 5.02 2.51	142 4.10
Not stated	269 44.4 14.4 −5.19	337 55.6 21.1 5.19	606 17.51
Column total	1867 53.9	1594 46.0	3461 100.0

$X^2 = 40.652$ with 3 df P $<$ 0.005

TABLE 8.5: Urban

Whom do you consider as ideal women?

Ideal Women	Male	Female	Row Total
Moderniser	517	542	1059
	49.0	51.1	50.7
	49.7	51.8	
Religious devotee	451	421	872
	51.4	48.3	41.80
	43.4	40.2	
Not stated	72	83	155
	46.5	53.5	7.43
	6.9	7.9	
Column total	1040	1046	2086
	49.86	50.14	100.0

$X^2 = 2.385$ with 2 df P $>.20$. As the X^2 test does not show significant association between the variables, analysis of residuals for the Table has not been done.

for each of the categories—modernisers and religious devotees, indicating a lack of association between sex and ideal womanhood in the urban area.

How are levels of education associated with types of idealised womanhood? Tables 8.6 (Rural) and 8.6 (Urban) provide us with some understanding of the association between levels of education and types of idealised womanhood.

Table 8.6 (Rural) shows a clear trend of association between levels of education and preference for the moderniser image of womanhood in the rural area. Illiteracy seems not to be significantly associated with modernising womanhood. But as the level of education increases the degree of its association with the modernising image seems also to increase, and middle and high levels of education seem to be significantly associated with the ideal of modernised womanhood. The religious devotee image, on the other hand, seems to have more significant association with primary level rather than with either illeracy or the upper levels of education.

Table 8.6 (Urban) indicates that in the urban area the modernised image of womanhood is more significantly associated with high education than with illiteracy or the lower levels of education, and that the degree of association between the devotee image and education decreases as the levels of education go up. Education seems to play a major part in the role perception of women by the Bangladeshis.

Islam and the Rights of Women in Bangladesh

Islam claims to be the first religion to have given women a full juristic personality and a status separate and distinct from that of man, and conferred upon her certain inalienable rights. Indeed, the Koran itself lists rights of

TABLE 8.6: Rural

Whom do you consider as ideal women?: by level of education

Ideal Woman	No Education	Class I–V	Class VI–X	Inter- mediate and above	Not Stated	Row Total
Moderniser	68	86	164	51	7	376
	18.0	22.8	43.6	13.6	1.9	10.9
	3.6	11.0	27.6	31.0	25.0	
	−15.14	0.20	14.38	8.47	2.41	
Religious devotee	1253	571	395	102	16	2337
	53.7	24.4	16.9	4.4	0.7	67.2
	66.1	73.4	66.0	62.0	57.1	
	−1.98	4.03	−0.65	−1.60	−1.17	
Both types	86	30	17	7	2	142
	60.6	21.1	12.0	4.9	1.4	4.1
	4.5	3.9	2.9	4.2	7.1	
	1.41	−0.38	−1.68	0.09	0.81	
Not stated	489	90	19	5	3	606
	80.7	14.9	3.1	0.8	0.5	17.6
	25.8	11.6	3.2	3.0	10.7	
	14.11	−4.93	−10.09	−5.01	−0.94	
Column total	1896	777	595	165	28	3461
	54.8	22.4	17.2	4.8	0.8	100.0

$\chi^2 = 501.252$ with 12 df P < 0.001

women. First the Koran details woman's inheritance of parental and husband's property. A female child gets a portion of parent's property equal to half of that of a male child. A wife inherits one-fourth of her husband's property if the husband dies without issue and gets one-eighth of the same if the husband leaves behind progeny (S. IV. 11–12).

Secondly, the Koran gives both husband and wife the right to divorce. The holy book emphasises the necessity of precautions against its abuse, urges that "part with them on equitable terms" (S.LXV.2).

The Western scholars sympathetic to Islam have long been pointing out that the rights guaranteed to women by the Koran had remained largely unimplemented in the Muslim world.[6] Thus, John L. Esposito concludes his study on women's rights in Islam:

> The implementation of *Qur'anic* reforms markedly improved her position in the family and society in the classical period. However, subsequent historical events as well as assimilated cultural influences at times seriously compromised her rights.[7]

Rounaq Jahan, a prominent woman academician in Bangladesh complains:

TABLE 8.6: Urban

Whom do you consider as ideal women?: by level of education

Ideal Women	No Education	Class I–V	Class VI–X	Inter- mediate and above	Row Total
Moderniser	9	17	302	731	1059
	0.8	1.6	28.5	69.0	50.7
	7.3	17.7	45.3	60.1	
	–9.99	–6.63	–3.43	10.83	
Religious devotee	105	72	312	383	872
	12.0	8.2	35.8	44.0	41.8
	84.6	75.00	46.7	32.0	
	9.98	6.75	3.15	–10.61	
Not stated	10	7	53	85	155
	6.5	4.5	34.2	54.8	7.4
	8.1	7.3	7.9	7.1	
	0.27	–0.05	0.61	–0.69	
Column total	124	96	667	1199	2086
	5.9	4.6	32.0	57.5	100.0

$\chi^2 = 207.600$ with 6 df P < 0.001

> *Sharia* laws grant Muslim women a number of limited rights but prevailing social norms prevent them from taking full advantage of even these limited rights.[8]

We asked our respondents (R49/U51) whether the rights guaranteed to women by Islam are established in Bangladeshi society. The answers are given in Tables 8.7 (Rural) and 8.7 (Urban).

As Tables 8.7 (Rural) and 8.7 (Urban) show, over 90 per cent of the respondents in the rural areas and around 80 per cent of the respondents in the urban areas hold the view that rights to property guaranteed to women by the Koran are established in Bangladesh. But about one quarter of the respondents in both rural and urban areas agree that women's right to divorce is only theoretical.

To probe further about the respondents' views on women's rights, we asked (R49/B-U51/B), "Do you agree with the following statement: In the context of the modern age, for the interest of women, women should be given more rights than what have been provided for them in Islam?" The answers to the questions are given in Tables 8.8 (Rural) and 8.8 (Urban).

As shown in Tables 8.8 (Rural) and 8.8 (Urban), while about one-fifth of the rural areas believe that women should be given more rights than what are provided for them in Islam, the percentage of people who demand more rights for women is as high as about 50 per cent in Dhaka City.

TABLE 8.7: Rural

Whether rights guaranteed to women are established in society

Rights	Established	Not Established	Not Stated	Total
Right to parental property	3314 95.8	125 3.6	22 0.6	3461 100
Right to husband's property	3330 96.2	106 3.1	25 0.7	3461 100
Right to divorce	2573 74.3	862 24.9	26 0.8	3461 100

TABLE 8.7: Urban

Whether rights guaranteed to women are established in society

Rights	Established	Not Established	Not Stated	Total
Right to parental property	1589 76.2	490 23.5	7 0.3	2086 100
Right to husband's property	1718 82.4	361 17.3	7 0.3	2086 100
Right to divorce	1549 74.3	530 25.4	7 0.3	2086 100

TABLE 8.8: Rural

Women should be given more rights than what have been provided for them in Islam

Category	Frequency	Percentage
Yes	667	19.3
No	2777	80.2
Not stated	17	0.5
Total	3461	100.00

TABLE 8.8: Urban

Women should be given more rights than what have been provided for them in Islam

Category	Frequency	Percentage
Yes	1036	49.7
No	1037	49.7
Not stated	13	0.6
Total	2086	100.00

TABLE 8.9: Rural

What should be additional rights for women equal with men?

Category	Frequency	Percentage
Abolition of dowry	22	0.6
Right to education	127	3.7
Right to freedom	15	0.4
Right to job	40	1.2
Equal rights	65	1.9
Others	105	3.0
Inapplicable	2772	80.1
Not stated	315	9.1
Total	3461	100.0

TABLE 8.9: Urban

What should be additional rights for women equal with men?

Category	Frequency	Percentage
Abolition of dowry	27	1.3
Right to education	173	8.3
Right to freedom	158	7.6
Right to job	180	8.6
Equal rights	459	22.0
Others	33	1.6
Inapplicable	1011	48.5
Not stated	45	2.2
Total	2086	100.00

What are these additional rights that are demanded for women? Tables 8.9 (Rural) and 8.9 (Urban) provide the answer.

Tables 8.9 (Rural) and 8.9 (Urban) indicate that abolition of dowry, right to education, right to freedom and the right to a job are among the new rights demanded for women. However, the percentage of respondents demanding more rights for women in the rural area is only about 10.8. The demand for more female rights is, however, quite widespread in the urban area. About 50 per cent of our urban respondents claim more rights for women, and 22 per cent among them seem to argue for the same rights for women and men in every sphere of life.

Who are these respondents who clamour for more rights for womenfolk? Is sex related to feminine demand? Tables 8.10 (Rural) and 8.10 (Urban) provide some answers to this question.

As could be expected, Table 8.10 (Rural) and 8.10 (Urban) show that in both urban and rural areas female respondents are more significantly associated with feminine demands than the male respondents.

TABLE 8.10: Rural

Women should be given more rights: by sex

Category	Male	Female	Row Total
Yes	255	412	667
	38.2	61.8	19.3
	13.7	25.8	
	−9.06	9.06	
No	1605	1172	2777
	57.8	42.2	80.2
	86.0	73.5	
	9.16	−9.16	
Not stated	7	10	17
	41.2	58.8	0.5
	0.4	0.6	
	−1.05	1.05	
Column total	1867	1594	3461
	53.9	46.1	100.00

$\chi^2 = 83.987$ 2 df P < 0.001

TABLE 8.10: Urban

Women should be given more rights: by sex

Category	Male	Female	Row Total
Yes	440	596	1036
	42.5	57.5	49.7
	42.3	57.0	
	−6.70	6.70	
No	596	441	1037
	57.5	42.5	49.7
	57.3	42.2	
	6.91	−6.91	
Not stated	4	9	13
	30.8	69.2	0.6
	0.4	0.9	
	−1.38	1.38	
Column total	1040	1046	2086
	49.9	50.1	100.0

$\chi^2 = 48.564$ 2 df P < 0.001

Is feminine libertarianism associated with religious belief? Let us look at Tables 8.11 (Rural) and 8.11 (Urban) to get an answer to this question.

The X^2 tests in Tables 8.11 (Rural) and 8.11 (Urban) show significant association between demand for more women's rights and types of religious belief. In rural areas demand for more female rights seems to be more significantly associated with modern and popular beliefs than with orthodox

TABLE 8.11: Rural

Women need more rights: by scales of religious beliefs

Category	Modern	Orthodox	Popular	Row Total
Yes	13	304	350	667
	1.9	45.6	52.5	19.3
	31.7	17.4	21.0	
	2.03	−2.89	2.46	
No	26	1439	1312	2777
	0.9	51.8	47.2	80.2
	63.4	82.1	78.7	
	−2.72	2.83	−2.25	
Not stated	2	9	6	17
	11.8	52.9	35.3	
	4.9	0.5	0.4	0.5
	4.04	0.19	−0.06	
Column total	41	1752	1668	3461
	1.2	50.6	48.2	100.0

$\chi^2 = 28.596$ 4 df P $<$ 0.001

TABLE 8.11: Urban

Women need more rights: by scales of religious beliefs

Category	Modern	Orthodox	Popular	Row Total
Yes	189	660	187	1036
	18.2	63.7	18.1	49.7
	75.3	51.0	34.6	
	8.66	1.52	−8.11	
No	62	627	348	1037
	6.0	60.5	33.6	49.7
	24.7	48.4	64.4	
	−8.44	−1.51	7.95	
Not stated	0	8	5	13
	0.0	61.5	38.5	
	0.0	0.6	0.9	0.6
	−1.33	−0.04	1.03	
Column total	251	1295	540	2086
	12.0	62.1	25.9	100.0

$\chi^2 = 116.185$ 4 df P $<$ 0.001

belief, while in the urban area this demand seems more to be the function of modern religious belief. In the rural area orthodox religious belief and in the urban area popular belief seem to have more significant association with the negative attitude to more extended female rights.

Is feminine demand for more rights associated with levels of education?

Tables 8.12 (Rural) and 8.12 (Urban) given below provide us with some understanding of this question.

The X² tests for both Tables 8.12 (Rural) and 8.12 (Urban) show significant association between feminine demand for more rights and levels of education. A look at the adjusted residuals in both the Tables shows a common trend of relationship between the two variables. As the level of education increases, the respondents' degree of association with feminine demand for rights also increases and vice versa, as the level of education goes up association with non-recognition of more women's rights decreases. In both rural and urban areas higher education seems to have clear association with more female rights.

Conclusion

Lack of sophistication of our data prevented us from understanding the micro decision-making process in the family and other primary groups in Bangladeshi society. However, our probe in this direction has led us to a significant finding. Faced with day-to-day problems, the vast majority of Bangladeshi Muslims seem to consult near relatives rather than people with secondary association. There seems still to be some influence of the village leaders in this regard. But in both rural and urban areas only a very small section of the people seem to seek guidance of religious leaders in temporal affairs.

With regard to the specific topic of this chapter—women's relationship with Islam in Bangladesh—we find a significant role played by women in the early religious socialisation of Muslim children, particularly in the urban area. As women seem to be associated more with popular religious belief, this role of women could be a factor in the persistent and widespread popular religious belief even in contemporary Bangladesh.

To understand the perception of the role of women by our respondents, we compared the appeal of Rokeya, a moderniser , and Rahma, Rabiʿa and Asiya, the religious devotees. While over two-thirds of the rural respondents favour religious devotees as ideals, about 51 per cent of urban respondents prefer the moderniser. In both urban and rural areas more educated people seem to admire the modernising role of women, and conversely, lesser-educated and illiterate people seem to admire the religious devotee types.

With regard to female rights to inheritance and divorce decreed by the Koran, most of our respondents seem to feel that these female rights are, by and large, established in Bangladesh. Dissenting opinion in this regard seems to be much larger in the case of the right to divorce than in inheritance.

The feeling about the inadequacy of rights granted to women by Islam and demands for more rights to women equal to those of men, does not seem to be strong in the rural area. These feelings and demands seem to be quite widespread in the urban area. We find that the female sex, modern religious belief and higher levels of education are associated with libertarian urges of womenfolk in Bangladesh.

TABLE 8.12: Rural

Women should be given more rights: by level of education

Category	No Education	Class I–V	Class VI–X	Inter-mediate and above	Not Stated	Row Total
Yes	352	135	125	53	2	667
	52.8	20.2	18.7	7.9	0.3	19.3
	18.6	17.4	21.0	32.1	7.1	
	−1.15	−1.52	1.18	4.28	−1.63	
No	1537	636	469	111	24	2777
	55.3	22.9	16.9	4.0	0.9	80.2
	81.1	81.9	78.8	67.3	85.7	
	1.34	1.28	−0.95	−4.28	0.73	
Not stated	7	6	1	1	2	17
	41.2	35.3	5.9	5.9	11.8	0.5
	0.4	0.8	0.2	0.6	7.1	
	−1.12	1.27	−1.23	0.21	5.05	
Column total	1896	777	595	165	28	3461
	54.8	22.5	17.2	4.8	0.8	100.0

χ^2 = 51.625 8 df P < 0.001

TABLE 8.12: Urban

Women should be given more rights: by level of education

Category	No Education	Class I–V	Class VI–X	Inter-mediate and above	Row Total
Yes	15	21	308	692	1036
	1.4	2.0	29.7	66.8	49.7
	12.1	21.9	46.2	57.7	
	−8.62	−5.57	−2.18	8.54	
No	104	74	356	503	1037
	10.0	7.1	34.3	48.5	49.7
	83.9	77.1	53.4	42.0	
	7.84	5.49	2.29	−8.24	
Not stated	5	1	3	4	13
	38.5	7.7	23.1	30.8	0.6
	4.0	1.0	0.4	0.3	
	4.97	0.53	−0.69	−1.95	
Column total	124	96	667	1199	2086
	5.9	4.6	32.0	57.5	100.0

χ^2 = 152.669 6 df P < 0.00001

NOTES

1 The percentage is derived from Table 3.05: Numerical and Percentage Distribution of 1981 Census Population adjusted for under count by age and sex, in *Statistical Pocket Book of Bangladesh 1986* (Dacca: Bangladesh Bureau of Statistics, 1986), p. 113.
2 See, for examples, "The Totality of Islam", in G.H. Jansen, *Militant Islam* (New York: Harper and Row 1979), pp. 17–30; and "Introduction" in J.L. Esposito (ed.), *Islam and Development: Religion and Social Change* (Syracuse: Syracuse University Press 1980), p. ix.
3 See Chapter III, pp. 62–3.
4 See Chapter IV, pp. 74–5.
5 See H. Joarder and S. Joarder, *Begum Rokeya—The Emancipator* (Dacca: Bangladesh Books International 1981).
6 See, for example, Chapter II, "The Status of Women in Islam", in R. Levy, *The Social Structure of Islam* (Cambridge: Cambridge University Press, reprinted 1979), pp. 91–134.
7 J.L. Esposito, "Women's Rights in Islam", *Islamic Studies*, Vol. XIV, 1975, p. 113.
8 R. Jahan, "Women in Bangladesh", in *Women for Women: Bangladesh 1975* (Dacca: University Press 1975), p. 27.

CHAPTER IX

ISLAM AND POLITICAL CULTURE IN BANGLADESH

The role of Islam in the politics of the Bangladesh area in the last four decades has been subjected to differing and contradictory interpretations. Islam was usually positively related to the partition of the subcontinent in 1947. Percival Spear, for example, wrote: "They [the Muslims] are sufficiently different to consider themselves as a separate nation: they differ from the Hindus not only in belief, but also in culture, traditions and, above all, in their sense of values".[1] This line of interpretation was challenged soon after the break-up of Pakistan in 1971. Rafiuddin Ahmed, writing after the emergence of Bangladesh, argued: "To categorize the Muslims all over India as a homogeneous entity, distinct from another homogeneous ethnic group, is of course grossly incorrect".[2] He went further: "In their ignorance, fanaticism and naivete they (the Mullahs) became willing instruments in the hands of the more powerful interest groups and helped give shape to an ideology which could only have a limited success, and that too for a brief period".[3]

For some scholars the collapse of the regime of Sheikh Mujibur Rahman, the "secular" founder-leader of Bangladesh, and the increasing use of Islamic slogans by the post-1975 military rulers proved the facile nature of Ahmed's interpretation of the role of Islam. Thus Mohammad Abdur Rashid writing in 1982 argued, following Aristotle and Brinton, that the secular Bangladesh revolution was like a fever afflicting the body politic of Bangladesh. As the revolutionary fever ended in August 1975, the Bangladesh polity regained its original traits and Islam, which was temporarily muted, reappeared on the Bangladesh political scene.[4]

There is, possibly, an inner logic in the seemingly diverse and contradictory roles of Islam in subcontinental politics in different periods during the last century or so. This logic is provided by the fact that the political role of Islam in each period was largely determined by its peculiar historical and socio-economic setting and the perception of the various groups of the Muslim elites of the time as to the degree of utility of the Islamic religious ideology for advancing their political and material interests. The particular historical-political conditions obtaining in British India in the 1930s and 1940s—prospect of the transfer of power to the natives by the British, and the Muslims' fear of subjugation by the economically and educationally advanced Hindu majority in free India—led the Muslim elite in Bengal to make a strategic coalition with the Muslim elites of the north and north-western parts of British India. These elites employed Islam as a means of fostering group identity to mobilise the Bengali Muslim masses. "So Muslim nationalism of the pre-independence [pre-1947] period", as Nasir Islam argues, "remained largely symbolic and differentiating in the sense that it distinguished Muslims from Hindus".[5]

The political and economic setting changed with the creation of Pakistan. With the fear of Hindu domination eliminated, conflicts over the share of political and economic power and the strategies and policies of the dominant West Pakistan and dominated East Pakistan became crucial factors in the Pakistan politics and provided the main dynamics for the ultimate break-up of Pakistan in 1971.[6] The policy of the power elite of the united Pakistan to use Islamic slogans to gain legitimacy for their domination over former East Pakistan and to destroy the cultural distinctiveness of East Pakistan through the imposition of Urdu as the only state language of Pakistan, forced the students and political leaders of East Pakistan to choose primordial and secular symbols, particularly language, in asserting their separate nationhood *vis-a-vis* Pakistan. This did not mean that Bengalis became less Muslim.[7] As we have stated earlier in Chapter VI,[8] secularism as propounded by the leaders of the Bangladesh nationalist movement was not directed against religion itself. As has been rightly pointed out by Joseph T. O'Connell, the Bengali word which these leaders used for secularism was *dharma-nirapeksata*, whose literal translation in English would be "neutrality in religion".[9] As Sheikh Mujibur Rahman explained:

> Secularism does not mean absence of religion. The 75 million people of Bengal will have the right to religion. . . . Our only objection is that nobody will be allowed to use religion as a political weapon.[10]

Besides, it was the administrative inexperience of Sheikh Mujibur Rahman and his colleagues, compounded by the radical forces generated by the Bangladesh liberation war of 1971, rather than secularism which brought about the collapse of the regime of Sheikh Mujibur Rahman.[11]

One should also be careful in finding too much of Islamic resurgence in Bangladesh in the post-1975 period. Military rulers of Bangladesh, suffering from an innate sense of illegitimacy, have been trying to gain popularity by resorting to Islamic slogans on the pattern of the power elite of the former united Pakistan. The Constitution of Bangladesh enacted by the Constituent Assembly in 1972 had, of course, been amended in 1979 to give it an Islamic character. But these changes were more cosmetic than substantial. The first change was the insertion of the Arabic phrase, "Bismillah-ar-Rahman-ar-Rahim" (In the name of Allah, the Beneficent, the Merciful) at the beginning of the Constitution. The second change was the substitution of "Absolute trust and faith in the Almighty Allah" in place of secularism in the Preamble to the Constitution.[12] Moreover, the constitutional changes were brought about by action "from the top"—through Presidential Proclamations under Martial Law.[13]

Following Trevelyan's dictum[14] that collection of the views, attitudes and orientations of each man and woman is necessary for understanding the forces of history at a particular period, we believe that our explorations in the present survey to understand the role of Islam in Bangladesh politics by asking relevant questions directly to the participating citizens in the area, will help us to find an interpretation that would be an addition and complementary to the interpretations suggested by scholars like Ahmed and Rashid, who have used mainly qualitative materials for their analysis.

Elements of Bangladesh National Identity

Any in-depth explanation of the role of Islam in the politics of Bangladesh would mean an understanding of how Islam is related to the political culture of Bangladesh. Basic to the question of political culture of any state are the elements that go together to shape the national identity of her people.[15] To understand the bases of national identity of Bangladesh, we asked our respondents.

R46/U48: Speaking generally, what are the things about your country that you are mostly proud of?[16]

The answers are categorised in Tables 9.1 (Rural) and 9.1 (Urban) given below.

The data collected in Tables 9.1 (Rural) and 9.1 (Urban) provide some common themes. Thus, the first eight variables in both the rural and urban tables—National Independence, National Flag, Citizen of Independent Country, Liberation War, Bengali Language, Bangladeshi, Bengali and

TABLE 9.1: Rural

Speaking generally, what are the things about your country that you are mostly proud of?

Category	Frequency	Percentage
National independence	220	6.4
National flag	9	0.3
Independent country	45	1.3
Liberation war	36	1.0
Bengali language	122	3.5
Bangladeshi	22	0.6
Bengali	59	1.7
National flower	3	0.1
Brave people	29	0.8
Agricultural product	410	11.8
Fertility of land	69	2.0
Islam	309	8.9
Tolerance of people	4	0.1
National beauty	14	0.4
Mineral wealth	5	0.1
Nothing to be proud of	277	8.0
Don't understand	1395	40.3
Others	88	2.5
Pride is not a good thing	9	0.3
Manpower	4	0.1
Not stated	332	9.6
Total	3461	100.0

TABLE 9.1: Urban

Speaking generally, what are the things about your country that you are mostly proud of?

Category	Frequency	Percentage
National independence	284	13.6
National flag	10	0.5
Independent country	89	4.3
Liberation war	148	7.1
Bengali language	226	10.8
Bangladeshi	38	1.8
Bengali	180	8.6
National flower	1	0.0
Brave people	49	2.3
Agricultural product	205	9.8
Fertility of land	30	1.4
Islam	283	13.6
Tolerance of people	14	0.7
National beauty	95	4.6
Mineral wealth	28	1.3
Nothing to be proud of	164	7.9
Don't understand	41	2.0
Others	119	5.7
Pride is not a good thing	2	0.1
Manpower	12	0.6
River resources	5	0.2
Do your duty	1	0.0
Not stated	60	2.9
Total	2086	100.0

National Flower—can be easily grouped under the category of secular nationalist feelings. The variables—agricultural products, mineral wealth, river resources, fertility of land, and national beauty—could be combined under a common heading, national resources and national beauty. The items—brave people and tolerance of people—can be categorised as qualities of the people. To help analyse our data and for examining the relation between elements of national identity and variables like religious beliefs and education, we have combined the relevant data of Tables 9.1 (Rural) and 9.1 (Urban) under the above common themes and prepared the collapsed Tables 9.2 (Rural) and 9.2 (Urban) on the following page.

The problem of the national identity of the Bangladeshi Muslims is usually formulated in the contradiction between the two major elements of their identity compound—religion and ethnicity (language, culture and race).[17] An examination of Tables 9.1 (Rural), 9.2 (Rural), 9.1 (Urban) and 9.2 (Urban) shows that most of the categories mentioned by our respondents as objects of national pride, express their secular nationalist feelings and their primordial loyalty to the land itself. In the rural sample, about 40 per cent of the respondents report that they do not understand the question (as we shall see below, the respondents with "no education" mostly state that they do not follow the question), 9.4 per cent do not answer, 8 per cent see nothing to be

TABLE 9.2: Rural

Short table on: Speaking generally, what are the things about your country that you are mostly proud of?

Category	Frequency	Percentage
Secular nationalist feelings	516	14.9
National resources and national beauty	507	14.6
Quality of people	33	1.0
Islam	309	8.9
Nothing to be proud of	277	8.0
Do not understand	1395	40.3
Others	97	2.8
Not stated	327	9.4
Column total	3461	100.0

TABLE 9.2: Urban

Short table on: Speaking generally, what are the things about your country that you are mostly proud of?

Category	Frequency	Percentage
Secular nationalist feelings	980	47.0
National resources and national beauty	376	18.0
Quality of people	64	3.1
Islam	283	13.6
Nothing to be proud of	164	7.9
Do not understand	41	2.0
Others	121	5.8
Not stated	57	2.7
Column total	2086	100.0

proud of, and 2.8 per cent give answers which cannot be grouped under any one heading. Out of the remainder—roughly 40 per cent—of respondents, about 9 per cent state that they are proud of Islam, while about 15 per cent mention secular symbols like national independence and liberation war, language, race (Bangladeshi, Bengali), and another 16 per cent cite categories expressing their pride in the country's resources and people. As for the urban sample, about 18 per cent of the answers fall under the headings—"Don't understand", "Nothing to be proud of", "Others", and "Not stated". Out of the remainder—about 82 per cent—answers, Islam accounts for 13.6 per cent, secular symbols for 47 per cent, and resources and people for 21 per cent.

The answers of the respondents in our survey indicate the dominance of the secular and primordial elements, as opposed to the religious element, in the present-day national identity complex of the Bangladeshi Muslims.

Our findings indicate the critical effects of the post-1947 political developments in the former East Pakistan on the formation of the present-day national identity of the Muslims of Bangladesh. S.M. Lipset has pointed out the decisive influence of the "syndrome of unique historical factors" in a country in the course of her political development.[18] The scholars on political change in former East Pakistan have all emphasised the movement for the establishment of Bengali as one of the state languages of Pakistan in the early 1950s as the watershed in the formation of a separate linguistic and cultural national identity of East Pakistan, vis-a-vis Pakistani identity as an Islamic state. As O'Connell writes:

> The process whereby East Pakistanis gradually became aware of themselves as a people distinct from West Pakistanis may be traced in their ongoing struggle to maintain Bengali as a national language, to thwart external efforts to deform the language, and to keep open communication with the literary springs of Bengali literature in the Indian West Bengal. The national holiday, the political ritual if you will, that was observed most spontaneously and solemnly before liberation and afterwards is February 21, the anniversary of the killing of several young men in a demonstration on behalf of the Bengali language. Language, blood and country became the emotive symbols of Bengali resistance.[19]

Increasing awareness among the East Pakistanis of regional economic disparity and internal colonialism helped further the growth of secular nationalism in East Pakistan.[20]

The state language movement became the model for subsequent Bengali resistance movements against West Pakistani domination—regional autonomy movements of 1954 and 1966, and the mass upheaval of 1969.[21] Lastly came the struggle for independence and the liberation war of 1971, which cost Bangladeshis enormously in "blood and gold".[22] All these traumatic developments left indelible impressions on the Bangladesh Muslim psyche, and it is no wonder that independence, the liberation war, language, and land are now the dominant motifs in the national identity complex of the Bangladeshi Muslims.

Islam and Elements of National Identity

How are the sources of national identity delineated by our survey related to Islamic religious beliefs? Tables 9.3 (Rural) and 9.3 (Urban) below provide some clues for answers to the above question.

The X^2 tests of both Tables 9.3 (Rural) and 9.3 (Urban) show significant association between types of Islamic religious beliefs and elements of Bangladeshi national identity. An examination of the adjusted residuals in both the Tables helps us to see the particular aspects of this relationship. As we expected, modern Islamic religious beliefs in both rural and urban areas seem to have significant association with secular nationalist symbols. But more importantly, orthodox religious beliefs also seem to have significant association with secular elements of Bangladesh national identity in both rural and urban areas, although in both the areas the degree of association between modern religious beliefs and secular nationalist feelings seems higher than the association obtaining between orthodox religious beliefs and secular

TABLE 9.3: Rural

Speaking generally, what are the things about your country that you are most proud of?
by religious belief

Elements of National Identity	Religious Belief			
	Modern	Orthodox	Popular	Row Total
Secular nationalistic feelings	17	294	205	516
	3.29	56.98	39.73	14.91
	41.46	16.78	12.29	
	4.80	3.13	−4.17	
Natural resources and national beauty	5	275	227	507
	0.99	54.27	44.73	14.53
	12.19	15.58	13.49	
	−0.44	1.76	−1.66	
Quality of people	0	17	16	33
	0.0	51.35	48.65	1.07
	0.0	1.08	1.08	
	−0.63	0.10	0.03	
Islam	2	198	109	309
	0.65	64.08	35.27	8.93
	4.88	11.30	6.53	
	−0.91	4.95	−4.76	
Nothing to be proud of	6	139	132	277
	2.7	50.18	47.65	8.0
	14.63	7.93	7.91	
	1.57	−0.15	−0.18	
Do not understand	9	604	782	1395
	0.65	43.30	56.05	40.31
	21.95	34.47	46.88	
	−2.41	−7.08	7.60	
Others	1	58	38	97
	1.03	59.79	39.18	2.80
	2.44	3.31	2.28	
	−0.14	1.83	−1.80	
Not stated	1	167	159	327
	1.03	51.07	48.62	9.44
	2.44	9.53	9.53	
	1.54	0.17	0.16	
Column total	41	1752	1668	3461
	1.18	50.62	48.19	100.0

$X^2 = 100.608$ with 14 df $P<0.001$

nationalist sentiments. None of the religious beliefs seems to have any particular association with answers reporting pride in natural resources and beauty of the nation, or reporting "Nothing to be proud of". Popular beliefs, rather than either modern or orthodox beliefs, seem to have more significant association with respondents stating that they do not understand the question in both rural and urban regions. None of the beliefs seem to be significantly associated with answers reporting pride in "Quality of people" in the rural

TABLE 9.3: Urban

Speaking generally, what are the things about your country that you are most proud of?
by religious belief

Elements of National Identity	Religious Belief			
	Modern	Orthodox	Popular	Row Total
Secular nationalistic feelings	150	633	197	980
	15.3	64.6	20.1	47.0
	59.8	48.9	36.5	
	4.32	2.22	−5.67	
Natural resources and national beauty	38	239	99	376
	10.1	63.6	26.3	18.0
	15.1	18.5	18.3	
	−1.26	0.65	0.21	
Quality of people	18	29	17	64
	28.1	45.3	26.6	3.1
	7.2	2.2	3.1	
	4.01	−2.80	0.12	
Islam	7	163	113	283
	2.5	57.6	39.9	13.6
	2.8	12.6	20.9	
	−5.31	−1.67	5.80	
Nothing to be proud of	17	106	41	164
	10.4	64.6	25.0	7.9
	6.8	8.2	7.6	
	−0.68	0.70	−0.27	
Do not understand	2	16	23	41
	4.9	39.0	56.1	2.0
	0.8	1.2	4.3	
	−1.42	−3.07	4.46	
Others	14	83	24	121
	11.6	68.6	19.8	5.8
	5.6	6.4	4.4	
	−0.16	1.52	−1.56	
Not stated	5	26	26	57
	8.8	45.6	45.6	2.7
	2.0	2.0	4.8	
	−0.76	−2.59	3.44	
Column total	251	1295	540	2086
	12.0	62.1	25.9	100.0

$X^2 = 118.795$ with 14 df $P<0.001$

area. Modern beliefs seem to be significantly associated with these answers in the urban sample. In the rural area orthodox beliefs rather than either modern or popular beliefs, seem to have more significant association with respondents reporting pride in Islam. In the urban sample it is the popular beliefs rather than either modern or orthodox beliefs which seem to have more significant association with pride in Islam.

Education and Bangladesh National Identity

As has been pointed out by some recent scholars on nationalism, national identity, to be stable and enduring, needs more than the feeling of one-ness. It has to be undergirded by modernising elements like education, industrialisation, urbanisation, modern means of communication and the like.[23] Nationalism is thus to a large extent a function of modernisation. One Bangladeshi scholar has argued:

> ... a degree of modernization of the society is necessary before a nationalist movement can develop fully. Despite the colonial type of exploitation of East Pakistan by West Pakistan, this crucial degree of modernization did take place in East Pakistan by 1966 especially because of the developmental efforts made by the Ayub government in the first half of the 1960s.[24]

Throughout this study we have taken modern education as the prime index of modernisation. How are the levels of education related to the dimensions of national identity in Bangladesh? Let us try to find out answers to this question by having a close look at Tables 9.4 (Rural) and 9.4 ((Urban).

The X^2 tests of both Tables 9.4 (Rural) and 9.4 (Urban) show significant association between levels of education and elements of national identity. A look at the adjusted residuals show that in the rural area the middle (Class VI–X) and high (Intermediate and above) levels of education rather than illiteracy and primary level of education seem to have significant association with secular nationalistic feelings, and the degree of association seems to be higher at the level of high education. In the urban area only high-level education seems to have significant association with secular symbols. While in the rural area primary and middle levels of education seem to have significant association with answers reporting pride in natural resources and national beauty, in the urban area only the middle level of education has significant association with such an answer.

In both rural and urban areas it is high education rather than illiteracy or lower and middle levels of education which seems to be more significantly associated with answers reporting pride in the "Quality of people". While in the rural area primary and middle levels of education, compared to illiteracy and high education, seem to be more significantly associated with respondents mentioning Islam as an element of national pride, in the urban area illiteracy as well as primary and middle levels of education, compared to high education, seem to have more significant association with such respondents. While illiteracy, or any level of education, does not seem to have any particular association with answers reporting "Nothing to be proud of" in the rural area, illiteracy in the urban area seems to have significant association with such answers. Illiteracy in the rural area and illiteracy as well as primary-level education in the urban region seem to have significant association with answers "Do not understand".

TABLE 9.4: Rural

Speaking generally, what are the things about your country that you are most proud of?
by level of education

Elements of National Identity	Level of Education					
	No Education	Class I–V	Class VI–X	Intermediate and Above	Not Stated	Row Total
Secular nationalistic feelings	132	113	174	89	8	516
	25.6	21.9	33.7	17.2	1.6	14.9
	7.0	14.5	29.2	53.9	28.6	
	−14.44	−0.32	10.78	14.42	2.03	
Natural resources and national beauty	193	136	152	22	4	507
	38.1	26.8	30.0	4.3	0.8	14.6
	10.2	17.5	25.5	13.3	14.3	
	−8.1	2.55	8.26	−0.48	−0.05	
Quality of people	18	6	4	5	0	33
	54.5	18.2	12.1	15.2	0.0	1.0
	0.9	0.8	0.7	3.0	0.0	
	−0.02	−0.59	−0.77	2.81	−0.52	
Islam	106	85	94	20	4	309
	34.3	27.5	30.4	6.5	1.3	8.9
	5.6	10.9	15.8	12.1	14.3	
	−7.5	2.23	6.45	1.47	0.99	
Nothing to be proud of	165	71	36	4	1	277
	59.6	25.6	13.0	1.4	0.4	8.0
	8.7	9.1	6.1	2.4	3.5	
	1.66	1.32	−1.92	−2.70	−0.86	
Do not understand	1046	264	73	6	6	1395
	75.0	18.9	5.2	0.4	0.4	40.3
	55.0	34.0	12.3	3.6	21.4	
	19.62	−4.08	−15.32	−9.84	−2.04	
Others	52	24	16	5	0	97
	53.6	24.7	16.5	5.2	0.0	2.8
	2.7	3.1	2.7	3.0	0.0	
	−0.23	0.54	−0.18	0.18	−0.90	
Not stated	184	78	46	14	5	327
	56.3	23.9	14.1	4.3	1.5	9.4
	9.7	10.0	7.7	8.5	17.9	
	0.56	0.63	−1.57	−0.43	1.52	
Column total	1895	777	595	165	28	3461
	54.8	22.5	17.2	4.8	0.8	100.0

$X^2 = 786.170$ with 28 df $P < 0.001$

Islam and the Will to Defend Bangladesh

The strength of the national identity of a people can possibly be best measured by the level of their determination to protect their independence in the face of external aggression. This determination is a *sine qua non* for the survival of a small state bordering on a large state. Historically rim states, that is small states bordering on large states, have suffered most from

TABLE 9.4: Urban

Speaking generally, what are the things about your country that you are most proud of?
by level of education

| Elements of National Identity | Level of Education | | | | |
	No Education	Class I–V	Class VI–X	Intermediate and Above	Row Total
Secular nationalistic feelings	20	22	320	618	980
	2.0	2.2	32.7	63.1	47.0
	16.1	22.9	48.0	51.5	
	−6.69	−4.86	0.53	4.67	
National resources and national beauty	18	21	148	189	376
	4.8	5.6	39.4	50.3	18.0
	14.5	21.9	22.2	15.8	
	−0.73	1.02	3.34	−3.26	
Quality of people	3	2	7	52	64
	4.7	3.1	10.9	81.3	3.1
	2.5	2.1	1.0	4.3	
	−0.31	−0.56	−3.68	3.86	
Islam	36	34	106	107	283
	12.7	12.0	37.5	37.8	13.6
	29.0	35.4	15.9	8.9	
	5.65	6.44	2.08	−7.32	
Nothing to be proud of	15	7	38	104	164
	9.1	4.3	23.2	63.4	7.9
	12.1	7.3	5.7	8.7	
	2.08	−0.20	−2.55	1.52	
Do not understand	20	6	11	4	41
	48.8	14.6	26.8	9.8	2.0
	16.1	6.3	1.6	0.3	
	12.18	3.10	−0.72	−6.28	
Others	1	1	21	98	121
	0.8	0.8	17.4	81.0	5.8
	0.8	1.0	3.1	8.2	
	−2.34	−2.03	−3.57	5.33	
Not stated	11	3	16	27	57
	19.3	5.3	28.1	47.4	2.7
	8.9	3.1	2.4	2.3	
	4.31	0.23	0.64	1.56	
Column total	124	96	667	1199	2086
	5.9	4.6	32.0	57.5	100.0

X^2 = 354.0441 with 21 df   P<0.001

violations of territory and sovereignty by their giant neighbours. Thus, Poland bordering on three great European powers—Russia, Prussia and Austria—had to undergo three partitions in one century. Belgium, Czechoslovakia and Finland all suffered repeated attacks by neighbouring great powers.[25] The Chinese invasion of Tibet in 1950–51; India's occupation of the major portion of Kashmir in 1947–49, and of Junagadh and Hyderabad

TABLE 9.5: Rural

What will you do if India attacks Bangladesh?

Category	Frequency	Percentage
Shall fight	2291	66.2
Do nothing	531	15.3
Government will fight	146	4.2
Look for Allah's help	105	3.0
Shall do whatever possible	122	3.5
Others	110	3.2
Not stated	156	4.5
Total	3461	100.0

TABLE 9.5: Urban

What will you do if India attacks Bangladesh?

Category	Frequency	Percentage
Shall fight	1509	72.3
Do nothing	261	12.5
Government will fight	106	5.1
Look for Allah's help	47	2.3
Shall do whatever possible	70	3.4
Others	54	2.5
Not stated	39	1.9
Total	2086	100.0

around the same time, India's "liberation" of Goa in 1961–62, and her annexation of Sikkim in 1975; Indonesia's annexation of East Timor in 1975–76, and the Vietnamese invasion of Cambodia in 1978–79—all indicate that the Third World big states are not likely to be different from the European great powers in their behaviour towards their small neighbours.[26]

The tyranny of geography over the security problem of Bangladesh is manifested by the fact that, except for a small border with Burma, Bangladesh is surrounded on three sides by Indian territory. Obviously any major threat to Bangladesh security is most likely to come from this giant neighbour.[27] To have a rough idea of the determination of the Bangladeshi Muslims to defend their independence against external aggression we asked our respondents:

Rural 23a/Urban 24a: What will you do if India attacks Bangladesh for any reason?

The answers are tabulated in Tables 9.5 (Rural) and 9.5 (Urban).

We can easily gauge the strength of the Bangladeshi national identity from the figures in Tables 9.5 (Rural) and 9.5 (Urban), where 66.2 per cent of the rural respondents and 72.3 per cent of the urban respondents state that they are prepared to shed their blood again to preserve their independent existence.

How is this determination to protect national identity related to religious beliefs? We shall examine Tables 9.6 (Rural) and 9.6 (Urban) to find out the answer to this question.

The X^2 tests of both Tables 9.6 (Rural) and 9.6 (Urban) show that categories of answers to the question, "What will you do if India attacks Bangladesh?" are significantly associated with types of religious beliefs. In the rural area the respondents stating that they would fight aggression seem

TABLE 9.6 Rural

What will you do if India attacks Bangladesh?
by religious beliefs

Category	Modern	Orthodox	Popular	Row Total
Shall fight	31	1206	1054	2291
	1.4	52.6	45.0	66.2
	75.6	68.8	63.2	
	1.28	3.32	−3.60	
Do nothing	2	222	307	531
	0.4	41.8	57.8	15.3
	4.9	12.7	18.4	
	−1.87	−4.41	4.82	
Government will fight	2	81	63	146
	1.4	55.5	43.2	4.2
	4.9	4.6	3.8	
	0.21	1.19	−1.24	
Look to Allah	0	54	51	105
	0.0	51.4	48.6	3.0
	0.0	3.1	3.1	
	−1.13	0.16	0.07	
Shall do whatever possible	2	51	69	122
	1.6	41.8	56.6	3.5
	4.9	2.9	4.1	
	0.47	−1.98	1.88	
Others	1	52	57	110
	0.9	47.3	51.8	5.2
	2.4	3.0	3.4	
	−0.27	−0.71	0.77	
Not stated	3	86	67	156
	1.9	55.1	42.9	4.5
	7.3	4.9	4.0	
	0.87	1.15	−1.34	
Column total	41	1752	1668	3461
	1.2	50.6	48.2	100.0

X^2 = 35.404 with 12 df   P<0.0004

TABLE 9.6 Urban

What will you do if India attacks Bangladesh?
by religious beliefs

Category	Modern	Orthodox	Popular	Row Total
Shall fight	204	936	369	1509
	13.5	62.0	24.5	72.3
	81.3	72.3	68.3	
	3.37	−0.08	−2.41	
Do nothing	15	158	88	261
	5.7	60.5	33.7	12.5
	6.0	12.2	16.3	
	−3.33	−0.54	3.08	
Government will fight	12	75	19	106
	11.3	70.8	17.9	5.1
	4.8	5.8	3.5	
	−0.23	1.88	−1.92	
Look to Allah	4	25	18	47
	8.5	53.2	38.3	2.3
	1.6	1.9	3.3	
	−0.75	−1.27	1.96	
Shall do whatever possible	6	43	21	70
	8.6	61.4	30.0	3.4
	2.4	3.3	3.9	
	−0.90	−0.11	0.79	
Others	6	44	4	54
	11.1	81.5	7.4	2.6
	2.4	3.4	0.7	
	−0.21	2.97	−3.14	
Not stated	4	14	21	39
	10.3	35.9	53.8	1.9
	1.6	1.1	3.9	
	−0.34	−3.40	4.02	
Column total	251	1295	540	2086
	12.0	62.1	25.9	100.0

X^2 = 54.405 with 12 df   P<0.00001

to be more significantly associated with orthodox religious beliefs. In the urban area the respondents expressing their will to fight seem to have a higher degree of association with modern religious beliefs. By contrast, the desire to remain inactive in the face of external threat seems to be significantly associated with popular beliefs in both rural and urban regions.

We have argued earlier in this chapter that it was the fear external to the Muslim community (fear from the Hindu majority in India) that helped the Muslims of India to get mobilised under the banner of Islam in the pre-1947 era. It has also been argued by some scholars on comparative Islam that "On the collective plane in its *external* aspect, Islam became an ideology of the nationalist type, mobilising the Muslim communities for defence against the non-Muslims, and in some cases, when circumstances were favourable, for aggression against the latter".[28] Here again a differentiation could be made between the types of Islamic religious beliefs. Our data suggest that the Muslims of modern and orthodox religious persuasions will be more readily available for mobilisation for meeting external threats than the Muslims with popular religious beliefs.

The relationship between categories of answers to the question, "What will you do if India attacks Bangladesh?" and levels of education is now in order for examination. Let us have a look at Tables 9.7 (Rural) and 9.7 (Urban).

TABLE 9.7 Rural

What will you do if India attacks Bangladesh?
by level of education

Category	Level of Education					Row Total
	No education	Class I–V	Class VI–X	Intermediate and above	Not Stated	
Shall fight	1068	547	503	149	24	2291
	46.6	23.9	22.0	6.5	1.0	66.2
	56.3	70.4	84.5	90.3	85.7	
	−13.50	2.81	10.39	6.70	2.19	
Do nothing	415	87	23	4	2	531
	78.2	16.4	4.3	0.8	0.4	15.3
	21.9	11.2	3.9	2.4	7.1	
	11.76	−3.64	−8.53	−4.71	−1.20	
Government will fight	59	50	30	5	2	146
	40.4	34.2	20.5	3.4	1.4	4.2
	3.1	6.4	5.0	3.0	7.1	
	−3.56	3.49	1.09	−0.77	0.77	
Look for Allah's help	77	18	9	1	0	105
	73.3	17.1	8.6	1.0	0.0	3.0
	4.1	2.3	1.5	0.6	0.0	
	3.87	−1.32	−2.37	−1.86	−0.93	
Shall do whatever possible	88	26	7	1	0	122
	72.1	21.3	5.7	0.8	0.0	3.5
	4.6	3.3	1.2	0.6	0.0	
	3.91	−0.30	−3.41	−2.08	−1.01	
Others	71	21	14	4	0	110
	64.5	19.1	12.7	3.6	0.0	3.2
	3.7	2.7	2.4	2.4	0.0	
	2.09	−0.85	−1.26	−0.56	−0.96	
Not stated	118	28	9	1	0	156
	75.6	17.9	5.8	0.6	0.0	4.5
	6.2	3.6	1.5	0.6	0.0	
	5.35	−1.37	−3.86	−2.47	−1.15	
Column total	1896	777	595	165	28	3461
	54.8	22.5	17.2	4.8	0.8	100.0

X^2 = 299.799 with 24 df $P<0.001$

TABLE 9.7 Urban

What will you do if India attacks Bangladesh?
by level of education

| Category | Level of Education | | | | Row Total |
	No education	Class I–V	Class VI–X	Intermediate and above	
Shall fight	77	62	472	898	1509
	5.1	4.1	31.3	59.5	72.3
	62.1	64.5	70.8	74.9	
	−2.62	−1.73	−1.10	3.03	
Do nothing	26	21	99	115	261
	10.0	8.0	37.9	44.1	12.5
	21.0	21.9	14.8	9.6	
	2.93	2.83	2.20	−4.68	
Government will fight	0	2	27	77	106
	0.0	1.9	25.5	72.6	5.1
	0.0	2.1	4.0	6.4	
	−2.65	1.36	−1.47	3.24	
Look for Allah's help	2	4	19	22	47
	4.3	8.5	40.4	46.8	2.3
	1.6	4.2	2.8	1.8	
	−0.49	1.29	1.25	−1.49	
Shall do whatever possible	2	5	27	36	70
	2.9	7.1	38.6	51.4	3.4
	1.6	5.2	4.0	3.0	
	−1.11	1.03	1.20	−1.04	
Others	2	0	12	40	54
	3.7	0.0	22.2	74.1	2.5
	1.6	0.0	1.8	3.3	
	−0.70	−1.63	−1.55	2.49	
Not stated	15	2	11	11	39
	38.5	5.1	28.2	28.2	1.9
	12.1	2.1	1.6	0.9	
	8.66	0.15	−0.50	−3.73	
Column total	124	96	667	1199	2086
	5.9	4.6	32.0	57.5	100.0

$X^2 = 132.281$ with 18 df $P < 0.001$

Table 9.7 (Rural) shows that in the rural area primary, middle and high levels of education rather than "No education" seem to have more significant association with the will to fight foreign aggression, and that the degree of association in this regard is higher at middle and high levels than at the primary level of education. In the case of the urban sample, high-level education seems to have significant association with the determination to fight external aggression. In both rural and urban regions, refusal to do anything seems to have significant association with the category of "No education". In the urban area we find the distinct trend of gradual decline of the desire to be inactive as the level of education rises to primary, middle and higher levels of education.

Bangladesh Islam and Separation of Religious and Political Leaderships

The last question that we want to discuss in this chapter is how Bangladesh Islam relates to the classical Islamic theory of the fusion of religious and political leadership. According to the tradition developed by the Prophet and the "four rightly-guided" Caliphs who succeeded him, religious and political leaderships were to be placed in the same hand. In the classical Islamic theory of political leadership there is no equivalent of the Christian doctrine: "Render therefore unto Caesar the things which are Caesar's, and unto God the things that are God's" (Matthew 22:21).

As has been pointed out by Wilfred Cantwell Smith, almost the whole of Islamic history from the beginning of the Umayyad rule has been a deviation from the pure classical form of union of religious and political leadership under the Prophet and the four pious Caliphs. The Umayyad, Abbasid and Ottoman emperors called themselves Caliphs but worked in practice less as "religious executives" than as "explicitly independent mundane power".[29] These Muslim rulers developed what Max Weber called patrimonial "sultanism"[30] rather than idealised "theo-democracy" of the classical Caliphate. The Ulema accepted the total control of political power by the emperors, developed the dogma of "absolute obedience to the ruler", and limited themselves to religious functions.[31] This bifurcation of religious and temporal power is being challenged by modern fundamentalist groups of various strengths in many Muslim states today. These fundamentalist groups not only repudiate the Western theory of separation of religion and politics, but also reject the post-classical Muslim history as unIslamic. They want to re-enact the pure classical Islamic past with unity of religious and political leadership.[32]

What type of political leadership do the Muslims of Bangladesh prefer? Do they like the unity of religious and political leaderships? Or do they want religious and political leaderships in separate hands? To elicit information on this score we asked the following question:

Rural 40/Urban 42: Out of these four types of people, which type would you select as your representative?
a) Alim/Maulvi/Pir Shaheb
b) Lawyer, teacher, doctor—English-educated, but to some extent religious
c) Businessman or landholder—rich, but to some extent religious
d) English-educated, but not religious.

Answers to these questions are tabulated in Tables 9.8 (Rural) and 9.8 (Urban).

As Tables 9.8 (Rural) and 9.8 (Urban) show, while 53.5 per cent of the

TABLE 9.8 Rural

What type of people would you elect?

Category	Frequency	Percentage
Alim/Maulvi/Pir Saheb	1360	39.3
Lawyer, teacher, doctor – English-educated, but to some extent religious	1851	53.5
Businessman or landholder – rich, but to some extent religious	76	2.2
English-educated, but not religious	17	0.5
Others	78	2.2
Not stated	79	2.3
Total	3461	100.0

TABLE 9.8 Urban

What type of people would you elect?

Category	Frequency	Percentage
Alim/Maulvi/Pir Saheb	139	6.7
Lawyer, teacher, doctor – English-educated, but to some extent religious	1627	78.0
Businessman or landholder – rich, but to some extent religious	46	2.2
English-educated, but not religious	101	4.8
Others	120	5.8
Not stated	53	2.5
Total	2086	100.0

rural respondents want to elect English-educated (and to some extent, religious) people as their representative, 39.3 per cent of these respondents want to vote for religious leaders—Alim/Maulvi/Pir. In the case of the urban sample, only about 7 per cent of the respondents indicate preference for religious leaders, while 78 per cent of them report their willingness to elect English-educated (and to some extent, religious) people as their representatives. Clearly the majority of the Muslims of Bangladesh do not want both religious and political power in the hands of religious leaders. How is this

Bangladeshi Muslims' belief in "two swords" related to religious beliefs? Tables 9.9 (Rural) and 9.9 (Urban) provide us some understanding of this question.

The X^2 tests of Tables 9.9 (Rural) and 9.9 (Urban) show significant association between religious beliefs and categories of answers to the question, "Which type of people would you elect?" A look at the adjusted residuals in Tables 9.9 (Rural) and 9.9 (Urban) shows that modern religious beliefs rather than orthodox or popular beliefs seem to have greater association with respondents stating that they would elect "English-educated but not religious" people. None of the beliefs in the rural area seems to have any particular association with either of the two major categories of answers, "Alim/Maulavi/Pir", or "Lawyer, teacher, doctor—English-educated, but to some extent religious".

TABLE 9.9 Rural

Which type of people would you elect?
by scale of religious beliefs

| Category | Religious Beliefs | | | |
	Modern	Orthodox	Popular	Row Total
Alim/Maulvi/Pir	11	678	671	1360
	0.8	49.9	49.3	39.3
	26.8	38.7	40.2	
	−1.64	−0.72	1.08	
Lawyer, teacher, doctor −	27	958	866	1851
English-educated, but	1.5	51.8	46.8	53.5
to some extent	65.9	54.7	51.9	
religious	1.59	1.43	−1.77	
Businessman or land-	1	40	35	76
holder − rich, but	1.3	52.6	46.1	2.2
to some extent	2.4	2.3	2.1	
religious	0.10	0.35	−0.37	
English-educated, but	2	9	6	17
not religious	11.8	52.9	35.3	0.5
	4.9	0.5	0.4	
	4.04	0.19	−1.06	
Others	0	30	48	78
	0.0	38.5	61.5	2.3
	0.0	1.7	2.9	
	−0.97	−2.17	2.38	
Not stated	0	37	42	79
	0.0	46.8	53.2	2.3
	0.0	2.1	2.5	
	−0.98	−0.68	0.89	
Column total	41	1752	1668	3461
	1.2	50.6	48.2	100.0

X^2 = 29.016 with 10 df   P<0.001

TABLE 9.9 Urban

Which type of people would you elect?
by scale of religious beliefs

| Category | Religious Beliefs | | | |
	Modern	Orthodox	Popular	Row Total
Alim/Maulvi/Pir	2	55	82	139
	1.4	39.6	59.0	6.7
	0.8	4.2	15.2	
	−3.97	−5.66	9.22	
Lawyer, teacher, doctor −	203	1045	381	1329
English-educated, but	12.5	64.1	23.4	78.1
to some extent	80.9	80.7	70.6	
religious	1.13	3.67	−4.91	
Businessman or land-	4	34	8	46
holder − rich, but	8.7	73.9	17.4	2.2
to some extent	1.6	2.6	1.5	
religious	−0.70	1.67	−1.33	
English-educated, but	22	63	16	101
not religious	21.8	62.4	15.8	4.8
	8.8	4.9	3.0	
	3.08	0.06	−2.36	
Not stated	20	98	53	171
	11.7	57.3	31.0	8.2
	8.0	7.6	9.8	
	−0.14	−1.34	1.59	
Column total	251	1295	540	2086
	12.0	62.1	25.9	100.00

X^2 = 105.491 with 8 df   P<0.001

An examination of the adjusted residuals of Table 9.9 (Urban) shows a clear pattern of association between different types of religious beliefs and categories of answers to the question, "Which type of people would you elect?" Popular religious beliefs seem to have greater association with the category of "Alim/Maulavi/Pir", orthodox beliefs with "Lawyer, teacher, doctor—English-educated and to some extent religious", and modern beliefs with "English-educated, but not religious".

The X^2 tests of both Tables 9.10 (Rural) and 9.10 (Urban) show significant association between levels of education of our respondents and the types of people they would elect. A look at the adjusted residuals of Table 9.10 (Rural) shows that illiteracy seems to be significantly associated with the desire to elect "Alim/Maulavi/Pir" and that the level of significance of this association decreases as the level of education increases. Middle and high levels of education seem to be significantly associated with answers indicating willingness to elect "English-educated, but to some extent religious people". Higher education seems to be significantly associated with answers preferring "English-educated but not religious people".

Table 9.10 (Urban) shows that in the case of the urban sample illiteracy as well as primary-level education has significant association with willingness to elect religious leaders, and that the level of significance of this association decreases as the level of education increases through higher levels of education. In Table 9.10 (Urban) we find middle-level education having significant relation with the desire to elect "English-educated, but to some extent religious" people. In this table we also see high-level education significantly associated with preference for election of "Businessman or landholder—rich, but to some extent religious", as well as "English-educated but not religious people", although the level of significance is much higher in the association between higher education and the desire to elect "English-educated but not religious people".

TABLE 9.10 Rural

What type of people would you elect?
by level of education

| Category | Level of Education | | | | | Row Total |
	No education	Class I–V	Class VI–X	Intermediate and above	Not Stated	
Alim/Maulvi/Pir	827	302	188	34	9	1360
	60.8	22.2	13.8	2.5	0.7	39.3
	43.61	38.9	31.6	20.6	32.1	
	5.73	−0.27	−4.22	−5.03	−0.77	
Lawyer, teacher, doctor – English-educated, but to some extent religious	941	412	366	115	17	1851
	50.8	22.3	19.8	6.2	0.9	53.5
	49.6	53.0	61.5	69.7	60.7	
	−4.99	−0.29	4.31	4.27	0.77	
Businessman or landholder – rich, but to some extent religious	34	20	15	5	2	76
	44.7	26.3	19.7	6.6	2.6	2.2
	1.8	2.6	2.5	3.0	7.1	
	−1.77	0.81	0.59	0.74	1.79	
English-educated, but not religious	7	4	2	4	0	17
	41.2	23.5	11.8	23.5	0.0	0.5
	0.4	0.5	0.3	2.4	0.0	
	−1.12	0.10	0.59	3.63	−0.37	
Others	39	22	13	4	0.0	78
	50.0	28.2	16.7	5.1	0.0	2.3
	2.1	2.8	2.2	2.4	0.0	
	−0.85	1.28	−0.12	0.15	−0.80	
Not stated	48	17	11	3	0	79
	60.8	21.5	13.9	3.8	0.0	2.3
	2.5	2.2	1.8	1.8	0.0	
	1.07	−0.20	−0.77	−0.40	−0.81	
Column total	1896	777	595	165	28	3461
	54.8	22.5	17.2	4.8	0.8	100.0

X^2 = 77.279 with 20 df   P<0.001

TABLE 9.10 Urban

What type of people would you elect?
by level of education

| Category | Level of Education | | | | Row Total |
	No education	Class I–V	Class VI–X	Intermediate and above	
Alim/Maulvi/Pir	36	30	43	30	139
	25.9	21.6	30.9	21.6	6.7
	29.0	31.3	6.4	2.5	
	10.29	9.88	−0.27	−8.86	
Lawyer, teacher, doctor – English-educated, but to some extent religious	75	59	569	926	1629
	4.6	3.6	34.9	56.8	78.1
	60.5	61.5	85.3	77.2	
	−4.88	−4.03	5.46	−1.10	
Businessman or landholder – rich, but to some extent religious	0	0	12	34	46
	0.0	0.0	26.1	73.9	2.2
	0.0	0.0	1.8	2.8	
	−1.72	−1.50	−0.86	2.27	
English-educated, but not religious	0	1	10	90	101
	0.0	1.0	9.9	89.1	4.8
	0.0	1.0	1.5	7.5	
	−2.58	−1.77	−4.87	6.59	
Not stated	13	6	33	119	171
	7.6	3.5	19.3	69.6	8.2
	10.5	6.3	4.9	9.9	
	0.95	−0.71	−3.70	3.34	
Column total	124	96	667	1199	2086
	5.9	4.6	32.0	57.2	100.0

X^2 = 287.836 with 12 df   P<0.001

Conclusion

To sum up our discussion in this chapter, the problem of the national identity of the Muslims of Bangladesh is usually formulated in terms of the contradiction between two major elements of their identity compound—religion and ethnicity (language, culture and race). Our survey indicates that secular symbols like national independence and liberation war, and primordial elements like language, land and race provide the main elements in the national identity compound of the present-day Bangladeshi Muslims. It seems to us that the traumatic political developments in the former East Pakistan largely explains this growth of secular and primordial symbols as the dominant motifs of the present national identity complex in Bangladesh.

It seems that the cataclysmic political developments in former East Pakistan and the accompanying social, economic and educational changes also transformed Bangladeshi Islam. Thus we find that modern and orthodox

Islamic religious beliefs as well as higher levels of education are significantly associated with secular and primordial nationalistic feelings in Bangladesh and with the determination of the majority of our respondents to fight for the preservation of their newly-won national independence.

Our survey reveals yet another aspect of the present-day Bangladeshi political culture. The majority of our respondents in both the rural and urban samples want to vest political power with English-educated-cum-religious-minded people, rather than with religious leaders—the Alims, Maulvis and Pirs. They seem thus to prefer separation of religion and politics, which is contrary to the classical political theory and practice of Islam. Consistent with our findings regarding the secular and primordial elements of Bangladeshi national identity, here again modern and orthodox religious beliefs and higher levels of modern education seem to be significantly associated with our respondents' inclination to separate politics from religious leadership.

Of course, the religious dimension of Bangladeshi national identity persists, albeit as the secondary element in the present-day Bangladeshi national identity compound. Revealingly, this element of Bangladeshi national identity seems to have significant association with popular religious beliefs, illiteracy and low education, which in turn seem to be correlates of unwillingness to fight against external aggression and inclination to vest political power with religious leaders.

NOTES

1   P. Spear, *India, Pakistan and the West* (London: Oxford University Press, 1949), p. 76.
2   R. Ahmed, *The Bengal Muslims 1871–1906: A Quest for Identity* (London: Oxford University Press, 1981), p. x.
3   *Ibid.*, p. 190.
4   M.A. Rashid, "Dharmo O Rajniti: Pakistan and Bangladesh" (Religion and Politics: Pakistan and Bangladesh), *Somaj Nirikhon* (Social Research) (Dhaka), September 1982, pp. 36–7.
5   N. Islam, "Islam and National Identity: The Case of Pakistan and Bangladesh", *International Journal of Middle East Studies*, Vol. 13, 1981, p. 57.
6   For two excellent analyses of the reasons for and the process of the disintegration of the former united Pakistan, see R. Jahan, *Pakistan: Failure in National Integration* (New York: Columbia University Press, 1972), and T. Maniruzzaman, *The Bangladesh Revolution and its Aftermath* (Dacca: Bangladesh Books International, 1980).
7   *Ibid.*, p. 241.
8   See Chapter VI, p. 96.
9   J.T. O'Connell, "Dilemmas of Secularism in Bangladesh", in B.L. Smith (ed.), *Religion and Social Conflict in South Asia* (Leiden: E.J. Brill, 1976), p. 65.
10 Quoted in T. Maniruzzaman, "Bangladesh Politics: Secular and Islamic Trends", in S.R. Chakravarty and V. Narain (eds.), *Bangladesh*, Vol. 1, *History and Culture*, (New Delhi: South Asian Publishers, 1986), p. 49.
11 For an analysis of the collapse of the regime of Sheikh Mujibur Rahman, see my article, "The Fall of the Sheikh Mujib Regime: An Analysis", *The Indian Political Science Review*, Vol. XV, No. 1, January 1981, pp. 1–19.
12 See K.M. Mohsin, "Trends of Islam in Bangladesh", in R. Ahmed (ed.), *Islam in Bangladesh: Society, Culture and Politics* (Dacca: Bangladesh Itihas Samiti, 1983), pp. 239–40.
13 T. Maniruzzaman, *The Bangladesh Revolution and its Aftermath*, p. 217. As to the most recent

attempt of General H.M. Ershad to declare Islam as the state religion of Bangladesh, the comments of *The Times* (London) are quite pertinent: "President Ershad's struggle to gain popular support for the power he seized six years ago this month has taken a dramatic, if desperate, turn. His original strategy was to secure a mandate through controlled elections, but the most recent of such elections—on March 3—failed to give him the credibility he sought. The opposition boycotted the polls and the turnout was low. Now the President has announced his intention of amending the Bangladesh constitution to make it an Islamic state conforming to Sharia Law. . . . What President Ershad's plan will not bring, however, is the one thing he most desires: the popular mandate that would make his rule legitimate. The most he can probably hope for is some respite in his struggle to survive". See editorial, "A New Islamic Republic?", *The Times*, 18 March 1988.

14   G.M. Trevelyan, *English Social History: A Survey of Six Centuries, Chaucer to Queen Victoria* (Harmondsworth: Pelican Books, reprint 1977), p. 10.

15   For more on this see L.W. Pye, "Identity and the Political Culture" in L. Binder *et al.*, *Crises and Sequences in Political Development* (Princeton: Princeton University Press, 1971), pp. 101–34.

16   We have borrowed this question from Gabriel A. Almond and Sidney Verba. Almond and Verba used this question to understand the "affect" of the citizens for their political systems in their classic cross-national survey, *The Civic Culture: Political Attitudes and Democracy in Five Nations* (Boston: Little, Brown, 1965), p. 64. We think that the question is equally good in tapping the bases of national identity of our respondents.

17   See, for example, A. Ghazi, "Muslim Bengal: A Crisis of Identity", in B. Thomas and S. Lavan (eds.), *West Bengal and Bangladesh* (East Lansing: Asian Studies Centre, 1973), pp. 147–61; T.N. Madan, "Two Faces of Bengali Ethnicity: Muslim Bengali or Bengali Muslim", *The Developing Economies*, Vol. 10, No. 1, March 1972, pp. 74–85; M.G. Kabir, "Post-1971 Nationalism in Bangladesh: Search for a New Identity", in M.A. Hafiz and A.R. Khan (eds.), *Nation-building in Bangladesh: Retrospect and Prospect* (Dhaka: Bangladesh Institute of International and Strategic Studies, 1986), pp. 40–62.

18   See S.M. Lipset, *Political Man: The Social Bases of Politics* (New York: Doubleday, paperback, 1963), p. 28.

19   J.T. O'Connell, *op. cit.*, p. 71. Badruddin Umar, former Chairman, Department of Political Science, University of Rajshahi, and a leading intellectual of Bangladesh, has written a detailed history of the state language movement in three volumes covering about 1,500 printed pages. See B. Umar, *Purba Banglar Bhasha Andalan O Tantkalin Rajniti* (Language Movement and Contemporary Politics in East Bengal), Vols. I and II (Dhaka: Mowla Brothers, 1970, 1983), and Vol. III (Chittagong: Bohi Ghar, 1985).

20   Islam, *op. cit.*, pp. 63–5.

21   For the details of these movements, see M. Ahmed, *Bangladesh: Constitutional Quest for Autonomy* (Dacca: University of Dacca Press, 1979).

22   See Maniruzzaman, *op. cit.*, p. 235. It should be pointed out here that both Muslims and Hindus of former East Pakistan together shed blood for the liberation of their land in 1971. It should also be pointed out here that those scholars who talks about the "thorny" problem of distinguishing the identity of Bangladeshis from that of the Bengali-speaking people of West Bengal in India, fail to understand the implications of the "syndrome of unique historical" antecedents of the area—the events of 1905, 1911, 1947 and 1971, and the great social, economic, political and psychological transformations accompanying those watersheds.

23   See, for example, K.W. Deutsch, *Nationalism and Social Communication* (Cambridge, Mass.: MIT Press, 1953).

24   See Chapter I, "The Politics of Group Interests: Insights from Pakistan and Bangladesh", in T. Maniruzzaman, *Group Interests and Political Changes: Studies of Pakistan and Bangladesh* (New Delhi: South Asian Publishers, 1982), p. 13.

25   For an excellent study of the problems of survival of European small states *vis-a-vis* their large neighbours, see D. Vital, *The Survival of Small States* (London: Oxford University Press, 1971).

26   See T. Maniruzzaman, *The Security of Small States in the Third World* (Canberra: The Strategic Defence Studies Centre, 1982), pp. 54–5.

27   It should be pointed out here that the euphoria of Indo-Bangladesh friendship generated by India's help in the liberation of Bangladesh in 1971 ebbed quickly. The transfer of arms and ammunition left by the Pakistani army in Bangladesh to India by the Indian army before it was withdrawn in March 1972, large-scale smuggling of Bangladesh jute, rice and other goods to India, the visible presence of Indian diplomats and bureaucrats in Bangladesh government circles led to a sharp rise in anti-Indian feelings in Bangladesh soon after independence. Lingering disputes between Bangladesh and India over the sharing of the Ganges water, delimitation of economic zones in the Bay of Bengal and Indian forcible occupation of an island claimed by Bangladesh continues to heighten concern of Bangladeshis for preserving national sovereignty. For more on this, see M. Ahmed, *Bangladesh: Era of Sheikh Mujibur Rahman* (Dhaka: University of Dhaka Press, 1983), pp. 181–94; M. Rashiduzzaman, "Changing Political Patterns in Bangladesh", *Asian Survey*, September 1977, Vol. XVII, No. 9, pp. 793–808; Kabir, *op. cit.*, pp. 50–3.

28   M. Rodinson, *Islam and Capitalism*, translated by Brian Pearce (London: Allen Lane, 1974), p. 225.

29   See W.C. Smith, *Islam in Modern History* (Princeton: Princeton University Press, 1957), p. 36.

30   See B.S. Turner, *Weber and Islam: A Critical Study* (London: Routledge and Kegan Paul, 1974), p. 172.

31   See F. Rahman, *Islam* (Chicago: Chicago University Press, 1979), p. 240.

32   For a discussion on these modern fundamentalist groups, see G.H. Jansen, *Militant Islam* (New York: Harper and Row, 1979), pp. 147–61; Rahman, *op. cit.*, pp. 222–3, 230–1. In Bangladesh the modern fundamentalist group is represented by Jamaat-i-Islami. For a discussion on the ideology, organisational techniques and limited appeal of the Jamaat-i-Islami, Bangladesh, see my "Jamaat-i-Islami: The Fundamentalist Islamic Movement in Bangladesh", a paper presented at the International Conference on "Islam, Communalism, and Modern Nationalism", at Bellagio, Milan, Italy, April 1981. Mimeographed copy of the paper is available from the author.

CHAPTER X

CONCLUSION

Anthropologists and sociologists usually point to the difficulty of understanding the "what, why and how" of religious change. Thus Clifford Geertz, a recent scholar on comparative Islam, writes:

> Of all the dimensions of the uncertain revolution in the new states of Asia and Africa, surely the most difficult to grasp is the religious. . . . It is not only very difficult to discover the ways in which the shapes of religious experience are changing, or if they are changing at all; it is not even clear what sorts of things one ought to look at in order to find out.[1]

How far have we been able to "grasp" the process of change in Bengal Islam—the first substantive issue that we have discussed in this study? Our evidence points to the conclusion that religious change is a concomitant and consequence of social change.

It is true that Islam in Bengal, unlike Protestantism in Europe and Buddhism and Jainism in India, did not originate entirely from conflicts internal to indigenous religions and society.[2] Islam had originated in Arabia and intruded into India and Bengal. But the "unique development" that Islam spread quickly and extensively in East Bengal while all surrounding areas remained heavily populated by Hindus points to the fact that major religious change is the function of a society in turmoil. Bengal society at the close of the twelfth century, unlike the Northern Indian Hindu society, was characterised by "disharmony and anomalous conditions". We have seen in Chapter I that the strains and stresses generated by prolonged and pervasive inter-religious conflict between Brahmins and Buddhists, intra-religious polarisation between Brahmins and non-Brahmins and inter-racial cleavage between Aryans and non-Aryans predisposed the bulk of the population in Bengal to accept a new faith. An extraordinary group of religious entrepreneurs, the Sufis, took advantage of this "prophetic break" in Bengal society and converted a major section of the Bengal population to Islam.

But religion is the sphere "where old wine goes as easily into new bottles as old bottles contain new wine",[3] and "a culture is no less a determinant in recasting and reformulating a religion than is a religion modifying a culture".[4] Thus the Sufis had to adapt Islam to local conditions and incorporate into Islam some of the local beliefs, rituals and practices to increase the appeal of Islam. Besides, the converts themselves retained some of their pre-Islamic beliefs and practices. Thus Islam in medieval Bengal developed its own distinctive character—partly exogenous and partly endogenous. This medieval Bengal Islam is usually described as popular, folk or syncretistic. The internal tension between the exogenous and endogenous "traditions" within this popular Islam combined with external forces provided much of the dynamics of later changes in it.[5]

Once established in Bengal, Islam as the ideology of the ruling political power and as a social force in itself began to affect religious and social change in Bengal society. With the patronage of the Muslim rulers, the Muslims built numerous mosques—madrassa complexes—which helped perpetuate Islamic beliefs and practices. But to strike permanent root in Bengal society, Islam needed a base in the landed class, the strategic social summit in a peasant society. In this regard too, the political power of the Muslim rulers was of great help for Bengal Islam. Successive Muslim rulers gradually supplanted the Brahminical *Samanta* (feudal) class by Muslim *jagirdars* and by the end of the sixteenth century the Muslims had achieved the predominant position in the Bengal landed class.

The century of the Mughal peace in Bengal (1612–1717) was, possibly, the golden age of Islam during the 550-year period of Muslim rule in medieval Bengal. Peaceful conditions brought fresh migrations of Sufis to Bengal, Muslim *jagirdars* provided "natural leadership" in the up-country regions, and Muslim rulers and officers, mostly drawn from metropolitan North India dominated the towns. Exogenous aspects of Bengal Islam were possibly gaining ascendancy over the endogenous elements.

One crucial consequence of the establishment of Muslim political power and the spread of Islam in Bengal having immense bearing on future subcontinental political configurations, was the growth of Bengali from an inchoate language into a lingua franca for the whole of Bengal. This development took place mainly under the independent sultanate, partly due to the sultans' need for effective control of their kingdom, and partly because of Islam's need for the vernacular medium to reach the Bengali people effectively.

The eighteenth century was the century of the most spectacular political transformation in Bengal (as well as in India)—the loss of political power by the Muslims to the British. But momentous economic and social change had already taken place in Bengal foreshadowing the loss of Muslim political power and having critical effects on Bengal Islam. At the beginning of the eighteenth century, Murshid Quli Khan, in a most unthinking manner, destroyed the Muslim landed aristocracy and created about twenty large Hindu *zamindar* houses that came to control almost all of the land in Bengal. A totally Hindu-dominated mercantile class had already grown in Bengal in the seventeenth century as a result of the flourishing of trade between Bengal and Europe during the days of the Mughal peace in India.

As the Hindus came to occupy the commanding heights of Bengal's society and economy, the Islamic socialising agencies like mosques, *madrassas* and *ulema* to some extent lost their effectiveness. The salience of the endogenous elements in Islam increased and additional Hindu beliefs, customs and rites intruded into Muslim society. The complete Hindu domination of the landed aristocracy particularly affected rural Islam in Bengal. Thus the first major wave of change that affected medieval Islam, the much talked about "degeneration, corruption and contamination" of Islam, reaching its zenith at the end of the eighteenth century, was the direct consequence of the loss of economic and political power by the Muslims in Bengal.

The process of social change in eighteenth-century Bengal also determined the leadership and character of the second major wave of change that swept Bengal Islam in the first half of the nineteenth century. As the Muslim aristocracy remained battered and moribund, and as the Muslims failed to take up English education, and thus could not yet develop a modern middle class, the leadership of Muslim society in Bengal (and in North India) fell to the religious leaders educated in orthodox religious schools and affected by the orthodox revivalist Wahhabi movement that had grown in Arabia in the later half of the eighteenth century. These orthodox leaders confused the effect with the cause, interpreting the decline of the Muslim power in terms of religious degeneration.

The orthodox revivalists, therefore, launched a massive campaign to "purify" Islam of what they regarded as "innovations", "accretions" and "deviations" in Bengal Islam. They enjoined the total and literal acceptance of the Koran and Hadith, strict observance of compulsory religious practices—believing in the one and only God, praying five times a day, fasting for one month a year, giving annual alms to the poor and making pilgrimage to Mecca. With their simplistic world view (interpretation of the rise and fall of society in terms of religious changes) and egalitarian proclamations, the revivalists appealed particularly to the bulk of Bengal's Muslim cultivators and other lower classes and mobilised, for the first time in Bengal history, a significant portion of them into social protest movements, albeit unsuccessful, directed against both the Hindus and the British.

One need not agree with the view of H.A.R. Gibb that the effects of the revivalist movements were more profound than the influences of Western liberal ideas in subsequent changes in Muslim society.[6] But the impact of the revivalist movements in nineteenth-century Bengal can hardly be underestimated. Religious reform is always an unending process and the campaign to "purify Islam" could only be partially successful. Yet the revivalist movements seemed to have altered the relative strengths of the exogenous and indigenous traditions as they had existed in Islam in the medieval period and transformed Bengal Islam, even in rural areas, beyond the stage of syncretistic development. The thrust of the movement has continued to the present time.

While the orthodox, revivalist and scripturalist movements continued, the gradual spread of English education among the Muslims brought about the third major wave of change in Bengal Islam. After the failure of the Sepoy Mutiny of 1857, the Muslim upper classes in North India and Calcutta began to reconcile themselves to British rule and earnestly took up English education. They felt the need to interpret Islam in the light of reason and advances in science and technology, to make it relevant to the new social order that had emerged in Europe and was being introduced in India by the British. The upper-class Muslim intellectuals like Sayyid Ahmad Khan and Syed Ameer Ali, deeply influenced by Western ideas, began to give rational interpretations of the Koran and Hadith. They sought to differentiate between the "essentials" and "accidentals" of Islam, and urged the adoption of the fundamental as opposed to the ancillary aspects of their religion. They highlighted the dynamic, creative and innovative spirit of Koranic teachings, and argued for imbibing the spirit as well as the performance of the religious practices enjoined by Islam.

The Muslims of Bengal were even later than their co-religionists in Central and Northern India in taking up Western education. The new modernist wave of change in Indian Islam thus came to affect Bengal significantly only at the beginning of the twentieth century, when a "new middle class" (lawyers, college and school teachers, doctors, government-service holders, university and college students, and the like) began to grow among the Bengali Muslims. Modernist Islamic literature, emphasising the "spirit" rather than the "letter" of the Koran, flourished in the twentieth century through the writings of scholars and litterateurs like Mohammad Akram Khan, Yakub Ali Choudhury, Mohammad Lutfor Rahman, Moham-mad Wajed Ali, Mohammad Barkatullah, S. Wajed Ali, Principal Ibrahim Khan and Abul Hashim. This literature has continued to grow in Bangladesh to this day.

Thus, after centuries of evolution, Bangladesh Islam in the 1980s does not stand as a unitary and monolithic structure of belief. There is a clear three-fold differentiation of religious beliefs—modern, orthodox and popular—within Bangladesh Islam today. A quantitative analysis of these three types of religious beliefs based on our rural and urban surveys is the second substantive aspect of our present study. We have developed an elaborate scale for measuring these three kinds of religious beliefs, and have roughly determined the extent of the spread of these beliefs in present-day Bangladesh. We find that while 50.6 per cent and 62.1 per cent of our rural and urban samples respectively hold orthodox religious belief, 48.2 per cent and 25.9 per cent of our rural and urban respondents respectively adhere to popular religious belief. Only 1.2 per cent of our rural sample and 12 per cent of our urban sample hold modern Islamic religious belief. The findings are indeed revealing. First, we see the astonishing power of survival of popular Islam. While orthodox Muslims now seems to constitute just the bare majority of the Muslim population of Bangladesh, popular Islam still seems to prevail among nearly half of Bangladesh Muslims. Secondly, although the modernist movement in Islam in Bangladesh areas has been going on for over a century, it has affected only a small minority of Bangladesh Muslims.

After having a rough idea of the distribution of modern, orthodox and popular religious beliefs we have tried to explore whether the existence of the three types of religious beliefs in present-day Bangladesh can be explained sociologically. We have thus examined the relationship between religious beliefs and several social variables—urbanisation, rurality, education, occu-pation, landownership and yearly income by using two statistical tests of association—the Chi-square test and analysis of residuals—widely used by social scientists to examine the relationship between two qualitative vari-ables. Through the thicket of tables, certain clear patterns of association between religious beliefs and social variables do emerge, indicating the inner logic between religious and social change, and the strength of the survey method is ferreting this out.

Illiteracy, poverty and low income seem to be the social correlates of popular religious belief in both urban and rural areas. In the urban area higher education, professional occupations and high yearly income seem to be highly associated with modern religious belief. High/middle-level education and middle-level income in the urban area seem to be correlates of orthodox belief. In the rural area, the middle level of education and the upper and middle levels of landownerships and incomes seem to have significant association with orthodox religious belief. Thus there seem to be distinct "social carriers" of Islamic religious beliefs in Bangladesh.

While statistical tests of association do not prove causal relationship between religious beliefs and their corresponding constellations of social correlates, the history of religious change in Bengal Islam helps us to understand the direction of the causal relation between them. We have seen that major religious changes in Bengal Islam had been the consequences of social change. We can thus argue that high levels of modernisation have continued to "modernise" Islam. Partial modernisation is fostering and nurturing orthodox religious belief, and low or absence of modernisation continues to nurture popular religious belief. Hence, we reach a Marxian rather than a Weberian conclusion that social conditions tend to determine Islamic religious beliefs in Bangladesh.

An analysis of Islamic religious practice in Bangladesh is the next major aspect of the present work. As in the case of religious belief, we developed an index for measuring the levels of observance of Islamic religious practice (high, medium, low). Using that index we find extensive observance of Islamic religious practice in contemporary Bangladesh. Less than 1 per cent of our rural sample and less than 4 per cent of our urban sample belongs to the category of low religious practice. On the other hand, 51 per cent of rural respondents and 49.6 per cent of urban respondents achieve the score of high religious practice. Besides, 47.8 per cent and 46.8 per cent of rural and urban samples respectively belong to the medium religious practice. Thus about half of the Bangladesh Muslim population have a more than casual interest in religious practice. The other half seems to comprise high religious practitioners.

In both the rural and urban samples high and medium levels of religious practice seem to have significant association respectively with popular and orthodox religious beliefs. Low religious practice seems to be more highly associated with modern religious belief. Significantly, and reinforcing the pattern of association between religious beliefs and levels of religious practice, the analysis of the social correlates of different levels of religious practice shows that different social environments that tend to produce modern, orthodox and popular religious beliefs also seem to be associated with low, medium and high levels of religious practice.

The fourth seminal issue which we have dealt with in this study is Islam's impact on the socio-economic development in present-day Bangladesh. We have seen that modern, orthodox and popular religious beliefs seem to have significant associations and common social bases respectively with low, medium and high levels of religious practice. More importantly, we seek to understand Islam's role as an ideational system in social change in

Bangladesh and compare this role with that of a rival intellectual force—modern education. Therefore, in discussing Islam's role in socio-economic development, we have been concerned exclusively with the impact of Islamic religious beliefs, so we have not examined the relationship between Islamic practices and social change.

Despite the criticism levelled against Max Weber's study on the Protestant ethic and the spirit of capitalism, his provocative hypothesis that religious belief can work as a major factor in social change by creating a work ethic among its adherents, deserves to be tested empirically. We have thus tried to find out whether Bangladeshi Muslims do have a work ethic; and if such a work ethic exists among them, whether it is associated with any of the Islamic religious beliefs.

Disproving the almost proverbial Bengali indolence, about 94 per cent of our respondents in both rural and urban samples state that they do not feel happy without work. More revealingly, 41 per cent of our rural respondents and 69 per cent of our urban respondents find pleasure in work because they want to achieve success in life. Idleness or lack of motivation on the part of the Bangladeshi Muslims do not seem to be the cause of the slow process of social and economic change in Bangladesh. With regard to the crucial question for our study—whether the work ethic of Bangladesh Muslims is especially associated with any particular type of Islamic religious belief—our survey shows that as far as the rural respondents are concerned, there is no association between pleasure-in-work and religious beliefs. In the case of the urban sample, however, pleasure-in-work seems to have a more significant association with modern Islamic religious belief than with either orthodox or popular beliefs.

We have taken the relationship between religious beliefs and family planning as the key test of Islam's role in facilitating or obstructing social change in Bangladesh for two reasons. First, family planning is an issue with a high religious susceptibility, even in highly secularised countries like the United States. Secondly, an individual's attitude to family planning is indicative of his overall belief about man's individual initiative in shaping his own destiny. Expectedly in both rural and urban samples modern religious belief seems to be associated with belief and practice in family planning. Strikingly in both the samples, orthodox religious belief also seems to be associated with belief in and acceptance of family planning programmes. Popular religious belief, by contrast, seems to be associated in both rural and urban samples with dependence on God for sustenance and non-adoption of a family planning programme.

Another index that we have used to examine the relationship between religious beliefs and social change is the question of granting additional rights to women, making them equal to men's rights. Women constitute 48.5 per cent of the population of Bangladesh. By Islamic laws, as well as because of social norms, women in Bangladesh do not enjoy equal rights with men. If women are given rights to education, freedom of movement, opportunities for employment and the like equal with men, the creative energies of about half the population could be fully released. Besides, because of the special role that women play in the socialisation process in general, and the Islamic socialisation of children in particular, increased rights for and a consequent attitudinal change in women would also mean an increasing pace of social as well as religious change. Modern religious belief in both the rural and urban samples seems to be associated with demand for more female rights. Orthodox belief in the rural area seems to be negatively associated with demand for increased rights for women, but seems to be neutral about it in the urban sample. Popular religious belief in the rural area seems to be neutral to the demand for more rights for women, but seems to be opposed to it in the urban area.

Another variable that we have taken as an index of social change is the adoption of modern methods of production in agriculture, and this item is used only for the rural sample. Here we find that popular religious belief seems to be more associated with the adoption of a modern irrigation system, and the use of manures and insecticides than either modern or orthodox beliefs. We have interpreted this association of popular belief with the adoption of modern methods of production in agriculture earlier in terms of the innate pragmatic rather than ideological character of popular religious belief. We can add here that social scientists make a distinction between the basic attitudinal change needed for sustained social change and the sheer imitation of modern techniques of pragmatic grounds which can bring only immediate and short-term development in any particular sector of society. We can possibly argue that association between popular belief with modern methods of production in agriculture could be more imitative than substantive.

In connection with our discussion on religious beliefs and social change, we have also tried to determine the level of inter-personal trust among the Bangladeshi Muslims and examine how religious beliefs are related to it. We have done so because some social scientists argue that a high level of inter-personal trust prevailing in a society increases the ability of its members to co-operate in developmental activities, and it is usually held by observers of the Bangladesh scene that Bangladeshis in general lack "associational sentiments". We find that the level of inter-personal trust in Bangladesh is not particularly high. We do not, however, find any common pattern of relationship between types of religious beliefs and levels of trust in Bangladesh in rural and urban samples. Islamic religious beliefs might not explain the general prevalence of the low level of trust in Bangladesh.

The conclusion that follows from our analysis of relationships between religious belief and social change in this study could not, therefore, be as provocative, unitary and deterministic as that of Max Weber's classic, *The Protestant Ethic and the Spirit of Capitalism*. Differentiated beliefs within Bangladesh Islam seem to have differential impacts on social change in Bangladesh. Far from being "intellectual confusion" and "paralysing romanticism", as H.A.R. Gibb called it,[7] modernist Islamic belief seems to be conducive to socio-economic development. Orthodox Islam is also found to be favourable to socio-economic change, although it seems to be less so than the modernist Islamic belief. As an ideational system popular religious belief, by contrast, seems to hinder development. With regard to the general work ethic of and inter-personal trust among Bangladeshis, Islamic religious beliefs do not seem to affect them much. In these respects, Bangladesh Islamic religious beliefs seem to be performing what has been called "negative enablement function" in social change.

The role of Islamic religious beliefs in the socio-economic development of Bangladesh comes into bold relief when we compare it with the role of modern education in this sphere. Higher education (Intermediate and above) seems to have a significant association with all the variables which we have taken as conducive to social change in this study—achievement orientation, belief in and practice of family planning, increased rights for women—in both rural and urban samples. Higher education also seems to be highly associated with the adoption of modern methods of agricultural production in the rural area. Middle-level education (Classes V–X) also seems to be significantly associated with achievement orientation, belief in, and practice and acceptance of family planning and adoption of modern methods in agriculture in the rural areas. By contrast, "no education" seems to have a significant negative association with all the variables that we have used as indices of modernisation in both urban and rural samples. As a matter of fact, we find the clear trend that as the level of education goes up, the level of significance of association of education with these modernising indices also increases. Thus modern education seems to be a clearer predictor of social change than any of the Islamic religious beliefs in Bangladesh. Indeed, since high and middle levels of education seem to be associated with modern and orthodox belief, the "transformative capacity" that we notice in these two types of religious belief might be due to their correlation with modern education. This conclusion suggests further that indigenous culture and belief systems need interaction by the intellectual forces emanating from the West before they can act as agents of social change.

An examination of the relation between Islam and Hinduism in contemporary Bangladesh is the next important line of inquiry that we have pursued in this study. The economic dominance that the Hindu upper classes exercised over the Muslims of the Bangladesh areas from the middle of the eighteenth until the first half of the twentieth century, has been eroded by the political and social changes of the 1940s to the present time. The Muslims now control almost exclusively the social, economic and political power in Bangladesh. The influence of Hinduism on Bangladesh Islam has naturally ebbed. Besides, the cumulative effects of the orthodox revivalist movements of the past two centuries has helped in the further dwindling of the Hindu influence in Bangladesh Islam. Our survey shows that the vast majority of Bangladesh Muslims do not share any saint, or god and goddess with the Hindus. The *pirs*, and gods and goddesses which, according to historians of Bengal, had been widespread among both Muslims and Hindus even as late as the first part of the nineteenth century, seem to have passed into legend, and now the legends themselves are fading away. We find that only 6.5 per cent of our rural respondents and 1.8 per cent of our urban respondents make votive donations to Hindu *pirs*; while 85 per cent of our rural sample and 81 per cent of our urban sample do not even watch the colourful Hindu *puja* celebrations. Thus, accretions from Hindu beliefs and practices do not seem to be a significant component of popular Islam in Bangladesh today. Popular Islam in contemporary Bangladesh centres mainly around the institutions of the Muslim *pirs* and *mazars*. These elements of popular Islam in Bangladesh represent folk religion which is the usual characteristic of any traditional peasant society,[8] and seem to be a common feature in other Muslim countries too.

The relationship between Islam and political culture is the last seminal theme we have tried to deal with in this work. Several aspects of this relationship are found particularly revealing. It is generally argued that the intermingling of religion and politics in most of the Muslim states takes place because Islam not only provides a total world view for its adherents, but also enjoins a complete code of life for Muslims.[9] However, we find that only 2.3 per cent of our rural respondents and 0.8 per cent of our urban respondents consult *maulanas* (persons educated in orthodox Islamic learning) for advice when faced with day-to-day problems. Bangladeshi Muslims, therefore, do not seem to be guided by religious considerations in their daily temporal affairs. They seem to distinguish between worldly and spiritual spheres of activities. This "two-sword" mindedness of Bangladeshis is conducive to the separation of religion and politics.

The Hindu-Muslim relation in Bangladesh that emerges from our study also seems favourable to the secularisation of politics. Bangladesh Islam, as a whole, seems to be tolerant of the Hindu minority. Sixty per cent of our rural respondents, and 79 per cent of our urban respondents, find the need for the Hindus to stay in Bangladesh on the grounds that the presence of diverse groups of people helps a nation to develop more fully. The level of a non-communal attitude in Bangladesh can be gauged from the fact that about 20 per cent of rural Muslims report friendship with Hindus, although Hindus constitute only 12.19 per cent of the rural population, and that 47 per cent of our urban respondents state that they have friendships with Hindus, when only 6 per cent of the population of Dhaka are Hindus. Political cleavages in Bangladesh in future are thus less likely to coincide with the religious division within the country, and this is likely to decrease the salience of religion in politics.

This conduciveness of Bengal Islam to the separation of religion and politics becomes manifest in our findings that 53.5 per cent of our rural respondents and 78 per cent of our urban respondents report their willingness to elect English-educated (to some extent religious) people as their representatives, while 39.3 per cent and 7 per cent of our rural and urban respondents respectively want to vote for religious leaders. Thus, in contradiction to classical political theory and practice, the majority of our respondents in both rural and urban samples want to vest political and religious leadership in separate hands.

Our step-by-step explorations in the relationship between Islam and political culture in Bangladesh in a unilinear way develops into the discussion of the most critical issue of Bangladesh's political culture—the strength and the determinants of Bangladeshi Muslims' national identity. The identity crisis, which is usually attributed to most of the developing nations of the Third World, does not seem to be an acute problem for contemporary Bangladeshi Muslims. A rough idea of the strength of their national identity can be gained from the fact that 66.2 per cent of the rural people and 72.3 per cent of our urban respondents state that they are prepared to shed their blood again to preserve their independent existence.

What are the elements of the national identity that the Bangladeshi Muslims seem to possess so strongly today? About 31 per cent of rural people and 68 per cent of our urban respondents mention secular symbols, such as national independence, liberation war, resources of the country, quality of the people, and primordial factors like language and race as their objects of national pride. It seems to us that the traumatic political developments in former East Pakistan largely explain this growth of secular and primordial symbols as the dominant motifs in the present national identity complex in Bangladesh.

Taking the strands of discussion on Islam and political culture given above all together, it seems that a largely secular political culture has developed in Bangladesh today. As in the sphere of socio-economic change, the different types of Islamic religious belief seem to have differing levels of association with this political culture of Bangladesh. Both modern and orthodox beliefs seem to have significant association with answers indicating separation of politics from religious leadership, while popular religious belief seems to be significantly associated with an inclination to vest political power with religious leaders. As expected, modern Islamic religious belief in both rural and urban samples seems to have a significant association with secular nationalist symbols. But more importantly, orthodox religious belief also seems to have a significant association with secular elements in national identity in both rural and urban samples, although in both the samples the degree of association between modern religious belief and secular nationalist feelings seems higher than the association obtaining between orthodox religious belief and secular nationalist sentiments. Orthodox belief in the rural area and popular belief in the urban sample seem to have a significant association with respondents reporting pride in Islam as the element of national pride.

Higher and middle level of education seem to be significantly associated with secular nationalist feelings and an inclination to separate religious and political leadership. Illiteracy and a lower level of education seem to have a significant association with answers reporting pride in Islam, and indicating a preference for the union of religious and political leadership. If secularisation of politics and symbols of national identity are regarded as political development, modernist as well as orthodox Islamic religious beliefs and modern education can be recognised as indices of political development in Bangladesh.

To sum up, as Bassam Tibi has stated, "Notwithstanding the claims of the fundamentalists that Islam is unchangeable, 'already perfect and pure, universal and for all times' students of Islam are familiar with the historically different patterns and cultural diversity of Islam".[10] We have thus seen that the Islam that spread and grew in medieval Bengal (1201–1757) was vastly different from the pristine Islam preached by the Prophet Mohammad in Arabia. We have seen how medieval Bengal Islam underwent major changes which were concomitant with social changes in Bengal Muslim society, first in the aftermath of the Bengal Muslims' loss of economic and political power in the eighteenth century and then with the spread of English education among the Bengal Muslims in the first half of the twentieth century. As the end result of these changes, three clearly differentiated patterns of religious belief have developed in contemporary Bangladesh Islam. We do not derive any monist conclusion about Islam and social change in contemporary Bangladesh. While modern and orthodox Islamic religious beliefs seem to be receptive to social change, popular religious belief seems to be a hindrance to it. Since the general process of modernisation, particularly the spread of modern education, seems to be associated with modern and orthodox beliefs, increasing modernisation, especially the wider spread of modern education in Bangladesh, is likely to render Bangladesh Islam in general more conducive to social and economic development.

We must, however, point out here that our study does not indicate that religious beliefs are purely dependent variables or mere epiphenomena— sheer reflections of social variables. Religious beliefs do seem to have a degree of autonomy. We have thus found that the pace of change in religious beliefs is extremely slow and that religious beliefs try to survive by accommodating to or absorbing external intellectual, economic and religious influences. Despite several centuries of existence, popular Islamic religious belief still holds sway over about half of the Muslim population of Bangladesh. In spite of the efforts of the most Westernised group of Muslims for a period covering about a century, only a very small portion of the Muslims of present-day Bangladesh seem to adhere to the modernist Islamic religious belief. One can even argue that Islam is trying to survive in the most modernised section of the Bangladesh Muslim population by transforming itself into what we have called the modernist Islamic belief. Contrary to all expectation, even ortho- dox religious belief, which today seems to have gained the allegiance of slightly more than half of the Muslim population of Bangladesh, seems to be responding to social and political changes showing itself, by and large, conducive to social change and even by reconciling to the largely secular identity of the Bangladesh nation. But at the same time, orthodox religious belief seems to have kept its moorings in scripturalism intact. Our study, therefore, seems to suggest that neither social variable nor religious belief is an absolute "given" or an independent variable. Religious belief and social variable seem mutually to condition each other. This paradigm suggests that the influence of religion will vary from socio-political context to socio-political context. Religion will be influential in one socio-political setting, but it will be inconsequential in another.

We find the relevance of this model of relative autonomy of religious and social factors and mutual influence of religious change and social change if we compare the political role of Islam in contemporary Bangladesh with that in some other present-day Muslim states. Recent observers of the Muslim world have all noticed the "resurgence of Islam" in many Muslim states, particularly those in the Middle East in the 1970s and 1980s.[11] It has generally been argued that the frustration of the Muslims at the failure of their Westernised modernising elites (whether civilian or military) to bring about quick economic development or establish social and economic justice led them to reject all foreign borrowings and to reassert their "identity and authenticity" in their indigenous religio-cultural heritage.[12] We have seen that such a frustration in self-fulfilment during the Pakistan period led the Bangladesh Muslims to reassert their "identity and authenticity" in language, land and ethnicity, and that both modernist and orthodox Islamic religious beliefs in Bangladesh seem to be supportive of this largely secular national identity of present-day Bangladesh. Since Islam does not seem to play the dominant role in the identity complex of present-day Bangladesh Muslims, and as the Hindu minority does not pose any threat to social, economic and political domination of Bangladesh Muslims, both the modernist and orthodox Muslims in Bangladesh seem to have developed a political culture favourable to separation of religion and politics. Islamic slogans in politics will still seem to have some appeal to the Muslims holding popular Islamic religious beliefs.

We have found that modernist and orthodox Muslims seem to be more associated with the educated upper and middle classes, while popular belief seems to prevail in the illiterate lower classes. As any observer of the Bangladesh scene can easily see, it is the educated upper and middle classes who provide the political activists in Bangladesh, and the uneducated lower classes who are usually politically apathetic and cannot be easily roused for sustained political activism. Thus the recent attempt by the present military ruler of Bangladesh, General Husain Muhammad Ershad, to gain credibility by appealing to the religious identity of Bangladesh Muslims by declaring Islam as the state religion of Bangladesh, is likely to have only limited success.[13] "Islamic Resurgence" thus does not seem to be the "wave of the future" in Bangladesh.

As John L. Esposito has pointed out, Islam is playing diverse political roles even in countries undergoing "Islamic Reassertion", like Saudi Arabia, Libya, Pakistan and Iran, because of the differing socio-political contexts prevailing in these countries.[14] Now we find in our present research that because of the unique socio-political developments in the Bangladesh area, especially during the period 1947–1971, Islam has lost much of its political salience in contemporary Bangladesh. Our study thus indicates, ". . . at least so far as the sociology of religion is concerned . . . there is no route to general knowledge save through a dense thicket of particulars".[15]

NOTES

1   C. Geertz, *Islam Observed: Religious Development in Morocco and Indonesia* (New Haven: Yale University Press, 1968), p. 22.

2   Gerhard Lenski has argued that the Protestant revolt itself seems to have had its origins in the internal conflicts of the Catholic Church, although the success of this revolt was undoubtedly dependent on peculiar features in the economic and political changes of sixteenth-century Europe. See G. Lenski, *The Religious Factor: A Sociological Study of*

Religion's Impact on Politics, Economics and Family Life (Westport: Greenwood Press, 1977), pp. 312–3. Buddhism and Jainism arose as a result of prolonged conflicts among the various castes, particularly between Brahmins and Kshatriyas, in Indian Hindu society. See R.C. Majumdar (ed.), *The History and Culture of the Indian People: The Age of Imperial Unity* (Bombay: Bharatiya Vidya Bhavan, second edition, 1953), pp. xiv–xv, 362–3.

3   Geertz, *op.cit.*, p. 1.

4   A. Roy, *The Islamic Syncretistic Tradition in Bengal* (Princeton: Princeton University Press, 1983), p. 249.

5   It seems that there was not a "fusion" of the exogenous and endogenous elements of the medieval Bengal Islam as Roy's syncretistic model would suggest. The formation of an Islamic party by Shaikh Nur Qutb Alam to force the resignation of the Raja Khans and to restore power to his son (who converted to Islam), provided an early example of the conflict between the "purists" and "the Bengal Muslim cultural mediators" in medieval Bengal Islam. See Chapter I above, p. 63.

6   H.A.R. Gibb, *Mohammedanism: An Historical Survey* (London: Oxford University Press, second edition, 1953), p. 166.

7   H.A.R. Gibb, *Modern Trends in Islam* (Chicago: The University of Chicago Press, 1947), p. 105.

8   For a general discussion on the question see Max Weber, *The Sociology of Religion*, translated by E. Fischoff (London: Social Science Paperbacks, 1965), pp. 80–4; H.H. Gerth and C.W. Mills, *From Max Weber: Essays in Sociology* (New York: Oxford University Press, 1958), pp. 283–4.

9   See G.H. Jansen, *Militant Islam* (New York: Harper and Row, 1979), pp. 17–30; J.L. Esposito (ed.), *Islam and Development: Religion and Social Change* (Syracuse: Syracuse University Press, 1980), p. ix.

10 B. Tibi, "The Renewed Role of Islam in the Political and Social Development of the Middle East", *The Middle East Journal*, Vol. 37, 1983, p. 11.

11 See, for examples, *ibid.*, pp. 3–13; R.H. Dekmejian, "The Anatomy of Islamic Revival: Legitimacy Crisis, Ethnic Conflict and the Search for Islamic Alternatives", *The Middle East Journal*, Vol. 34, 1980, pp. 1–12; M. Ayoob (ed.), *The Politics of Islamic Reassertion* (New York: St. Martin's Press, 1981); A.E.H. Dessouki (ed.), *Islamic Resurgence in the Arab World* (New York: Praeger, 1982); J.L. Esposito (ed.), *Voices of Resurgent Islam* (Oxford: Oxford University Press, 1983).

12 See, J.L. Esposito, "Islam and Politics: Review Article", *The Middle East Journal*, Vol. 36, 1982, pp. 415–20.

13 For a discussion on General Ershad's attempt to gain popular support by appealing to the religious identity of the Bangladesh Muslims, see the editorial, "A New Islamic Republic?", in *The Times*, 18 March 1988; see also Amanullah, "A People Bewildered", *Holiday*, (Dacca), 14 April 1988.

14 Esposito, *op.cit.*, p. 419.

15 Geertz, *op.cit.*, p. 22.

BIBLIOGRAPHY

Abdullah, M., *Sir Syed Ahmad Khar Dharmo O Samajik Chintadhara* (Religious and Social Thought of Sir Syed Ahmed) (Dhaka: Islamic Foundation, 1982).

———, *Muslim Jagorane Kabi-Shahityik* (Some Poets and Litterateurs in Muslim Reawakening) (Dhaka: Islamic Foundation, 1980).

Adnan, S. and Rahman, H.Z., "Peasant Classes and Land Mobility: Structural Reproduction and Change in Bangladesh", *Studies in Rural History* (Dhaka: Bangladesh Itihas Samity, 1979).

Abu-l-Fazl, *The Ain-i Akbari*, translation by H.S. Jarret (New Delhi: Oriental Book Reprint Corporation, third reprint, 1978).

Ahmed, A., *Studies in Islamic Culture in the Indian Environment* (Oxford: Clarendon Press, 1964).

Ahmed, M., *Bangladesh: Constitutional Quest for Autonomy* (Dhaka: University Press, 1979).

———, *Era of Sheikh Mujibur Rahman* (Dhaka: University Press, 1983).

Ahmed, N., *Islamic Heritage of Bangladesh* (Dacca: Department of Films and Publications, Government of Bangladesh, 1980).

Ahmed, R., *The Bengal Muslims 1871–1906: A Quest for Identity* (Delhi: Oxford University Press, 1981).

Ahmed, R. (ed.), *Islam in Bangladesh: Society, Culture and Politics* (Dhaka: Bangladesh Itihas Samity, 1983).

Ahmed, S., *Muslim Community in Bengal, 1884–1912* (Dacca: Oxford University Press, 1974).

Ali, A.K.M. Ayub, *History of Traditional Islamic Education in Bangladesh* (Dhaka: Islamic Foundation, 1983).

Ali, M.W., *Moroo Bashkar* (The Desert Son) (Calcutta: Bulbul House, 1941).

Ali, S., *Jiban Nirabichchinna* (Life is Uninterrupted) (Dhaka: Islamic Foundation, 1980).

Ali, S.W., *Jibaner Shilpa* (The Art of Life) (Calcutta: Gulista Publishing House, 1941).

Almond, G.A. and Verba, S., *The Civic Culture: Political Attitudes and Democracy in Five Nations* (Boston, Mass.: Little, Brown, 1965).

Arnold, T.W., *The Preaching of Islam: A History of Propagation of the Muslim Faith* (Lahore: Shirkati-Qalam, 1961).

Azam, G., *Bangladeshe Islamic Andolon* (Islamic Movement in Bangladesh) (Dacca: Islamic Publications, 1978).

Azraf, M., *Jiban Samashyar Samadhane Islam* (Problems of Life and Their Solutions as put forward by Islam) (Dhaka: Islamic Foundation, 1985).

Banfield, E.C., *The Moral Basis of a Backward Society* (Chicago: The Free Press of Glencoe, 1958).

Bangladesh Bureau of Statistics, Dacca, *1986 Statistical Year Book*

———, *Bangladesh Population Census, 1981: Report on Urban Area*

Banu, U.A.B. Razia Akter, "The Fall of the Sheikh Mujib Regime: An Analysis", *The Indian Political Science Review*, Vol. XV, No. I, January 1981.

———, "Jamaat-i-Islami: The Fundamentalist Islamic Movement in Bangladesh", Paper presented at the International Conference on "Islam, Communalism and Modern Nationalism", at Bellagio, Milan, Italy, held in April 1981.

Barkatullah, M., *Parasya Prativa* (The Talents of Persia) (Calcutta: Bengal Press, 1924).

Beveridge, H., *Translation of Akbar Nama of Abu-l-Fazl* (Delhi: ESS Publications, second edition, 1977).

Bhattacharya, S.N., "State of Bengal under Jahangir", "Conquests of Islam Khan (1608–1613)", and "Last Achievements of Islam Khan", in J.N. Sarkar, *History of Bengal*, Vol. 2, *Muslim Period (1200–1757)* (Dacca: University of Dacca, 1948).

Binder, L., *et al.*, *Crises and Sequences in Political Development* (Princeton: Princeton University Press, 1971).

Blau, P.M. (ed.), *Approaches to the Study of Social Structure* (London: Open Books, 1976).

Blalock, H.M., Jr., *Social Statistics* (New York: McGraw-Hill, second edition, 1980).

Blondel, J., *Voters, Parties and Leaders: The Social Fabric of British Politics* (Baltimore: Penguin Books, 1967).

Campbell, A. & Katona, G., "The Sample Survey: A Technique for Social Science Research", in L. Festinger and D. Katz (eds.), *Research Methods and Behavioral Science* (New Delhi: Amerind Publishing Company, 1970).

Chakravarty, S.R. and Narain, V. (eds.), *Bangladesh*, Vol. I, *History and Culture* (Delhi: South Asian Publishers, 1986).

Chattopadhyaya, A.K., *Introduction to Ancient Bengal and Bengalis* (Howra: Locknath Pustikalaya, 1957).

Chattopadhyaya, D. (ed.), *History and Society* (Calcutta: K.P. Bagchi, 1978).

Choudhury, A.M., "Aspects of Ancient Bengal Society and Socio-religious Attitudes: Tradition and Continuity", *The Dacca University Studies*, Vol. XXXVII, December 1982, pp. 148–60.

Choudhury, Y.A., *Manab Mukut* (The Crown of Men) (Calcutta: Nowroj Library, 1926).

Coleman, J.S. (ed.), *Education and Political Development* (Princeton: Princeton University Press, 1966).

Davis, W., "Religion and Development: Weber and the East Asian Experience", in M. Weiner and S.P. Huntington (eds.), *Understanding Political Development* (Boston, Mass.: Brown, 1987).

Dekmejian, H.R., "The Anatomy of Islamic Revival: Legitimacy Crisis, Ethnic Conflict and the Search for Islamic Alternatives", *The Middle East Journal*, Vol. 34, 1980.

Deutsch, K.W., *Nationalism and Social Communication* (Cambridge, Mass.: MIT Press, 1953).

de Vylder, W., "Urban Bias in Development in Bangladesh", *The Journal of Social Studies*, No. 4, July 1979.

Eaton, R.M., "The Profile of Popular Islam in the Pakistani Punjab", *Journal of South Asian and Middle Eastern Studies*, Vol. II, No. 1, Fall, 1978.

Esposito, J.L., "Women's Rights in Islam", *Islamic Studies*, Vol. XIV, 1975.

——, *Islam and Politics* (Syracuse: Syracuse University Press, 1984).

Esposito, J.L. (ed.), *Islam and Development: Religion and Social Change* (Syracuse: Syracuse University Press, 1980).

——, *Voices of Resurgent Islam* (Oxford: Oxford University Press, 1983).

Everitt, B.S., *The Analysis of Contingency Table* (London: Chapman and Hall, reprinted 1980).

Faaland, J. and Parkinson, J.R., "A Development Perspective for Bangladesh", *The Bangladesh Development Studies*, Vol. IV, No. I, 1976.

——, *Bangladesh: The Test Case of Development* (New Delhi: S. Chand, 1977).

Festinger, L. and Katz, D. (eds.), *Research Methods in Behavioral Science* (New Delhi: Amerind Publishing Company, 1970).

Franda, M.F., "Moral Implications of Bangladesh", *Asia Supplement* I, Fall 1974.

——, "Fundamentalism, Nationalism and Secularism among the Indian Muslims", Paper presented at the International Conference on "Islam, Communalism and Modern Nationalism" at Bellagio, Milan, Italy, held in April 1981.

——, *Bangladesh: The First Decade* (New Delhi: South Asian publishers, 1982).

Gaborieau, M., "The Cult of Saints among the Muslims of Nepal and North India", in S. Wilson (ed.), *Saints and Their Cults: Studies in Religious Sociology, Folklore and History* (Cambridge: Cambridge University Press, reprinted 1985).

Gafur, A., *Shwashwata Nabi* (The Eternal Prophet) (Dhaka: Islamic Cultural Centre, 1980).

Geertz, C., *Islam Observed: Religious Development in Morocco and Indonesia* (New Haven: Yale University Press, 1968).

Geertz, C. (ed.), *Old Societies and New States: The Quests for Modernity in Asia and Africa* (New Delhi: Amerind Publishing Company, 1971).

Gellner, E., *Saints of Atlas* (Chicago: University of Chicago Press, 1969).

Gerth, H.H. and Mills, C.W., *From Max Weber: Essays in Sociology* (New York: Oxford University Press, 1958).

Ghazi, A., "Muslim Bengal: A Crisis of Identity", in B. Thomas and S. Lavan (eds.), *West Bengal and Bangladesh* (East Lansing: Asian Studies Center, 1973).

Gibb, H.A.R., *Modern Trends in Islam* (Chicago: University of Chicago Press, second impression, 1950).

——, *Mohammedanism: An Historical Survey* (London: Oxford University Press, 1953).

Gilsenan, M., *Saint and Sufi in Modern Egypt: An Essay in Sociology of Religion* (Oxford: Clarendon Press, 1973).

Gosh, B., *Bangali O Bangla Shahitya* (Bangalee and Bengali Literature) (Calcutta: New Age Publishers, 1981).
Government of Pakistan, Karachi, *Census of Pakistan, 1951, Population according to Religion (Table 6), Census Bulletin 2.*
———, *Population Census of Pakistan, 1961, Bulletin No. 2.* Government of the People's Republic of Bangladesh, *The Constitution of the People's Republic of Bangladesh (as modified up to 28 February 1979)* (Dacca: Government Printing Press, 1979).
Haberman, S.J., "The Analysis of Residuals in Cross-classified Tables", *Biometrics*, 29 March 1973.
Habibullah, A.B.M., "Husain Shahi Dynasty", in J.N. Sarkar, *History of Bengal*, Vol. 2, *Muslim Period (1200–1757)* (Dacca: University of Dacca, 1948).
Hafiz, M.A. and Khan, A.R. (eds.), *Nation-building in Bangladesh: Prospect and Retrospect* (Dhaka: Bangladesh Institute of International and Strategic Studies, 1986).
Hagen, E.E., *On the Theory of Social Change: How Economic Growth Begins* (Homewood: the Dorsey Press, second printing, January 1963).
Hai, M.A. and Pasha, A., *Charya Gitika* (in Bengali) (Dhaka: Mowla Brothers, 1968).
Haq, M.E., *A History of Sufi-ism in Bengal* (Dacca: Asiatic Society of Bangladesh, 1975).
———, *Nawab Bahadur Abdul Latif: His Writings and Related Documents* (Dacca: Samudra Prakashani, 1968).
Hashim, A., *The Creed of Islam* or *The Revolutionary Character of the Kalima* (Dacca: Islamic Foundation, third edition, 1980).
Hunter, W.W., *The Indian Musalmans* (Dacca: Banalipi Mudrayon, Bangladesh edition, 1975).
Islam, N. and Haq, Z.S., *Population and Migration Characteristics in Khulna City: Final Report on Population and Migration Survey of Khulna Master Plan Area Conducted in 1980 for Khulna Development Authority* (Dacca: Centre for Urban Studies, 1981).
Jackson, K.D., *Traditional Authority, Islam and Rebellion: A Study of Indonesian Political Behavior* (Berkeley: University of California Press, 1980).
Jafar, A. (ed.), *Maulana Akram Khan* (in Bengali) (Dhaka: Islamic Foundation, 1986).
Jahan, R., *Pakistan: Failure in National Integration* (New York: Columbia University Press, 1972).
———, "Women in Bangladesh", in *Women for Women Bangladesh 1975* (Dacca: University Press, 1975).
———, "Members of Parliament in Bangladesh", *Legislative Quarterly*, Vol. I, August 1976.
Jannuzi, F.T. and Peach, J.T., *Report on the Hierarchy of Interests of Land in Bangladesh, based on the 1977 Land Occupation Survey of Rural Bangladesh* (Washington, D.C.: United States Agency for International Development, 1977).
Jansen, G.H., *Militant Islam* (New York: Harper and Row, 1979).
Joarder, H. and Joarder, S., *Begum Rokeya: The Emancipator* (Dacca: Bangladesh Books International, 1981).
Kabir, M.G., "Post-1971 Nationalism in Bangladesh: Search for a New Identity", in M.A. Hafiz and A.R. Khan (eds.), *Nation-building in Bangladesh: Prospect and Retrospect* (Dhaka: Bangladesh Institute of International and Strategic Studies, 1986).
Karim, A., *Social History of the Muslims in Bengal (down to AD 1538)* (Dacca: the Asiatic Society of Pakistan, 1959).
Karim, A.K.N., *The Changing Society in India, Pakistan and Bangladesh* (Dacca: Nowroz Kitabistan, 1976).
Kashem, A., *Bigghan, Samaj, Dharma* (Science, Society and Religion) (Dhaka: Islamic Foundation, 1987).
Khaleque, A., *Jano Shankha Bishphoron-O-Bangladesh* (Population Explosion and Bangladesh) (Dhaka: Adhunik Prokashani, 1981).
Khan, A.A., "Rural-Urban Migration and Urbanization in Bangladesh", *Geographic Review*, Vol. 72, No. 4, October 1982.
Khan, Akram M., *Mustafa Charit* (Character of Mohammad) (Calcutta: Mohammadi Press, 1926).
———, *Tafsirul Koran* (Exegesis of the Koran), Vols. 1 and 2 (Calcutta: Mohammadi Publishing Company, 1930), Vols. 3–5 (Dhaka: Mohammad Badrul Anam Khan, 1959).
Khan, I., *Islamer Marmakatha* (The Essence of Islam), delivered as a speech at the meeting held in remembrance of Raja Ram Mohan Ray in Tangail in 1934.

Khan, M.U.A., *History of Faraidi Movements in Bengal* (Dhaka: Islamic Foundation, second edition, 1984).

———, *The Islamic Reform Movement in Bengal in the Nineteenth Century: Meaning and Significance*, Paper presented to the Symposium on "Islam in Bangladesh: Society, Culture and Institutions", Dacca, 24–26 December 1982.

Konijn, H.S., *Statistical Theory of Sample Survey Design and Analysis* (Leiden: North Holland Publishing Company, 1973).

Latif, N.A., *Short Account of My Public Life* (Calcutta: Newman, Dalhousie Square, 1885).

Levy, R., *The Social Structure of Islam* (Cambridge: Cambridge University Press, reprinted 1979).

Lewis, B. (ed.), *The World of Islam: Faith, People and Culture* (London: Thames and Hudson, 1976).

Ling, T., "Buddhist Bengal, and After", in D. Chattopadhyaya (ed.), *History and Society* (Calcutta: K.P. Bagchi, 1978).

Lipset, S.M., *Political Man: The Social Bases of Politics* (New York: Doubleday, paperback, 1963).

———, "Social Structure and Social Change", in P.M. Blau (ed.), *Approaches to the Study of Social Structure* (London: Open Books, 1976).

Lyon, P. and Manor, J. (eds.), *Transfer and Transformation: Political Institutions in the New Commonwealth* (Leicester: Leicester University Press, 1983).

Madan, T.N., "Two Faces of Bengal Ethnicity: Muslim-Bengali or Bengali-Muslim?", *The Developing Economies*, Vol. 10, No. I, March 1972.

Malik, H., *Muslim Nationalism in India and Pakistan* (Washington, D.C.: Public Affairs Press, 1963).

Malik, L., "Measuring Consensus in Pakistan", *Journal of South Asian and Middle Eastern Studies*, Vol. VI, No. I, Fall, 1982.

Mallick, A.R., *British Policy and the Muslims in Bengal (1757–1856)* (Dacca: Bangla Academy, 1977).

Maloney, C., *Why does Bangladesh Remain so Poor?* Part II, *Eight Answers UFSI Reports*, 1985/No. 34 (Indianapolis: Universities Field Staff International).

Maniruzzaman, T., *The Bangladesh Revolution and its Aftermath* (Dacca: Bangladesh Books International, 1980).

———, *Group Interests and Political Changes: Studies of Pakistan and Bangladesh* (New Delhi: South Asian Publishers, 1982).

———, *The Security of Small States in the Third World* (Canberra: the Strategic Defence Studies Centre, 1982).

———, "Bangladesh Politics: Secular and Islamic Trends", in R. Ahmed (ed.), *Islam in Bangladesh: Society, Culture and Politics* (Dhaka: Bangladesh Itihas Samity, 1983).

Maududi, A.A., *Islamic Law and Constitution*, translated by K. Ahmad (Lahore: Islamic Publications, fourth edition, 1969).

Majumdar, R.C. (ed.), *Bangladesher Itihas: Dyitio Khando: Maddhaya Jug* (History of Bengal, Part 11, Medieval Period) (Calcutta: General Printers and Publishers, 1946).

———, *The History of Bengal*, Vol. I, *Hindu Period* (Dacca: University of Dacca, second impression, 1963).

———, *The History and Culture of the Indian People: The Age of Imperial Unity* (Bombay: Bharatiya Vidya Bhavan, second edition, 1953).

May, L.S., *The Evolution of Indo-Muslim Thought after 1857* (Lahore: Sh. Muhammad Ashraf, 1970).

Mohsin, K.M., "Trends in Bangladesh Islam", in R. Ahmed (ed.), *Islam in Bangladesh: Society, Culture and Politics* (Dhaka: Bangladesh Itihas Samity, 1983).

Morrison, B.M., *Political Centers and Cultural Regions in Early Bengal* (Delhi: Rawat Publications, 1980).

Moser, C.A. and Kalton, G., *Survey Methods in Social Investigation* (London: Heinemann Educational Books, second edition, 1971).

Newcomb, T.M., "The Interdependence of Social Psychological Theory and Methods: An Overview", in L. Festinger and D. Katz (eds.), *Research Methods in Behavioral Science* (New Delhi: Amerind Publishing Company, 1970).

O'Connell, J.T., "Dilemmas of Secularism in Bangladesh", in B.L. Smith (ed.), *Religion and Social Conflict in South Asia* (Leiden: E.J. Brill, 1976).

Pye, L.W., *Politics, Personality and Nation-building* (New Haven: Yale University Press, 1963).

Qanungo, R.R., "Bengal under the House of Balban", in J.N. Sarkar (ed.), *The History of Bengal*, Vol. II, *Muslim Period (1200–1757)* (Dacca: University of Dacca, 1948).

Rahim, M.A., *Social and Cultural History of Bengal*, Vol. I, (1201–1576) (Karachi: Pakistan Historical Society, 1963).

———, *Social and Cultural History of Bengal*, Vol. II (1576–1757) (Karachi: Pakistan Publishing House, 1967).

———, *The Muslim Society and Politics in Bengal* (Dacca: University of Dacca, 1978).

Rahim, M.A., et al., *Bangladesher Itihas* (History of Bengal) (Dhaka: Nowroz Kitabistan, third edition, 1987).

Rahman, F., "Islamic Modernism: Its Scope, Method and Alternatives", *International Journal of Middle East Studies*, Vol. I, 1970.

———, *Islam* (London: Chicago University Press, second edition, 1979).

Rahman, M.L., *Manab Jiban* (Man's Life) (Calcutta: Mohammadi Book Agency, 1936).

Rahman, M.M., *Bangla Vashai Koran Charcha* (Culture of the Holy Koran in the Bengali Language) (Dhaka: Islamic Foundation, 1986).

Rashid, M.A., "Dharma O Rajniti: Pakistan and Bangladesh" (Religion and Politics: Pakistan and Bangladesh), *Samaj Nirikhon* (Social Research), Dhaka, September 1982.

Ray, N., *Bangalir Itihas: Adi Parbo* (History of Bengal: The Ancient Phase) (Calcutta: Lekhak Somobay Samati, 1950).

Revell, R., "Possible Future of Bangladesh", *Asia*, No. 29, Spring 1973.

Rodinson, M., *Islam and Capitalism*, translated by Brian Pearce (London: Allen Lane, 1974).

Roy, A., *The Islamic Syncretistic Tradition in Bengal* (Princeton: Princeton University Press, 1983).

Roy, N.B., "Bengal under Imperial Afghan Rule", in J.N. Sarkar (ed.), *The History of Bengal*, Vol. II, *Muslim Period* (Dacca: University of Dacca, 1948).

Rubbee, K.F., *The Origin of the Musalmans of Bengal* (Calcutta: Thacker, Spink and Company, 1895).

Saklayen, G., *Bangladesher Sufi-Shadhak* (Saint-Devotees of Bangladesh) (Dhaka: Islamic Foundation, third edition, 1982).

Sarkar, J.N. (ed.), *History of Bengal*, Volume 2, *Muslim Period (1200–1757)* (Dacca: University of Dacca, 1948).

Sarkar, J.N., "Transformation of Bengal under Mughal Rule", in J.N. Sarkar (ed.), *The History of Bengal*, Vol. 2, *Muslim Period (1200–1757)* (Dacca: University of Dacca, 1948).

Sayeed, K.B., "Religion and nation-building in Pakistan", *The Middle East Journal*, Vol. 17, No. 3, Summer 1963.

———, *The Political System in Pakistan* (Boston, Mass.: Houghton Mifflin, 1967).

Shaikh, A.I., *Pir Dudu Miyan* (in Bengali) (Dacca: Islamic Foundation, 1980).

Smith, B.L. (ed.), *Religion and Social Conflict in South Asia* (Leiden: E.J. Brill, 1976).

Smith, D.E. (ed.), *South Asian Politics and Religion* (Princeton: Princeton University Press, 1966).

Smith, W.C., *Modern Islam in India* (London: Gollancz, second edition, 1946).

———, *Islam in Modern History* (Princeton: Princeton University Press, 1957).

Spear, P., *India, Pakistan and the West* (London: Oxford University Press, 1949).

Stepanek, J.F., *Bangladesh — Equitable Growth?* (New York: Pergamon Press, 1979).

Thomas, B. and Lavan, S. (eds.), *West Bengal and Bangladesh* (East Lansing: Asian Studies Center, 1973).

Tibi, B., "The Renewed Role of Islam in Political and Social Development of the Middle East", *The Middle East Journal*, Vol. 37, 1983.

Titus, M.T., *Islam in India and Pakistan* (Madras: Christian Literature Society; first published in 1930, revised and reprinted in 1959).

Trevelyan, G.M., *English Social History: A Survey of Six Centuries, Chaucer to Queen Victoria* (Harmondsworth: Pelican Books, reprint, 1977).

Trimingham, J.S., *Islam in West Africa* (Oxford: Clarendon Press, 1959).

Turner, B.S., *Weber and Islam* (London: Routledge and Kegan Paul, 1974).

Umar, B., *Purba Banglar Bhasha Andolon O Tantkalin Rajniti* (The Language Movement and Contemporary Politics in East Bengal), Vols. I and II (Dacca: Mowla Brothers, 1970, 1980), and Vol. III (Chittagong: Bohi Ghar, 1985).

Vital, D., *The Survival of Small States* (London: Oxford University Press, 1971).

Voll, J.O., *Islam: Continuity and Change in the Modern World* (Boulder: Westview Press, 1982).

Watt, W.M., *Islam and the Integration of Society* (London: Routledge and Kegan Paul, fourth impression, 1970).

Weber, M., *The Sociology of Religion*, translated by E. Fischoff (London: Social Science Paperbacks, 1965).

————, *The Protestant Ethic and the Spirit of Capitalism*, translated by T. Parsons (New York: Charles Scribner's Sons, 1958).

————, *The Religion of China: Confucianism and Taoism*, translated by H.H. Gerth (New York: Free Press, 1951).

————, *Ancient Judaism*, translated by H.H. Gerth and D. Martindale, (New York: Free Press, 1952).

————, *The Religion of India: The Sociology of Hinduism and Buddhism*, translated by H.H. Gerth and D. Martindale (New York: Free Press, 1958).

Weiner, M. and Huntington, S.P. (eds.), *Understanding Political Development* (Boston, Mass.: Brown and Company, 1987).

Wilson, A.J. and Dalton, D. (eds.), *The States of South Asia: Problems of National Integration* (London: C. Hurst, 1982).

Wilson. S. (ed.), *Saints and their Cults: Studies in Religious Sociology, Folklore, and History* (Cambridge: Cambridge University Press, reprinted 1985).

Zaman, H., *Samaj, Sangskriti, Sahitya* (Society, Culture and Literature) (Dacca: Islamic Cultural Centre, 1980).

INDEX

Abdullah, M. 52n
Adalat, 17
Adnan, Shapan, 79n
Afghanistan, 1
Ahmed, A., 25n, 29n
Ahmed, Nazimuddin, 31n
Ahmed, Rafiuddin, xiii, 53n, 55, 63n, 147, 169n
Aisia, Bibi, 135
Akbar, 2, 28
Al-Hasan of Basra, 15
Ali, A.K.M.A., 53n
Ali, Inayet, 39
Ali, Keramat, 41
Ali, Syed Ameer, 46
Ali, Wajed, 48, 43n, 175
Ali, Wilayat, 39
Almond, Gabriel, 124, 130n, 170n
Alpine Aryans, 5
Arnold, T.W., 2
Aristotle, 147
Aryans, 5
Aurangzeb, 2
Austro-Asiatic people, 5
Azam, Ghulam, 53n
Azra, M., 53n

Babar, 23
Baljon, J.M.S., xvii
Balk, 12
Balkhi, Shah Sultan, 13
Banu, U.A.B. Razia Akter, 169n
"*Bara Bhuiyans*", 19-20
Barbosa, 4
Barkatullah, M., 53n, 175
Bayabahara Sastras, 8
Bengali Culture, xii
Beverly, 3
Beveridge, H. 31n
Binder, L., 170n
Bistan, 12
Blondel, J., 79n
Brahmins, 5
Brinton, 147
Buddhism, 6-8
Bukhara, 15
Byzentium, 1

Calvinists, 109
Chandidas, 11

Change in Islam, 59
Charyapodas, 10, 11, 30n
Chattopadhyaya, 29n
Choudhury, A.M., 29n
Choudhury, Yakub Ali, 175
Chi-Square Test, 69
Christianity, 2, 4
Coleman, J.S., 129n
Constitutional Changes, 148
Conversion Theory, 3-4
Cornwallis, Lord, 21
Cottam, Richard W., xvi
Creevey, L.E., 95n

Dargah, 15, 17
Darul Harb, 41, 43
Davis, Winston, 110, 128, 129n
Dekmejian, R.H., 184n
Delhi, 2, 12
Dessouki, A.E.H., 184n
Deutsch, K.W., 170n
Dijkema, F.Th., xvii
Dahakosa, 10, 30n
Durga, 5

Eaton, R.M. 107n
Engels, Friedrich, xviii
Ershad, General H.M., 160, 170n, 183
Esposito, J.L., xviiin, 138, 183

Faaland, Just, xviiin, 129n
Fahien, 6
Faraidi Movement, 35-37
Fazal, Abul, 23, 32n
Fischoff, E. 184n
Franda, Marcus F., xvi, 129n, 130n
Freund, J., xviiin
Functionalist, 4

Gaboriev, M., 107n
Gafur, Abdul, 53n
Gallagher, Charles, xvi
Gellner, Ernest, xvi, 107n
Gerth, Hans, F., xviiin, 129n
Geertz, Clifford, 130n, 172, 183n, 184n
Ghazi, A., 170n
Ghazi, Shah Ismail, 14
Ghori, Muhammad, 1
Ghos, B., 29n
Ghuzz, 1

INTERNATIONAL STUDIES
IN
SOCIOLOGY AND SOCIAL ANTHROPOLOGY

EDITED BY K. ISHWARAN

21. FUSÉ, T. (ed.). *Modernization and Stress in Japan.* 1975.
ISBN 90 04 04344 6

22. SMITH, B.L. (ed.). *Religion and Social Conflict in South Asia.* 1976.
ISBN 90 04 04510 4

23. MAZRUI, A.A. (ed.). *The Warrior Tradition in Modern Africa.* 1977.
ISBN 90 04 05646 7

25. SMITH, B.L. (ed.). *Religion and the Legitimation of Power in South Asia.*
1978. ISBN 90 04 05674 2

31. LELE, J. (ed.). *Tradition and Modernity in* Bhakti *Movements.* 1981.
ISBN 90 04 06370 6

32. ARMER, J.M. *Comparative Sociological Research in the 1960s and 1970s.*
1982. ISBN 90 04 06487 7

33. GALATY, J.G. & P.C. SALZMAN (eds.). *Change and Development in
Nomadic and Pastoral Societies.* 1981. ISBN 90 04 06587 3

34. LUPRI, E. (ed.). *The Changing Position of Women in Family and Society. A
Cross-National Comparison.* 1983. ISBN 90 04 06845 7

35. IVERSON, N. (ed.). *Urbanism and Urbanization. Views, Aspects and Dimensions.* 1984. ISBN 90 04 06920 8

36. MALIK, Y.K. *Politics, Technology, and Bureaucracy in South Asia.* 1983.
ISBN 90 04 07027 3

37. LENSKI, G. (ed.). *Current Issues and Research in Macrosociology.* 1984.
ISBN 90 04 07052 4

38. ADAM, H. (ed.). *South Africa: the Limits of Reform Politics.* 1983.
ISBN 90 04 07484 8

39. TIRYAKIAN, E.A. (ed.). *The Global Crisis. Sociological Analyses and
Responses.* 1984. ISBN 90 04 07284 5

40. LAWRENCE, B. (ed.). *Ibn Khaldun and Islamic Ideology.* 1984.
ISBN 90 04 07567 4

41. HAJJAR, S.G. (ed.). *The Middle East: from Transition to Development.*
1985. ISBN 90 04 07694 8

43. CARMAN, J.B. & F.A. MARGLIN (eds.). *Purity and Auspiciousness in Indian Society.* 1985. ISBN 90 04 07789 8

44. PARANJPE, A.C. *Ethnic Identities and Prejudices.* 1986.
ISBN 90 04 08111 9

45. ABU-LABAN, B. & S. MCIRVIN ABU-LABAN (eds.). *The Arab
World. Dynamics of Development.* 1986. ISBN 90 04 08156 9

46. SMITH, B.L. & H.B. REYNOLDS (eds.). *The City as a Sacred Center. Essays on Six Asian Contexts.* 1987. ISBN 90 04 08471 1

47. MALIK, Y.K. & D.K. VAJPEYI (eds.). *India. The Years of Indira Ghandi.* 1988. ISBN 90 04 08681 1

48. CLARK, C. & J. LEMCO (eds.). *State and Development.* 1988. ISBN 90 04 08833 4

49. GUTKIND, P.C.W. (ed.). *Third World Workers. Comparative International Labour Studies.* 1988. ISBN 90 04 08788 5

50. SELIGMAN, A.B. *Order and Transcendence. The Role of Utopias and the Dynamics of Civilization.* 1989. ISBN 90 04 08975 6

51. JABBRA, J.G. *Bureaucracy and Development in the Arab World.* 1989. ISBN 90 04 09194 7

52. KAUTSKY, J.H. (ed.). *Karl Kautsky and the Social Science of Classical Marxism.* 1989. ISBN 90 04 09193 9

53. KAPUR, A. (ed.). *The Diplomatic Ideas and Practices of Asian States.* 1990. ISBN 90 04 09289 7

54. KIM, Q.-Y. (ed.). *Revolutions in the Third World.* 1991. ISBN 90 04 09355 9

55. KENNEDY, C.H. & D.J. LOUSCHER (eds.). *Civil Military Interaction in Asia and Africa.* 1991. ISBN 90 04 09359 1

56. RAGIN, C.C. (ed.). *Issues and Alternatives in Comparative Social Research.* 1991. ISBN 90 04 09360 5

57. CHOUDHRY, N.K. (ed.). *Canada and South Asian Development. Trade and Aid.* 1991. ISBN 90 04 09416 4

58. RAZIA AKTER BANU, U.A.B. *Islam in Bangladesh.* ISBN 90 04 09497 0

59. JABBRA, J.G. & N.W. JABBRA (eds.). *Women and Development in the Middle East and North Africa.* ISBN 90 04 09529 2, in the press